CU00546371

THE

# VOCABULARY

OF

# EAST ANGLIA;

AN ATTEMPT TO RECORD

THE VULGAR TONGUE OF THE TWIN SISTER COUNTIES,

## NORFOLK AND SUFFOLK,

AS IT EXISTED

𝕴𝖓 𝖙𝖍𝖊 𝖑𝖆𝖘𝖙 𝕿𝖜𝖊𝖓𝖙𝖞 𝖄𝖊𝖆𝖗𝖘 𝖔𝖋 𝖙𝖍𝖊 𝕰𝖎𝖌𝖍𝖙𝖊𝖊𝖓𝖙𝖍 𝕮𝖊𝖓𝖙𝖚𝖗𝖞,

AND STILL EXISTS;

WITH PROOF OF ITS ANTIQUITY FROM ETYMOLOGY AND AUTHORITY.

Antiquam exquirite matrem.—VIRGIL.

BY THE LATE REV. ROBERT FORBY,

RECTOR OF FINCHAM, NORFOLK.

IN TWO VOLUMES.

VOL. I.

## LONDON:

PRINTED BY AND FOR

J. B. NICHOLS AND SON, 25, PARLIAMENT STREET.

AND SOLD BY MATCHETT AND STEVENSON, AND WILKIN, NORWICH;
RAW, IPSWICH; SLOMAN, YARMOUTH; DECK, BURY;
LODER, WOODBRIDGE; SWINBORNE, WALTER, AND TAYLOR,
COLCHESTER; GUY, CHELMSFORD; AND DEIGHTON, CAMBRIDGE.

1830.

iii

# CONTENTS.

# PREFACE.

It may be expected from the Editor, that he should give some account of the book which he now offers to the public ; but the extracts from Mr. Forby's Correspondence in the following Memoir are so full and explicit upon this subject, as to render any observations on the design and nature of the work unnecessary. Some explanation, however, may be required of one passage in the correspondence referred to; in which (after detailing the plan of the work) it is stated, that it would " conclude with an Essay on the remarkable prevalence of Anglo-Saxon nomenclature in the Topography of East Anglia." It might be supposed from this passage, that some part of Mr. Forby's materials had been suppressed, or that the book had been abridged of one of its members in the present publication. But this is assuredly not the case. Whatever might have been the Author's original intention, it is probable that he soon changed his views, and abandoned his design : at any rate, it is quite certain, that neither in his letters to the Editor, nor in several conversations which they had on the subject of his book a few months before his death, did he ever mention this Essay. Indeed there appears to have been no provision made for it in any of the papers which came into the Editor's possession, except a collection of the names of a few parishes; but without any notice of the purpose for which they were brought together, or the slightest sketch from which the plan of the proposed Essay could be conjectured. It may not be improper perhaps, in this place, to mention in what degree of forwardness the work was left by Mr. Forby.

The Introduction and the two first Essays were entirely finished, and copied out fairly for the press. The Vocabulary had been for some time in an equally forward state of preparation, and had been repeatedly revised. These parts may therefore be said to have received the Author's final correction. The " Essay on the Grammar of the East-Anglian Dialect" was composed subsequently, and was copied out fairly for more than three parts of its length. The remainder was supplied by the Editor from a rough copy, which, however, he was not always able exactly to decipher; and he suspects it was not quite finished by the Author. For the Appendix there were some materials, of which the Editor has availed himself.

Such was the state of the work, when the Author was, by the will of Providence, suddenly snatched away, and his book left incomplete. It was still, however, the opinion of his friends (of whom the Editor avows himself to have been one)

that, incomplete as it was, it ought not to be lost
to the world: and, as the Executors declined the
printing, it was finally agreed that the work should
be published by subscription. It is certainly not improbable that the judgment of Mr. Forby's friends
may have been biassed by their affection for him: and
most undoubtedly the work would have appeared
to much greater advantage, if the Author had been
spared to put the finishing hand to his composition, and to superintend its publication. But the
Editor still entertains a hope that the opinion of
himself and his friends may be confirmed by the
Public; and that the Book, with all its disadvan-
tages, may not be found unworthy of the patronage
it has received. But, however this may be, he
trusts that it will meet with the indulgence usually
shown to posthumous publications, and that he may
be allowed to bespeak it in the language of the
poet:

Orba parente suo quicunque volumina cernis,
 His saltem vestrâ detur in urbe locus.
Quòque magis faveas, *non hæc sunt edita ab illo,*
 Sed quasi de domini funere rapta sui.
Quicquid in his igitur vitii rude carmen habebit,
 Emendaturus, si licuisset, erat.   OVID, Trist. Eleg. 6.

GEORGE TURNER.

*Kettleburgh, Nov.* 16, 1829.

# NAMES OF SUBSCRIBERS.

HIS GRACE THE DUKE OF GRAFTON.

HIS GRACE THE DUKE OF NEWCASTLE.

THE RT. HON. WILLIAM HENRY EARL OF ROCHFORD.

THE RIGHT HON. GEORGE EARL OF ASHBURNHAM.

THE RIGHT HON. GEORGE JOHN EARL SPENCER, K. G.

THE RIGHT HONORABLE JOHN EARL OF STRADBROKE.

THE RIGHT HON. ARCHIBALD EARL OF GOSFORD.

THE RIGHT HON. LORD VISCOUNT ACHESON.

THE RIGHT HON. DOWAGER LADY SUFFIELD.

THE RIGHT HONORABLE AND REV. LORD BAYNING.

THE RIGHT HONORABLE LORD WODEHOUSE.

THE HONORABLE JOHN WODEHOUSE,
Lieutenant, Vice Admiral, and Custos Rot. of the Co. of Norfolk.

THE RIGHT HONORABLE LORD HENNIKER.

THE RIGHT REVEREND THE LORD BISHOP OF ELY.

THE RIGHT REV. THE LORD BISHOP OF NORWICH.

THE VERY REVEREND THE DEAN OF NORWICH.

THE VERY REVEREND THE DEAN OF ELY.

THE REVEREND THE DEAN AND CHAPTER OF ELY.

SIR THOMAS GERY CULLUM, BART.

SIR WILLIAM PARKER, BART.

SIR CHARLES BLOIS, BART.

SIR THOMAS SHERLOCK GOOCH, BART., M. P.

SIR SAMUEL FLUDYER, BART.

SIR W. H. B. FOLKES, BART.

SIR W. F. MIDDLETON, BART.

SIR EDMUND K. LACON, BART.

Henry Alexander, Esq. CorkStreet.

John Alexander, Esq. 3, Knights-
bridge Terrace.

Miss Alexander, Ely.

Rev. Wm. Allen, Narburgh.

Thomas Amyot, Esq. F.R.S. Treas.
S.A. James-st. Buckingham-gt.

John Angerstein, Esq. 2 copies.

Rev. Geo. Anguish, Gislebarn,Suff.

Andrew Arcedeckne, Esq. M.P.
Glevering Hall.

Walter Arcedeckne, Esq.

Rev. Dr. Bacon, Fring Parsonage.

Rev. Samuel Hadely.

Rev. Edward Barlée.

Rev. William Barlée.

George Barlée, Esq.

C. F. Barnwell, Esq. British Mus.

Nathaniel Barthropp, Esq. Ha-
cheston.

Rev. Rob. Bathurst, Norwich.

Rev. Thomas Beauchamp.

Rev. Edward John Bell, Wickham
Market.

Rev. Philip Bayles, Rector of St.
Mary at the Walls, Colchester.

Rev. Philip Bell, Stow.

Rev. J. W. Bellamy, Head Master
of Merchant-taylors' School.

H. B. Bence, Esq.

Mr. H. Bennington.

Mrs. Berney, Morton.

David Bevan, Esq. 5 copies.

Robert Bevan, Esq. Rougham.

John Bidwell, Esq. London.

L. S. Bidwell, Esq. Thetford.

Rev. George Bidwell, Standon.

J. Blackburne, Esq. St. John's
College, Cambridge.

Rev. T. C. Blofeld, Hoveton.

Giles Borrett, Esq. Yarmouth.

Mrs. Borthwick, Upper Park Cottage, Dedham.

Rev. J. D. Borton, Blofield.

Rev. Joseph Bosworth, Vicarage,
Little Horwood.

John Brightwen, Esq. Yarmouth.

Rev. Tho. Breadhurst, Brandeston.

J. T. Brockett, Esq. F.S.A. Newcastle.

Rev. Charles Brooke, Ufford Place.

Mrs. J. Brooke, East Bergholt,
Dedham.

Miss Brooke, Hemel Hempstead.

Rev. James Brown, Norwich.

Rev. Thomas Brown, Hemingston.

Mrs. Brown, ditto.

Rev. Lancelot R. Browne, Kelsale.

Rev. Wm. Browne, Marlesford.

Mrs. Browne, Elsing.

Rev. Chas. Cambell, Weasenham.

The Ven. G. O. Cambridge, Archdeacon of Middlesex and Prebendary of Ely.

Mrs. George Cambridge, Twick-
enham Meadows.

Rev. George Capper, Wherstead.

Miss Cappers, Beacon Hill, Mart-
lesham.

J. S. Cardale, Esq. Leicester.

Rev.Wm. Carr, B.D. BoltonAbbey.

Rev. Joseph Carter.

Rev. Thos. Carthew, Woodbridge.

Rev. Thomas Catton, St. John's
College, Cambridge.

Rev. Dr. Chafey, Master of Sidney
Sussex College, Cambridge.

Rev. Edw. Chaplin, Camden Town.

Rev. Dr. Chevallier, Aspall Hall.

Charles Chevallier, Esq. ditto, ditto.

Rev. C. Chevallier, Badingham.

Rev. John Clarke, Woodbridge.

Miss Clough, Feltwell.

Rev. Edward Cobbold, Watlington.

John Cobbold, Esq. Ipswich.

Rev. S. Cobbold, Woolpit.

T. W. Coke, Esq. M. P. Holkham.

H. Colby, Esq. Yarmouth.

Rev. Samuel Colby, Ellingham.

Rev. William Colby.

Rev. A. Collett, Heveningham.

Rev. N. Colville, Livermere.

James Colvin, Esq. Grove, Little
Bealings, near Woodbridge.

R. Crawshay, Esq. Honingham.

Francis Cresswell, Esq. Lynn.

Rev. Thomas Crompton..
Charles Crowe, Esq. Coddenham.
Rev. Henry Crowe, Bath.
Philip Crowe, 45, Montagu-squ.
W. H. Crowfoot, Esq. Beccles.
Rev. B. Cubitt, Stoley.
Rev. W. Dalton, Swaffham.
William Dawes, Esq. Bank of England.
Capt. Davy, R. N. Mount Amelia, Ingoldisthorpe.
Rev. Charles Davy, Barking.
Mrs. Davy, Barking.
Miss Davy, Barking.
Miss C. Davy, Barking.
Miss M. D. Davy, Barking.
D. E. Davy, Esq. Ufford.
Rev. F. Daubeney, Bexwell.
Rev. J. Day, Hethersett.
Mr. Deck, bookseller, Bury.
Charles Devon, Esq. Loudham Hall, near Woodbridge, 2 copies.
Rev. W. F. Drake, Norwich.
Rev. Philip Durham, Ely.
M. Edgar, Esq. Ipswich.
Rev. A. Edwards, Great Cressingham.
Rev. Edward Edwards, Lynn.
Edmund Elsden, Esq. Lynn.
Mr. Etheridge, Stoke.
H. R. Evans, Esq. Ely.
W. Everard, Esq. Lynn.
Mrs. Everard, Dedham.
Rev. Henry Fardell, Prebendary of Ely.
Rev. Dr. Fawssett, Minister of Brunswick Chapel, St. Mary-le-bone.
T. Fisher, Esq. Cambridge.
Mr. W. S. Fitch, Ipswich.
John Fitz-Gerald, Esq. M. P. Wherstead Lodge.
Andrew Fountaine, Esq. Narford Hall.
Henry Francis, Esq. Norwich.
Mrs. Francis, Norwich.
Rev. Dr. French, Master of Jesus College, Cambridge.

Rev. —— French, Bedingham.
John Gage, Esq. Director S.A. Lincoln's Inn.
J. Garden, Esq. Redisham Hall.
Mr. Garner Gill.
S. H. L. N. Gilman, Esq. Hingham.
Rev. Theophilus Girdlestone, Baconsthorpe.
Rev. W. E. Girdlestone, Ke ling.
Mrs. Girdlestone, Kelling Hall.
Rev. W. Girling, Scarning.
Mr. John Andrew Girling, jun. 45, West Smithfield, London.
Rev. John Glasse, Burnham Westgate.
Robert Gooding, Esq. Southwold.
Rev. John Griffith, Ely.
E. H. Grigson, Esq. Saham.
Rev. Wm. Grigson, Saham.
Rev. John Hindes Groome, Earl Soham.
John Gunn, Esq. Lincoln's-Inn.
Rev. W. Gunn, Smallburgh.
Daniel Gurney, Esq. North Runcton.
Mrs. Henrietta Gurney, Norwich.
Hudson Gurney, Esq. M. P. 2 copies.
Rev. Robert Hamond, Swaffham.
Miss Hamond.
Rev. R. Hankinson, Bilney.
Rev. W. Hardwicke, Outwell.
Thomas Harvey, Esq. Northwold.
Mrs. Harvey, Watton.
Miss Harwood, Ely.
Rev. B. G. Heath, Creeting All-Saints.
Miss Helsham, Burnham.
Mr. George Helsham, Ely.
Rev. Cuthbert Henley, Rectory, Rendlesham.
Rev. Edward Hibgame, Jesus College, Cambridge.
Rev. Martin Hogge, Southacre.
Rev. Gervas Holmes, Copford.
W. J. Hooker, LL. D. Glasgow.
Rev. James Hoste, Litcham.

Hon. and Rev Frederick Hotham, Dennington.

Rev. Edward J. Howman, Hockering.

Rev. R. F. Howman, Beccles.

Rev John Humfrey, Wroxham.

J. B. Huntington, Esq. Hethel.

W. Hustler, Esq. Registrar of the University of Cambridge.

Mr. Ingle, Lynn.

Hugh Jackson, Esq. Wisbech.

Rev. S. Jackson, Blakenham.

W. Rhodes James, Esq. Barking.

H. N. Jarratt, Esq. Great Bromley.

Edmund Jenney, Esq. Hasketon.

Rev. George Jenyns, Prebendary of Ely.

Rev. Richard Johnson, Statham.

Rev. T. Kerrich, Principal Librarian, Cambridge University.

Rev. W. Killett, Kenninghall.

Rev. Geo. King, Prebendary of Ely.

Tho. W. King, Esq. Heralds College.

Rev. W. Kirby, F. L. S. &c. Rector of Barham.

John Kitson, Esq. Norwich.

F. Lane, Esq. Lynn.

James Lawson, Esq. London.

Rev. James Layton, Catfield.

Rev. William Layton, Ipswich.

Rev. W. C. Leach, Ely.

J. F. Leathes, Esq. Herringfleet Hall.

Rev. J. Lewis, Gillingham.

Mr. J. Loder, bookseller, Woodb.

Rev. John Longe, Coddenham.

John Longe, Esq. Coddenham.

Rev. Robert Longe, Coddenham.

Rev. R. Lucas, Oxburgh.

Lynn Subscription Library.

Rev. Thomas Mack, Tunstead.

Rear-Admiral Manby, Northwold.

Matthew Manby, Esq. Kettlestone.

Miss H. L. Marcon, Swaffham.

Jonathan Matchett, Esq. Lakenham.

Rev. John Metcalfe, Canterbury.

Rev. Wm. Metcalfe, Foulmire.

Rev. Thomas Methold, Prebendary of Norwich.

Rev. George Millers, Ely.

Rev. W. Millers, Rector of Aberdaron, 2 copies.

Major Edw. Moor, Bealings Hall.

J. Morse, Esq. Swaffham.

Mr. E. Muggridge, bookseller, Lynn, 2 copies.

Rev. T. C. Munnings, Gorgate.

Rev. W. Newcome, Hockwold Hall.

Rev. T. Newman, Little Bromley.

Norfolk and Norwich Literary Institution.

Rev. Henry North, Ringstead.

Mr. John Notcutt, Ipswich.

Rev. James Oakes, Tostock.

The Venerable J. Oldershaw, Archdeacon of Norfolk.

W. W. Page, Esq. Woodbridge.

Francis Palgrave, Esq. F. S. A. 26, Duke street, Westminster.

Rev. Benj. Parke, Prebend. of Ely.

Rev. John Partridge, Cranwich.

Rev. George Peacock, Fellow of Trinity College, Cambridge.

Wm. Pearce, Esq. Weasenham Hall.

Rev. Charles Penrice, Plumstead, 10 copies.

George Penrice, M.D Yarmouth.

John Penrice, Esq. Hobland Hall.

Mrs. Penrice, Yarmouth.

Henry Petrie, Esq. Keeper of the Records, Tower.

Rev. Daniel Pettiward, Onehouse.

Rev. Richard Pillans, Larlingford.

W. P. Pillans, Esq. Swaffham.

Rev. R. Pointer, Southery.

Rev. George Preston, M.A. Rector of Lexden.

Rev. Joseph Procter, D.D. Master of Catherine Hall, and Prebendary of Norwich

Rev. Rede Rede, Colchester.

Robert Reeve, Esq. Lowestoft.

F. R. Reynolds, Esq. Yarmouth.

Rev. J. P. Reynolds, Munden Rectory.

J. Robinson, Esq. Carbrook.

Mrs. Robinson, Carbrook.

Rev. John Romney, Whitestock Hall, Lancashire.

Rev. James Royle, Wereham.

Rev. John Royle, Rector of Compton Martin, co. Somerset.

Mr. Salmon, Stoke.

Col. Say, Downham.

Christopher Sayers, Esq. Yarmouth.

Mr. Seppings, Syderstone.

R. N Shawe, Esq. Keagrave.

Rev. Thomas Shelford, Tutor of Corpus Christi Coll. Camb.

Rev. Revett Sheppard.

Mr. John Shipp, Bookseller, Blandford.

Rev. — Singleton.

Robert Smirke, Esq. Stratford Pl.

Edward Smirke, Esq. Temple.

Sydney Smirke, Esq. F.S.A. 4, Carleton Chambers.

Rev. Joshua Smith, Holt.

Rev. T.C. Smith, Rector of Denver.

The Worshipful J. H. Sparke, Chancellor of the Diocese of Ely, and Prebendary of Ely.

H.P.Standly, Esq. Paxton, St.Neots.

Rev. John Standly, Diddington, 2 copies.

Mr. Steele, Stoke.

S. W. Stevenson, Esq. Norwich.

William Steward, Esq. Yarmouth.

Francis Steward, Esq. Yarmouth.

Rev. Mr. Stratton, Boughton.

Mrs. Styleman, Snettisham.

Rev. Dr. Sutton, Norwich.

George Swaine, Esq. Broxbourn, Herts.

Robert Swallow, Esq. Watton.

Swinborne and Co. booksellers, Colchester.

Rev. Ralph Tatham, B.D. Public Orator of the University of Cambridge.

Rev. Geo. Frederick Tavel, Campsey Ash.

Rev. Geo. Taylor, LL.D. Dedham, Essex.

Mr. P. Thomson, Bookseller, New Road, London.

Rev. E. Thurlow, M.A. Prebendary of Norwich.

Rev. H. Tilney, Hockwold.

Rev. H. J. Todd, Settrington

Rev. W. G. Townley, Beaupre Hall.

Dawson Turner, Esq. 5 copies.

Rev. G. T. Turner, Kettleburgh.

Rev. Richard Turner, B.D. Yarmouth, 2 copies.

Thomas J. Turner, Esq. Colchester.

C. Tyrell, Esq.

Samuel Tyssen, Esq. Narburgh.

Rev. Edward Valpy, Norwich.

Sir C. B. Vere, K.C.B. Brooke Hall, near Ipswich.

H. Villebois, Marham House.

Rev. Ellis Wade, Blaxhall.

Mrs. Agnes Waddington, Ely.

Rev. George Waddington, Northwold.

Mrs. Thomas Waddington, Bury St. Edmund's.

Mr. Robert Wales, Fincham.

Miss Warburton, Dedham.

William Watson, Esq. Wisbech.

Frederick White, Esq. Bredfield House.

Rev. J. Neville White, Norwich.

Rev. Walter Whiter, Hardingham.

Roger Wilbraham, Esq. Stratton Street.

Robert Whincop, Esq. Lynn.

Rev. J. Whitmore, Polstead.

Mr. S. Wilkin, Norwich, 2 copies.

E.Wodehouse, Esq.M.P. Norwich.

Mr. Samuel Woodward, Norwich.

Yarmouth Monthly Book Club.

The Worshipful W. Yonge, Chancellor of the Diocese of Norwich.

Rev. T. Young, Necton.

# MEMOIRS

OF THE

# REV. ROBERT FORBY.

THE very first letter which I chanced to open upon my return from Italy, at the close of the year 1825, announced to me the death of the subject of these Memoirs. Four months only had elapsed since I had left him in the enjoyment of perfect health; and it had been fixed that he should pay me a visit immediately on my coming home, in order that whilst the impression was still fresh upon my mind, I might detail to him the principal treasures of nature, of art, and of learning, which I had seen in the magic regions beyond the Alps, and might thus at once gratify a man eminently qualified to receive pleasure from the recital, while I corrected any hasty or erroneous opinion of my own by the extensive knowledge, the sound judgment, and the good sense which I well knew that he possessed. But the grave had already closed upon one of

VOL. I.       b

the earliest, the kindest, and the best of my friends.

The letter which communicated to me this intelligence was from his brother in law, the Rev. George Millers, a Minor Canon of the Cathedral at Ely, under date of December 21; and it ran in the following terms:

" It becomes my melancholy and painful duty to acquaint you with the sad event which has thrown us all into the greatest distress and affliction. Yesterday morning, Mr. Waddington called upon our good friend, Mr. Forby, about one o'clock, while he was taking his bath, as usual. After waiting a considerable period, the family became alarmed; and, upon opening the door, they found that he had fainted in the water, and had been suffocated, and had evidently been dead some time. The news was immediately communicated to me at Ely; and, without losing a moment, I set out, and arrived at Fincham this morning. I need not say that it is a most bitter affliction and irreparable loss to us all. It will, however, be a source of much consolation, when the mind becomes composed, that, though his death has been awfully sudden, yet his religious and exemplary life leaves us every hope that he was fully prepared for the change, and will not fail to receive the reward of his proved service."

It were easy to dilate in panegyric upon the deceased, or in expression of the regret of numerous surviving friends: more difficult by far is the task of giving interest to the biography of an individual, whose days were passed in the quiet retirement of a village, most usefully indeed to society, and most honourably to himself, in the education of youth, the exercise of domestic duties, and the occupations of a parish priest; but unmarked by any of those occurrences which may claim to be recorded. The life of a literary man is seldom more than the catalogue of his publications: they indeed may remain, and may delight or instruct posterity; but it commonly happens that the "fallentis semita vitæ," trodden by the individual who composed them, presents an insuperable obstacle to our obtaining any intimate acquaintance with the author. The very time devoted to composition intimates seclusion; and seclusion is in every respect the contrary of notoriety. A portrait may make known " quæ membra, quis illi vultus erat," and a fac-simile of an autograph may acquaint us with the character of his hand-writing; and, from either the one or the other of these, ingenious persons may speculate upon the supposed talents or moral properties of the man; but the transactions and the occurrences of his life will remain unknown; or, if known, will only be matter

of interest to those, who, from knowledge of the
individual while living, love to dwell with affection
upon his memory. I speak, of course, of literary
men in the mass: in this, as in every other case,
there are of necessity exceptions which prove the
rule; when minds, cast in the highest mould, while
they distinguish themselves by their writings, have
still sufficient energy to take part in the more active
scenes of life; or when writings are impressed with
such a stamp of genius as to render the every-day
table-talk of the author, his opinions upon miscellaneous subjects and upon the events of the passing
hour, objects of general inquiry and interest.

To neither of these classes did Mr. Forby belong; and, excepting for the following publication,
he is scarcely even entitled to be ranked among
the number of authors. Nearly the whole that had
previously appeared from his pen, consisted only
of a letter to the Bishop of Norwich,*—a single
sermon,†—an antiquarian dissertation, printed with
his name, — and a few election squibs without
it; but equally known to have originated from

---

* "Letter to the Bishop of Norwich, on some passages in the Re-
ports of two Speeches, said to have been addressed by his Lordship
to the Church Missionary Association and Bible Society," 1815, 8vo.

† "A Sermon preached in the parish church of St. Peter at Man-
croft in the city of Norwich, on Good Friday, April 14, 1797, for the
benefit of the Charity Schools in that city." 4to.

him. The latter are designated by that playful
humour which strongly characterized the conversation and habits of the man. It will be sufficient
here to introduce, by way of specimen, the following epigram, which appeared at the time when the
late Mr. Windham came forward, in conjunction
with Mr. Coke, as candidate for the representation
of the county of Norfolk, and when his adversaries
strove to excite the popular feeling against him, by
charging him with the numerous changes in his
public career. It was entitled,

### THE POLITICAL WEATHERCOCK,

OR,

### THE WHITE COCKADE.

" When opticians a sunbeam dissect,
    Pure and white as it comes from the sun,
What plain folks would never suspect,
    They can shew seven tints mixed in one :
There's red, yellow, green, orange, and blue,
    For Tories or Whigs, both or neither,
Each to choose his appropriate hue,
    And then change, if they please, like the weather.
But such emblems, so stale and deceiving,
    Philosophical Windham derides,
And by white, which includes all the seven,
    Demonstrates that he's on all sides."

I could adduce many others of a similar description; but, meritorious as they may appear in the

eyes of one party, and harmless in those of both, I cannot consent to exhibit my departed friend in the light of a busy meddler in county elections. The minister of the religion of the Blessed Jesus has a different and a far more exalted character to maintain. The very magisterial office, however important their services may be in it, is barely compatible with the real interests of a clergyman. If it does not, as too often happens, excite angry feelings between himself and his flock, it causes them to regard him in a new light, as exalted above them, and thus in a manner estranged from them. Such a man, I speak generally, for I know many most honourable exceptions, can rarely become one of those, to whom the poet alludes, when he says that,

> " The service past, around the pious man,
> With ready zeal, each honest rustic ran;
> E'en children followed with endearing wile,
> And plucked his gown, to share the good man's smile.
> His ready smile a parent's warmth expressed,
> Their welfare pleased him, and their care distressed :
> To them his heart, his love, his grief were given;
> But all his serious thoughts had root in Heaven."

I dwell with the more earnestness upon the subject, as the circumstance of his having been placed in the Commission of the Peace was a source of the bitterest anxiety and sorrow to my friend. Warm, generous, open hearted, and unsuspicious,

and, to use the words of Horace, " uni æquus vir-
tuti atque ejus amicis," he acted from the impulse
of a heart that he knew to be right; but he did not
always give time to his judgment to temper his
conduct; nor did he always allow himself to weigh
the importance of self-controul and deliberate
judgment.

Hence he was led into errors, which, venial in
themselves, exposed him to the venomed shafts of
others, who exulted and triumphed over foibles,
which the good man would have viewed with regret
and pardoned, and the generous man would have
respected and defended.

More than five and thirty years have now elapsed
since I quitted Mr. Forby's parsonage at Barton,
to enter upon the busy scenes of active life; and it
is no less a subject of pride than of the most heart-
felt gratification to me to be able to say, that,
during all that time, nothing ever occurred to in-
terrupt the friendly feeling between us. The vir-
tues and the abilities, which, as a boy, I admired in
my tutor, I no less respected and loved, as a man,
in my friend; and the sentiments which I here
express, I am persuaded, are shared by the great
majority of those, who, like me, were indebted to
him for their education, as I am sure they are by a
large circle of surviving parishioners and friends:

Ευδευ· ἀλλ' οὐ σειο λελασμενοι ἐσμεν, ἐταιρε,
Ου μεν δη ζωοντος ἀκηδεες οὐδε θανοντος.

Mr. Forby was born of respectable, but far from opulent parents, at Stoke Ferry, in the county of Norfolk, and was educated at the free school at Lynn, under the care of the Rev. Dr. Lloyd, of whom he always spoke with esteem and gratitude, as an excellent master and an accomplished scholar. He had here the good fortune to have among his companions some men of distinguished ability, the Rev. Henry Lloyd, the son, of his master, Professor of Hebrew at Cambridge; the Rev. Thomas Catton, Senior Fellow of St. John's College, in the same University; the Rev. Thomas Carpendale, Master of the college at Armagh; and, though last, not least, the friend and preserver of shipwrecked sailors, Captain G. W. Manby, the man who above all others of our times has distinguished himself by his exertions in the cause of humanity. With all these he maintained more or less of intimacy throughout life. By Dr. Lloyd himself he was particularly esteemed and regarded, as a scholar of whom he had reason to be proud. I remember, while I was his pupil at Barton, an application to him on the part of his old master, to furnish an inscription for a drinking cup, made from the stem of a mulberry-tree, which had grown in the school play-ground at the time he lived there, but had then recently fallen from age. The following is a copy of what he sent; and it is the only one I now remember of many similar productions which were once in my possession. I regret that I have not preserved more; for, trifles as they are, I feel that they were particularly qualified to convey a correct idea of that neatness of taste and feeling which in an eminent degree marked his classical acquirements.

> " Me quondam viridi comâ decoram
> Noras, tu virides vigens per annos :
> Mori sis, utinam, memor vetustæ ;
> Lapsæ relliquias tenes ; senectus
> Oppressit, cecidi ; cades et ipse.
> Dum tempus sinit invidum bibendum est."

I may, I hope, be allowed to quote another trifle of the same character, which the late Dr. Sayers has preserved in the last edition of his " Dissertations." The ancient font belonging to the church of Burnham Depedale had been removed from its place; and its stones would have been dispersed and lost, had not Mr. Forby collected them, and rebuilt in his garden that very curious monument " antiquæ laudis et artis." This done, he added to it the following inscription:

> ." NE PEREAT INDIGNUM PERIRE,
> NE QUO TURPI CONTAMINETUR USU,
> HOC BAPTISTERIUM,
> ARTIS ANGLO-SAXONICÆ OPUS,
> A STUDIOSIS NOVITATIS

LOCO PROPRIO DETURBATUM,
HIC POSITUM, A. D. M.DCCCVII.
ID SALTEM ANTIQUI JURIS OBTINET,
UT NON NISI CŒLESTEM AQUAM CAPIAT."

From Lynn Mr. Forby was removed to Caius College, Cambridge, where he graduated in 1781, and soon after became a Fellow; and where he would have continued to reside, but that the late Sir John Berney, in an evil hour, induced him to resign his fellowship and abandon his prospects in College, for the sake of retiring into the country and undertaking the education of his sons. He received from Sir John the small living of Horningtoft, in Norfolk; but all other expectations from that quarter were frustrated by misfortunes on the part of the Baronet. Mr. Forby, who, in the full confidence that he had now found his harbour, and bidden farewell to hope and fortune, had fixed himself at Barton Bendish, in the immediate vicinity of his intended patron, and had taken his mother and sisters to reside there with him, was obliged to have recourse to pupils for his sustenance. Shortly after this time, my connection with him commenced in the year 1790: he begun with the intention of receiving two scholars, and before I left him in 1793 the number had increased to six. The diffusion of his well-merited celebrity caused even this number in a few years to be nearly doubled, till in

1297 he found it necessary to engage a larger residence, and removed from his confined parsonage at Barton to Wereham. Two years subsequently, the death of his uncle, the Rev. Joseph Forby, wholly altered his situation and his views. He came into possession of the valuable living 'of Fincham, an adjoining parish, the presentation to which belonged alternately to his family and to the Crown; and he fixed himself there, never again to move, in 1801. Pupils he still continued to take, but they were no longer necessary to furnish him with daily bread; and every one who has been conversant, in however slight a degree, with education, knows that the daily and hourly annoyances necessarily attendant upon it are such, that no motive can ever thoroughly reconcile the mind to the irksome task, except the spur of more irksome necessity.

Hence vexations arose, of which, in a letter, written to me about this time, he thus feelingly complained: " The father of one of my pupils lately took upon himself to address to me a sort of language which I was not disposed to brook; for I am proud, you know; a mighty good sort of a man, but of no great amplitude or elevation of mind, he thought fit to descant much on my *pecuniary* obligations to him. I found myself obliged to tell him that I did not desire any man to send his son to me who did not think the obligation perfectly mutual; and this unexpected and incomprehensible remark producing language more affronting still, I added, that I should feel uneasy in having the care of a pupil whose father did not feel entire confidence and satisfaction; and, as that did not seem to be the case with him, I wished him to remove his son. The lad and I parted on the best and most friendly terms; he did all he could to induce his father to relent, but in vain: he will speak kindly and gratefully of me. I have also lost another pupil. I have neither room nor disposition to enlarge on the very unhandsome manner in which I have been treated in this case. The fact is this; my having *an usher* gives offence. It is to no purpose to observe, that if I be fit to be trusted at all, I am fit to be trusted with the choice of an assistant, and that I know best whether my assistant answers my purpose or not. Education being one of those subjects which every body understands intuitively, my experience and skill go for nothing in this matter; and, except I will do every thing myself, I am not to be confided in. I expect more attacks of this sort, and have no doubt, *entre nous*, that my numbers will dwindle, perhaps rapidly: so let them; I *will* have an assistant as long as I am persuaded in conscience I want one; and when I have no more boys than I can abso-

lutely attend to in every point myself, I will dis-
miss him."—I have indulged myself in this long
extract, not so much to show the situation, as the
feelings, of the man; but he nevertheless continued
to take pupils for above ten years more, and at
last relinquished them with regret, so thoroughly
does use grow into a second nature. At the time
the complaints just alluded to were made, Mr.
Forby had added to his very important duties at
home more than one of a public nature, which,
however they might contribute to his importance
in the scale of society, were but little calculated to
extend the sphere of his real usefulness; and he
soon felt the burthen oppressive. In writing to
me upon the subject in 1803, he says, " Indeed,
till you have experienced the heavy drudgery of an
acting Justice, Deputy Lieutenant, and Commis-
sioner of the Land Tax, one of two on whom the
burthen of a large district lies, you will not readily
conceive the fatigue they cause to the mind. Of
the fatigue of my daily domestic occupations you
are a competent judge: this is to be added to the
other; and, when I have left home soon after
breakfast, and return at 5 o'clock to a solitary dinner, which I abhor, with my head full of parish
rates, surveyor's accounts, vagrants, rnn-away-
husbands, assaults, petty larcenies, militia lists and

substitutes, tax duplicates and distress warrants,
some or all of these jumbled together in a horrid
confusion; and, my dinner dispatched, sit down to
have my aching head split by prosaic verses, bald
themes, or abominable lessons, tell me is it wonderful if I take up any slight amusement that lies in
my way, kick off my shoes, and lounge by the fireside,
or try to win sixpence of my mother at cribbage?"

I have already spoken cursorily of Mr. Forby as
a scholar, and upon this point it were of course as
easy as it were agreeable for me to dilate. Whether he was what would in the present day be regarded as a profound and critical Grecian, I cannot presume to consider myself competent to decide. I have heard Dr. Parr say that he was not;
but every one who knew that most learned and
extraordinary man, knows that his judgment was so
affected by strong and unchecked feeling, that im-
plicit reliance was by no means to be placed upon
his opinions, when the object of them was an individual who might by any accident be brought into
collision with himself, or who was opposed to
his favourite doctrines. That Mr. Forby was far
from a contemptible scholar may, I flatter myself,
fairly be inferred from a "Dissertation upon the
different uses of the middle Verb in Greek," written when he had scarcely attained to the age of

twenty. This Dissertation, addressed to his friend
the Rev. Charles Davy, the present rector of Barking, in Suffolk, displays extensive reading and great
ingenuity; and, if it is not entirely satisfactory, I
will venture to say that its not being so is in no
small degree attributable to the subject itself. It
was printed by Mr. Davy's father, himself a Suffolk
clergyman and of the same name, in two volumes
of "Letters upon Subjects of Literature," a work
full of erudition, strong sense, good feeling, and
genuine piety, but by no means known as it deserves, being principally devoted to one of those
topics the most difficult to be explained and understood, the Music of the Greeks. For the same gentleman Mr. Forby afterwards composed the following epitaph, which, in speaking of his classical at-
tainments, cannot be considered out of place, as
serving to display them in another point of view.
It has never, I believe, appeared in print,* and in
sending it to me he observed, that nobody would
know whence it came, indeed that he was very diffi-
dent of his skill in these matters:

Carolus Davy, A. M.

Rector hujus ecclesiæ,

et ecclesiæ de Topcroft in com. Norf.

* I do not even know if it was ever used for the purpose for which
it was designed; for Mr. Forby at the same time sent another, which
it is probable, was preferred, as being much shorter; or probably his
advice was adopted, to take one in English, in preference to either.

vir bonus, pius, ingeniosus, eruditus,
verae Religionis et studiis et moribus cultor,
artium elegantiorum subtilis judex,
doctrinarum quoque severiorum non mediocriter peritus,
Paralysi correptus,
vitae aerumnosae taedium,
aegro et debilitate corpore,
sed mente inconcussâ,
sex annos fortiter et piè perpessus est ;
altero tamen et saeviore ictu
afflictus needum oppressus,
egregiis animi dotibus per alterum sexennium superstes,
tandem occubuit
octavo die Apr. An. Dom. M.DCC.XCVII,
septuagesimum et quintum annum agens.
Talem virum dum ademptum flemus,
tantis ereptum malis laetamur.

Even those who have read Mr. *Davy's Letters* may be ignorant that the Dissertation just mentioned was written by Mr. Forby; for it is only signed with his initials, and his name is not once mentioned in the work. Nothing more of his classic compositions was ever printed. I wish they had been; for I am sure they would have done him credit. Of my own knowledge I can venture fearlessly to affirm that it would be difficult to find any man who was more sensibly alive to the beauties of style, especially in poetry, and that few were more conversant with the most esteemed authors of Greece and Rome. His memory was stored, his

mind was tinctured, and his conversation was enriched with them: he studied them himself with
intense delight, and he equally delighted in des-
canting upon the varied excellencies of each to his
pupils.   Nor were the seeds always scattered upon
ungrateful soil;  for, of the comparatively small
number of those educated under his care, the names
of three are to be found upon the rolls of fame at
Cambridge, as distinguished in their academical
career by the highest of classical honours, the having obtained the Chancellor's medal.   He was no
less conversant with the classical writers of our own
country, among whom, as Theocritus, Horace, and
Virgil, among the ancients, he had studied Chaucer, Shakspeare, and Pope, with particular attention, and had often amused himself with annotating
upon them.   But every memorandum of this description appears to have perished with him, as did
his correspondence, whence I might otherwise have
drawn curious and copious materials for this Memoir, for the present scantiness of which I cannot
too much apologize.

The favourite amusement of Mr. Forby's leisure
hours was the study of Botany and Architectural
Antiquities, the one naturally congenial to a mind
accustomed no less by taste than by duty to "look
through nature up to Nature's God," nor like the

brutes that perish, content " pinguescere glandibus,
neque arborem aspicere unde ceciderit fructus;"
the other scarcely less naturally springing from the
habit of conversing with the authors of days long
past. To botany he was more particularly attached
during the time which I spent with him; and it was
no less my pleasure and my pride to accompany
him in his botanical rambles, than it is at present
to acknowledge that I am indebted to his precepts
and example for any proficiency which I may have
myself made in this delightful pursuit. The following extract will tend to give some idea of the ar-
dour with which he cultivated it: " Be it known
that I feel myself more eager and alert about
botany now than I have ever done. Almost every
day since my return home I have done something.
Do not, however, suppose that I have done much,
and am speedily coming forth to immortalize myself by new discoveries. Remember how miserably
low my collection is, even in common plants, and
in what confusion. I have *stumped* into that ex-
quisite spot, Shouldham Common, and made discoveries: none, indeed, extremely rare: among
them *Teucrium Scorodonia* on the edge of a fen-
ditch, very luxuriant and shrubby; *Hypericum
humifusum* and *Galium procumbens.* Apropos: not
the *Galium spurium;* where does it grow? I have

for you a specimen of *Orobus tuberosus* and *Lathy-
rus Aphaca.* *Oenanthe crocata* I have found for
you; but it dries most intractably. I wish you
would gather me two or three dozen seeds of *Ononis
repens :* 1 have two reasous; I should like to sow
it in my garden, to try how it will keep its character; and I wish to compare its seeds with those of
the other two species, if such they be, which I find
abundantly here. I am in some hopes of detecting
a specific difference between *arvensis* and *spinosa*
in the seeds. If this occult difference be ascertained, then are the thorns a sufficient *primâ facie*
character, and the business is done at once."

The letter just quoted was written prior to the
year 1798, at which time Mr. Forby was elected a
Fellow of the Linnæan Society, the only literary
or scientific distinction which he ever obtained.
His decided taste for antiquities commenced subsequently to that period, and had its origin in the
comparative failure of his eye-sight, which to a
great degree disqualified him for botany. " You
have heard, it seems," he says to me in 1805, " of
my lately acquired taste for antiquities. It is impossible to say how much I am amused by it.
Never did I examine a new plant found at length,
at the expence of much fatigue, with more delight.
The plain fact is this; my eyes are by no means

good enough to be trusted with the examination of microscopic objects; and it is a very foolish thing to play tricks with eyes. I am therefore come to a sort of *stand still* in botany. Architectural antiquity fell in my way accidentally, and I much delight in it."

Nearly at the same time an application was made to Mr. Forby to assist Mr. Miller, then engaged in reprinting Blomefield's History of Norfolk, with an additional volume, supplying those points in which our county historian is notoriously deficient, and bringing down the succession of property, &c. to the date of the publication. The proposal was so much to his taste that he would readily have joined any other in the task, though he himself shrank from the responsibility of general editor. On the same ground he resisted a similar application to write an introductory Essay to " Cotman's Architectural Antiquities of the County." " I am very willing," said he, " to communicate to Mr. Miller any thing I know upon the subject, and I should be truly glad to assist Mr. Cotman, who was lately for a day or two in my house, and to whom I pointed out several things in the neighbourhood, with which he will enrich his collection. I am much pleased with what he has done: so far as I have been able to follow him, he is very accurate, a main point with all who design

for your antiquaries, who are humdrum matter-of-
fact folks, very fond of accurately discriminating,
and very much afraid of being led astray by the
picturesque. As to Mr. Miller, to tell you the
truth, I have occasionally amused myself with an
indistinct intention of doing something to serve as
a sort of supplement to the History of Norfolk in
that particular in which it is most deficient. Neither Blomefield nor his continuator seems to have
had discriminative taste or judgment in architectural antiquity. Indeed, how should they? it is in
a manner new ground, opened since their time,
and indefatigably beaten. Our remains of ancient
art (and among them, I believe, an unusual proportion of very ancient ones) are yearly dwindling
away, by stupid disregard, by perverse innovation,
by wanton mischief, and even by dishonest depre-
dation. It seems therefore that a man would not
·waste his time in recording the actual state of
things, not with minute descriptions, which would
spread into immeasurable length, but as compre-
hensively and distinctly as possible. Such a survey
would, in a very short time, cease to be a view of
the present, and become a history of the past, and
would therefore progressively increase in interest
and value. I had thought of throwing our
·Churches into their several classes of round-arched

style, and three separate orders of pointed-arched, leaving (perhaps a greater number) those unclassed, which bear no certain mark of their age; under them to mention towers, fonts, crosses, stalls, monuments, and other subordinate points: such I mean as are distinct; to notice briefly the present state and quantum of remains of monastic edifices, and to pay attention to castles, such as Rising; castellated mansions, as Caistor; and manor houses, as Arminghall. Now, it is plain, that, with a series of engravings to refer to, the two things, *conjurando amicè*, would make an interesting publication. But my life is so far advanced that in all probability the idea will end where it has begun. The friendly solicitude you express for my literary character only causes me to smile. You are asked, you tell me, "what has he done?" And does such a question gall you? indeed it makes me laugh; and, let me tell you, a strong spice of contempt is mixed with my merriment. The next time the question is proposed, tell the querist (I do not desire to know who it is) he has laboured honestly and, in some cases, successfully, to make others better men and better scholars than himself. But I suppose to *do* means *print :* to be sure it is a word of very extensive import, and I think this meaning of it is almost as ludicrous as any of those which my poor old friend, Dr. Smith, of Caius College, attached to it, who used it on all occasions. Let me tell you that most of the very best teachers, public and private, to whom I am as nothing, have *done nothing*, because they have had something else to do. I tell you again that I think I could *do* such a book as I have just mentioned, and it is not impossible but I may. But I also tell you again, as I have told you before, that if I were to *do* any thing which will really tend to raising my literary character *in public*, it will be professional. In the mean while, whatever is in private, such let it remain; I am satisfied, and read my books, and converse with my friends, and write to them now and then, and take my snuff at perfect ease, and utterly regardless of the foolish questions which are asked about me by prating puppies, who do not know me, and whom I do not desire to know."

With this extract I would conclude my remarks upon Mr. Forby's literary pursuits, did I not feel it necessary to say a few words with more particular reference to the volume which this memoir is intended to precede. Deprived as that work has been of its preface, and even of a portion of its intended contents, by the sudden death of the author, it is only by his letters, and perhaps only by those addressed to myself, that the full scope of his de-

sign can be made known.   I well remember, when
I was his pupil in 1792, the interest he took in collecting specimens of what he called the Doric dialect of his parishioners.   The first allusion which
I find to the subject in our correspondence, is in
1809, on the occasion of my sending him Jamieson's Scottish Dictionary.   " Thank you," says he,
" again and again for this book.  I have really never
met with so agreeable a Scotchman.  It would have
answered to have hired a cart to bring him.  Whatever becomes of his hypothesis that English and
Scottish are distinct from each other, and co-de-
scendants of Anglo-Saxon and other Gothic
tongues, to which I think objections may be taken,
it is certain there is a much stronger family likeness than I could have expected between the Cale-
donian and the Icenian languages.  Of about 1300
or 1400 words, which I have from time to time collected, I find above 250 in Jamieson.  If ever I
were to methodize and discuss and print my collection, this comparison would form a valuable part
of it, and would strongly illustrate what I have always thought."

The idea of methodizing, discussing, and printing, here casually mentioned, appears from this
time forward to have continually occupied a place
in Mr. Forby's mind, and gradually to have ac-

quired "decided form and feature." Reference is
made to it in the greater number of the letters
which I received from him. In June 1821 he en-
tered upon the subject more at large. "In the
long evenings and some of the foul days in winter,"
he says, "I may probably prepare myself to talk to
you to some purpose on my collection of Icenisms.
It is certainly very copious, but in a state of such
confusion and illegibility that it would be to no
purpose whatsoever to give you the perusal of it,
which you seem to wish. I agree with you that
such collections are not only curious but useful, and
might be made of public and general interest; are,
in fact, worth reading; and too good to be left for
an executor or administrator to throw into the fire
among other waste papers. And certainly that is
likely to be their fate, if they be not arranged by the
collector himself; for nobody else would be able,
if he were both willing and qualified. On looking
into my farrago, I find myself in possession of not
fewer than 2000 words and phrases. Some of them,
no doubt (say 500, but I think it is saying too much,)
might be classed as instances under general observations on pronunciation, perversion of authentic
words, &c.; but the rest would be fair provincialisms, to be arranged in alphabetical order, explained, derived, &c. Now, if I were ever to get

them into order, it would be my main object to explain and derive as much as possible: to prove
them to have been legitimate parts of the English
language, in a now obsolete state of it. I have a
very considerable number of etymologies, chiefly
from Somner, Junius, Skinner, and Jamieson. I
find a prodigious deal of Saxon and the connected
Northern languages. I am most to seek in French
derivations, of which I suspect many that I cannot
ascertain. Cotgrave indeed furnishes me some
good ones, and the Norman Dictionary a few more;
but this Dictionary was compiled for the especial
use of lawyers, to enable them to understand old
statutes, pleadings, deeds, &c., while all legisla-
tive, forensic, and what we now call diplomatic business, was conducted in that language; so that it
only incidentally contains the name of common
things, and general vernacular or vulgar phraseology. Our great strength certainly lies in Saxon:
I have a notion our Icenian ancestors got no important share of those "integra verborum plaustra,"
which Chaucer is absurdly said to have introduced,
writing, forsooth, his popular poems in a language
fresh imported, and which consequently nobody
could understand. When I cannot get derivations, I put down authorities; some from Chaucer,
Shakspeare, and the writers of former times who

have been raked out of their ashes. This at least proves antient usage. Indeed this *tracing back* seems the only way to turn such collections to use. Those who have previously made them, Grose for instance, seem to be satisfied with merely giving a catalogue of the words they have picked up, as they picked them up, without caring what they were."

With only one more extract I will close what remains to be said respecting the Icenian Glossary. The extract in question contains internal evidence of having been written shortly before Mr. Forby's death. He had been telling me that he had sent a *sample* of his vocabulary to our mutual excellent friend the Rev. George Turner, of Kettleburgh, and he proceeds to say, " To him and to you I am under different sorts of obligation ; to you for black-letter, &c. and to him for large and valuable con-tributions of materials. He and I agree exactly in our conception of what ought to be done; and we have exchanged many letters, in which he has sent me his approbation of this small part of my task in terms much stronger than I looked for. And yet, in reading what he writes over and over again, I am obliged to believe that he means what he says, and that our coincidence of opinion upon this sub-ject produces his approbation. I had better, I

think, give you the outline of what is intended.
The title will be this, or something to the same
effect, written out not in form but so as to econo-
mize room, " A General View of the popular East
Anglian Dialect of the English Language, as it existed in the last twenty years of the Eighteenth
Century, and still exists in what has hitherto passed
of the Nineteenth Century, consisting of, first, an
Introduction and three preliminary Essays, on the
origin and progress, on the principal characteristics
of pronunciation, and on the chief peculiarities of
grammar in that dialect: secondly, a Vocabulary,
with etymologies, ancient authorities, modern coincidences, occasional explanations, and examples of
usage: thirdly, an Appendix containing such matters as could not be conveniently arranged under
any leading words, as proverbial phrases, anomalous sayings, memorial reliques, quaint similes, su-
perstitious notions, or customs, still existing or
scarcely extinct, as far as they are connected with
language.   With a concluding Essay on the remarkable and almost universal prevalence of Anglo-Saxon Nomenclature in the Topography of
East Anglia.   By a Native East Anglian.   'Antiquam exquirite matrem.'   This, I think, gives you
a farther insight than you have had before; and the
extent is greater than you suppose, certainly

greater than I originally contemplated. No such view, as far as I know, has yet been taken of provincial or popular English ; and, as many of the materials are undeniably curious, if they be tolerably put together, it must be an accession to English Literature in one particular part of it. Whatever may be thought of its importance, it cannot fail to illustrate the history of the language. Now let me tell you generally what has been done. The introduction and preliminary matter, as far as the mode of pronunciation; grammar, not put together yet, but plenty of materials, though at present, "rudis indigestaque moles."—In the vocabulary, I have come to the end of R. For the appendix I have very considerable materials, but have begun no arrangement ; indeed for every part there will be need of much revision, correction, omission, and in some respects new disposition ; but I have the great comfort that what I have done is to a certain degree α που στω; and my hope is to have all my prefatory matter and all my vocabulary ready in three months time, when I purpose visiting you." —The three months passed, the visit was paid, and the incompletion of the work afforded but another proof of the "vanity of human wishes and human expectations !"

Having thus spoken of Mr. Forby generally, and

d 3

as a man of letters, and more particularly in reference to this work, a short but most pleasing portion of my task remains, and one which I might
aptly preface with the Virgilian "paullo majora
canamus.". I allude to the moral character of the
man. On this subject I feel I cannot do better than
adopt, with a few alterations, the eulogium pronounced by one of the most accomplished scholars
of the age upon another friend of mine, deceased
just twenty years ago; and I appeal with the full-
est confidence to every one who knew Mr. Forby,
whether what was said by Mr. Mathias of Mr.
Nicholls, may not with the strictest truth be applied to him.

"Of his high and important professional duties
he was neither unmindful nor neglectful. He was
regular in the discharge of his sacred offices as a
clergyman in his parish in which he constantly resided. There was a peculiar propriety and deco-
rum in his manner of reading; and in his sermons
he was eloquent, impressive, affecting, and always
perspicuous. To the poor his house was ever
open; and not only were they benefited by his precepts and example, but they were sure to find a
friend in their need, a comforter in their sorrows,
and a benefactor and physician in the hour of ill-
ness. He loved his country, he loved her laws, her

ordinances, her institutions, her religion; and her government; for he knew that they have made and still make England to be what it is. He abhorred the troubler of the state, the spurious reformer, the obstreperous tyrannic demagogue, and the disorganizing sophist. He dreaded also the influence and the principles of the Romish Church; and, however they may be softened or explained away by modern sophists, he deprecated their encouragement or their revival amongst us; but he loved that toleration and freedom, which the Church and Constitution of England, steering between opposite extremes, grant with evangelical discretion to every sect of Christians: in a few words, ' nullius obscuravit gloriam, nullius obstitit commodis, nullius obstrepuit studiis, dignitates non ambivit, quæstum non venatus est.' "

The same resemblance which thus prevailed in general traits of character was very strikingly marked in a particular one, filial piety to their mothers. In that sacred and bounden duty which is owing from a son to a parent they were alike eminently exemplary. Both lost their fathers at a very early period of life; and both were not only singularly affectionate, unremitting and unvaried in their attention and reverential attachment to their widowed mothers, but devoted themselves to

celibacy, that they might the more entirely perform
that duty. Both too had the satisfaction of seeing
their mothers live under their roof to a very advanced age. Mr. Forby lost his but one year before his own death at the age of ninety-three,
favoured beyond the common lot of humanity, not
so much in prolonged existence, as in having been
allowed to preserve the entire possession of her
faculties to a period so far exceeding the ordinary
life appointed to man. I make no apology for sub-
joining a portion of his letter to me upon the subject of her death; for, as I am sure that the sentiments there expressed, will at once be felt to be
highly honourable to the writer, and to be the genuine effusions of an unsophisticated heart, so I am
persuaded that the greater part of my readers will
regard them with a peculiar pleasure, at the respon-
sive glow in their own bosoms, which recognizes
the existence of similar feelings in themselves.
" You touch me sensibly," says he, "in the exact
conception and recollection you have of the nature
of my domestic protection of my venerable mother,
and of her gentle and beneficent character. But
of the origin and extent of that more than usually
close and lasting connection of parent and child
you can know nothing; and there are circumstances
which strengthen the case very much. Almost

from my earliest childhood I was sensible of her
sorrows and sufferings, and of the patience and
calmness with which she endured them. Reduced, I
may say, to poverty by the misconduct of my unfortunate father, she and her family were indeed relieved
and supported by near connections on either side ;
but on both sides she had to deal with harsh and
ungentle spirits, who knew not, or would not know,
how to treat a mind so mild and benign as hers ;
and who, in the very acts of their kindness, made
her feel much bitterness of spirit. Among my very
earliest recollections is a resolution to take charge
of my mother ; perhaps at as early an age as I was
capable of entertaining such a thought. I availed
myself of the very first opportunity, stopping short
in my probably more promising career in College,
and accepting a small benefice, with the curacy
and little parsonage-house at Barton. There began your knowledge of us ; from that time we enjoyed together the moderate comforts and conve-
niences of life, certainly not unmixed with its cares
and sorrows ; but tempering and alleviating them
to each other. I am persuaded that I both cheered
and lengthened her life ; and I am sure that she
soothed and calmed many vexations and anxieties
to me. We lived together in that mutual and
tender attachment, of which you are so sensible,

more years than could have been calculated; and
at length we are separated by a sickness and death
borne in a manner most consonant to the whole
tenor of her life; that ευθανασια, about which proud
philosophy prates, but which only humble simple
Christianity effects. And now, besides the high
and holy hope of meeting again, which cannot and
must not be indulged without trembling, does not
all I have said tend to suggest much consolation?
And there is another consideration which also yields
much of it, that my earnest wish (though I never
dared to make it my prayer) that I might not leave
her behind me in the world, has been accomplished.
Yet, after all, I severely feel my loss: even were it
not of one so reverenced and beloved, the loss of
one's constant companion for thirty-six years, and
the consequent total subversion of daily domestic
habits during so very large a portion of life, cannot
but be painful. This, however, must be overcome,
and a new set of habits formed; but it must be by
a very gradual process, and the result of effort."

With this, I close my memoir: it cannot but be
doubted that he who wrote the above, appealing
for the truth of what he said to one so well acquainted with the circumstances, was a good son;
and to be a good son involves in itself the being
a good man; for, independently of the command

from Heaven, that we should "honour our parents," what Cicero so beautifully said of our country is hardly less applicable to filial love, that " omnes omnium charitates mater amplectitur." Though many examples therefore of the virtue of the man occur to me, to multiply them were but to weaken what has been already adduced.

Again, then, to borrow the words of Mr. Mathias, " while I am conscious that my pen has been guided by a pious and disinterested affection, I trust that those friends into whose hands these few pages may fall, will either approve or excuse this little memorial of a most valuable man, whom I loved and esteemed while living, and whose departure I most seriously and most deeply regret."

D. T.

# INTRODUCTION.

FROM a writer who offers to the public a volume on a *Provincial Dialect*, and ventures to announce his intention of confirming, by *authority* and *etymology*, the strange words and phrases he is about to produce, some introductory explanation of his design may reasonably be required. The very mention of such an undertaking is likely to be received with ridicule, contempt, or even disgust ; as if little or nothing more could be expected, than from analysing the rude jargon of some semi-barbarous tribe ; as if, being merely oral, and existing only among the unlettered rustic vulgar of a particular district, *Provincial Language* were of little concern to general readers, of still less to persons of refined education, and much below the notice of philologists.

However justly this censure may be pronounced on a fabricated farrago of cant, slang, or what has more recently been denominated *flash language*, spoken by vagabonds, mendicants, and outcasts; by sharpers, swindlers, and felons; for the better concealment of their illegal practices, and for their more effectual separation from the " good men and true " of regular and decent society; it certainly is by no means applicable to

any form whatsoever of a *National Language*, constituting the vernacular tongue of any province of that
nation. Such forms, be they as many and as various
as they may, are all, in substance, remnants and derivatives of the language of past ages, which were, at
some time or other, in common use, though in long
process of time they have become only locally used and
understood.

Such is the general character of *Provincial Language*,
and to prove it on behalf of a very considerable district
of this country is the object of the present undertaking.
Whatever may be the value of the following collection
of *provincialisms* (which is for the public to determine),
it is undeniably far more copious than has ever yet been
made by any of the few writers who have given their
attention to the subject, and the discussion of it is also
much more particular. It is desirable that the reader
should conceive as clear a notion as can be previously
conveyed to him of the contents of this Vocabulary.
The best way of communicating it will be in a short
account of the origin and progress of the present collection, and of the determination, at length formed, of
submitting it to the public. The first hint was suggested to the author by observing, in his occasional
perusal of some of the old poets, and especially Shakspeare, many words and phrases in current use among
his rustic neighbours, and therefore readily intelligible
to him, though they seemed very much to puzzle the
annotators. Indeed, after much prolix and elaborate
criticism, a difficulty often remained as it was found,
which an East Anglian clown would have solved at
first sight or hearing. The commentaries themselves.

afford more opportunities of the same sort, in the mul, titude of quotations from old plays, poems, and pamphlets, not likely to be otherwise brought within the reach of general readers.

These archaisms, found to be still alive, though supposed utterly extinct, were thought worthy to be noted; at first in the margin of the book, but that being found inconvenient, a sort of common-place book was soon provided, and kept always at hand, to receive such additions as might offer themselves, lest matter so easily evaporable should escape. The collection increased; and, together with that increase, the wish to enlarge it still farther. An additional inducement was felt to dip into old books or pamphlets, in verse or prose, as opportunity presented. Living words and phrases were also noted with more vigilance and attention. This spirit of collecting was not, indeed, always and equally active through so many years, but it was never entirely dormant. Upon the whole the accumulation became considerable. And not inconsiderable were the opportunities and facilities of enlarging it. The author has announced himself a native East Angle. In fact, he has passed all his days, now not a few, within the boundaries of this ancient kingdom. He was not sent out of it for his school education. He was for some few years on the foundation of a college in our East Anglian University. He passed a few of his earlier years in Suffolk, and during the large remainder he has resided in Norfolk; always an inhabitant of villages, and by natural disposition, as well as by his profession, led into habits of familiar conversation with persons of different ranks in village society. Some months ago, a few literary friends, acquainted with the existence and the nature of his philological stores, repeated, with more earnestness, representations often made before, that by a little necessary preparation and arrangement they might be made no unacceptable offering to the public; at least to that proportion of it which is likely to feel an interest in any light thrown upon the history of our language. One of those friends who had long amused himself by forming a similar collection, principally in the county of Suffolk, powerfully supported his representation by frankly communicating it. It will readily be conceived that the two collections in great measure coincided. The additions, however, thus made to the original stock, were very considerable. If it should not be thought necessarily to result from this statement, the author thinks proper explicitly to declare, that every individual word and phrase inserted in the following Vocabulary has been in actual use within the time mentioned in the title-page. For the great majority of them he is himself responsible. To the accuracy of his principal contributor, or rather coadjutor, he implicitly trusts. And, with respect to those other contributions, which at different times have been incidentally received from many other quarters, he has been very minute and particular in his inquiry. Nothing has been admitted on vague rumour, or helped out by fancy.

But this summary account of the origin, progress, and completion of the East Anglian Vocabulary, does not seem to be all that is required as introductory to it, and explanatory of the true design and purport of the work. The author hopes he shall not be thought

to overwhelm it with introduction. He will be on his
guard lest he do so; but he is well aware that he is
about to incur some risk of that sort. It is the duty,
however, of every advocate to make out the best case
he can for his client, though he be obliged sometimes
to run into considerable length. The plaintiffs in this
case, claim to be legitimately descended from various
branches of a very ancient and honourable family.
Like many other members of good families, by the
changes and chances of a long course of years, they
have fallen in the world, and are now excluded from
that society in which they had a right to appear, and
utterly hopeless of being restored to it. But they are
still laudably tenacious of the honour of their high descent, and are anxious the world should know, that,
though degraded, they do not feel themselves dis-
graced; and still retain so much decent pride, as for-
bids them to associate and level themselves with a vulgar rabble of blackguards and raggamuffins, of spurious, ignoble, or unknown extraction. If their advocate
repeat what has been said before, and perhaps better
said, he ventures to hope that, he shall at least exhibit
some things in a new light; that nothing will be found positively "stale and unprofitable," or which has not a proper and sufficient bearing on the subject. If, on the contrary, he should say, what does not, in some particular
points, coincide with what has been said by writers of
the highest authority, he trusts that he shall never appear to violate the respect due to them from him; and
is ready most frankly to acknowledge, that it was the
strong light thrown upon the subject by them, which
may have led him, in some instances, to somewhat

different conclusions. And he persuades himself it will not be unobserved, that though he is in private duty bound only to vindicate his native dialect from the opprobrious charge of barbarous fabrication, he will at the same time, be virtually offering a like defence of *Provincial English* in general. With a view to making our introductory matter, as orderly and as distinctly intelligible as may be, and to confining it within due bounds, it is proposed to arrange it in the form of three Preliminary Essays. But before we enter upon them, it is proper, if not necessary, to convey some general notion of what is meant by the etymologies and authorities which have been mentioned. The first of these words may possibly be thought of ominous import, as intimating the danger of bewildering a reader in those intricate mazes of meaning, in which etymologists delight to expatiate. The author hastens to give assurance that no such danger is to be apprehended. Mr. Whiter may trace through half the languages of mankind, the "primordia vocum," till he finds them at length on the very threshold of Babel. While it is impossible not to admire the boldness and magnitude of his plan; the copiousness and variety of erudition, which, with perfect facility, he brings to bear upon it; the acuteness of his reasonings, and the aptness of his illustrations; we must consider it as far beyond our limited scope, and entirely beside our humble and modest purpose. Mr. Horne Tooke may, with consummate skill, dissect particles till he lays open their very component fibres. We may be delighted with the "Diversions of Purley," and gratefully acknowledge the utility of that work, to those

who are desirous of becoming acquainted with the mi-
nutest niceties in the structure of their mother tongue.
Yet still we must consider it as of very little concern
to us in our plain straight forward inquiry. All we
have to do is, simply, to refer certain words in a modern language, to what we conceive to be their arche-
types in an ancient one. This easy and direct process
is no more than to take some East Anglian word, in
actual modern use, and to trace its identity or near connexion with some word in the Anglo-Saxon language,
as that language is embodied in the great works of
Somner and Lye. In case of failure in this attempt,
to seek it in some one of the kindred Gothic tongues,
or dialects; the Teutonic, Belgic, Islandic, Suio-Gothic,
or Danish, * as they are to be found in the works of
our old etymologists, Minshew, Skinner, Junius, &c.
or in a great modern etymological work, Dr. Jamieson's Dictionary of the Scottish Language ; which has
very numerous points of coincidence or near connexion with our East Anglian. If no direct proof can be
found on behalf of a modern word, that it descends
from some branch of the Gothic stock ; yet some trace
of family likeness may still exist ; some particular
combination of letters, perhaps, or other characteristic
feature, which may pretty satisfactorily point out its
remote ancestry, though the actual pedigree be not

---

* It may be proper to observe, that to all the words cited from
the old etymologists are invariably affixed the Latin interpretations
found with them. This may be taken as a pledge, that ancient words
are not adjusted to our modern ones, merely by sound, or in any other
fanciful manner.

producible.\* If neither positive proof, nor reasonable presumption, can be adduced of such exalted extraction, a word may still be shewn to come of a very an-

---

* A particular account of these characteristic marks would be too digressive, if inserted in the text, and too cumbrous in a note. Many of the most important may be found in Wallis's Gram. Ling. Angl. Edit. Bowyer, 1765, pp. 164, &c. The learned author says that, of all the languages with which he was acquainted, the Anglo-Saxon abounds most in congruences of sound and sense; and that in one monosyllable more is often expressed than in other languages by compound or decompound words, or by periphrases. He shews this by comparing certain initial and final combinations of letters, with the ideas generally conveyed by words in which they occur; and adds examples. The initial combinations are *cl. cr. gr. scr. shr. sk. sl. sm. sp. sq. st. str. sw. thr. wr.* The final combinations are *ash. ambl. angl. imbl. ing. ingl. ink. inkl. umbl. ush.* Certainly more might have been given. And these are rather to be considered as a sample, than as an enumeration. On the same principle, an instance or two of these connexions of sound and sense may suffice here, and the reader, who wishes to examine more particularly, may follow the reference, given above, to Wallis's Grammar. Words beginning with *cl.* are said to have in general a signification of close contact, adherence, or tenacity; and that those terminating in *ash*, imply some mode of harshness, or sharpness. An instance of the former may be *clammy*, of the latter *dash*, of both jointly *clash*. To all these words Wallis's observation is applicable. In some, it is not so distinct, or perhaps fails. It is general, not universal. It may be further observed, that these combinations of letters, whether initial or final, but especially the latter, are peculiar to the northern languages; and if some of the former be found also in those of southern Europe, it is by no means improbable that they were left there by the Goths in their inroads. So that our words in which they occur, may, in default of proof positive, be reasonably presumed to have descended, either directly from our own Anglo-Saxon, or else, more or less indirectly, from some kindred Gothic dialect.

cient family, long settled in this country, and longer
still in some other, from which it came to contribute
to the riches of our multifarious tongue. In such cases,
also, weight may sometimes be allowed to family likeness. A word may be thought to have a strikingly
French air, yet none of its kindred be found in the old
French dictionaries.

After all, words may sometimes, perhaps very rarely,
be found, of which such an etymologist as the author
may feel reluctantly constrained to say, that they are
" nullis majoribus orta." Still he may be able to
shew " vixisse proba," nay, even " honoribus aucta,"
and that they were to be seen in the best company, at
different times, from five hundred to one hundred
years ago.* It seems necessary to fix the lowest limit
of antiquity somewhere; and upon that principle, what
the Roman critic says of a writer is here transferred
to a word.

Est vetus atque probum centum quod perficit annos.

This is all the author means by *etymology* and *autho-*

---

* The mode of referring to these authorities seems to require
some apology. It is as general as possible; for the most part only
by initial letters of which a table is prefixed. Very few actual cita-
tions are given, excepting those from Shakspeare. The references to
Dictionaries must of course be exact, the word itself being a sufficient
guide. In all other instances the insufficiency arises necessarily from
the mode in which the collection has been made. It was enough for
the collector, having satisfied himself, to put down the initial letter or
letters of an old author's name, or even o. e. for old English. Now
he comes before the public, he has only to express his hope, that his
accuracy, under such circumstances may be trusted. Were it even
possible, it would be very tedious and laborious, to go over the
ground again, in order to be more precise.

*rity.* When he has proved any one of these points, he has done all that can be fairly required of him, as it is all that he has undertaken to perform. He has shewn that his native dialect is genuine English, and was not manufactured at home for private use. And he cannot forbear figuring to himself some plain, unpretending, old fashioned East Anglian yeoman, unmercifully rallied upon his Norfolk or Suffolk talk, by some one very little qualified to correct him, lighting by chance upon this book, and discovering that he speaks a great deal more good English, than either he or his " corrector Bestius," was aware of. No doubt he would very naturally express his satisfaction at the discovery; ludicrously enough, perhaps, but more rationally than the Bourgeois, in Molière, who was so astonished and delighted to find that he had been talking prose all his life long.

# ESSAY I.

*On the Origin and Progress of Popular Language, with
a particular view to that of East Anglia.*

Quinctilian says that " Consuetudo sermonis est con-
sensus eruditorum."   Many passages to the same purport might be cited from many authors, ancient and
modern; but we may rest satisfied with the authority
of the great Rhetorician, and take his words as our
fundamental proposition.  On that foundation stands all
Language, provincial as well as national ; popular not
less than philosophical or poetical.  If a popular Provincial Dialect be avowedly the peculiar subject of
discussion, it cannot be considered separately on its
own merits, for how shall it be disentangled from the
National Language of which it is a part.  The most
that can be done for it is to have it always in view, and
never to lose sight of its peculiar claims to attention.
This is what is intended here.

To imagine that the vulgar fabricate language for
their own ordinary use is an absurdity.  They neither
do, nor can think of any such process.  They take and
use whatsoever is provided for them; and that provision is made, varied, and improved by the learned of
successive ages.  From them it goes downward,.
stamped with authority, which may very properly be.

called *classical*. A satirical poet, indeed, speaks con-
temptuously of

"The classics of an age which heard of none."

Pope, Dunc.

It is certainly true that many ages of mankind have
passed away without hearing of any classics. Yet all
had them. They were unacknowledged because their
influence was unperceived, though always efficiently
operating. We commonly give the distinctive appellation of *classic* to the great writers of Greece and
Rome. It is too confined a term, and does not appear
to be of much longer standing in our language than
a century. Before that time, the word was used in a
much wider sense, comprehending all those who fixed
the standard, or set the fashion of language, in any
age or country, rude or refined, learned or illiterate.
On this point, respect is certainly due to the opinion
of Roger Ascham. He says of Chaucer, that he
"valued his authority of as high estimation, as he did
that of Sophocles or Euripides, in Greek." Chaucer
died about 100 years before the birth of Ascham.
Within that period, no writer appeared who could pretend to any share of the high authority attributed by
the great "Scholemaster" to the father of English
poetry, whose age was certainly a brilliant æra in the
history of the English language. Improvement was,
however, tacitly progressive during that period, though
it be impossible to trace * it step by step. Contemporary

---

* "In order to trace with exactness the progress of any language,
it seems necessary — first, that we should have before us, a continued
series of authors; secondly, that those authors should have been
approved, as having written at least with purity; and thirdly, that

with Ascham, there were writers of indisputably *classic* authority. On comparing passages of Chaucer's Persone's Tale, or Tale of Melibeus, or of Wickliffe's contemporary Translation of the New Testament, with passages from the writings of Sir Thomas More, Arch. bishop Cranmer, Ascham himself, or even with the homely style of " Maistre Hugh Latymer," it must appear that much improvement had taken place in the construction of English prose. And with respect to poetical composition, we certainly find in the poems of Surry, Wyatt, and Spenser, " versiculos magis fac- tos, et euntes mollius." From that time to this, under a succession of eminent writers, the farther progress of improvement has been uninterrupted; but it is not necessary here to go into particulars of it.

It will be more to our purpose, to go back for a while to the age of Chaucer, and from that point of eminence and elevation, take a retrospective* view,

their writings should have been correctly copied. In the English language we have scarce any authors within the first century after the conquest; of those who wrote before Chaucer, and whose writings have been preserved, we have no testimony of approbation from their contemporaries or successors; and lastly, the copies of their works, which we have received, are in general so full of inaccuracies, as to make it often very difficult for us to be assured that we are in possession of the genuine words of the author." Tyrwhitt's " Essay on the Language and Versification of Chaucer," London, 1775. The same observations may be extended, in nearly equal force, a century after Chaucer, till the art of printing had not only been discovered, but improved.

* In this *retrospect*, the observations quoted from Tyrwhitt in the preceding note, acquire additional force at every step beyond their limit, the Conquest; till all traces whatsoever are lost in darkness palpable.

however indistinct and unsatisfactory it may be, in
order to dispatch at once, all that is intended to be
said on the present topic of discussion—the influence
exercised, more or less in all ages, by the learned and
refined, on the *popular* language of their respective
times. Our intended retrospect is covered with mists
and fogs which soon become quite impenetrable. The
writers of those dark ages were all monks; their subjects were almost entirely History, Theology, and
Legendary Biography; and they wrote in barbarous
Latin. Those who wrote in their native language,
such as it then was, were too few and too far asunder,
to constitute any thing like a series of native *classics*.
The only two, perhaps, who can be discerned with
tolerable distinctness, are Piers Plowman, and Robert of
Gloucester.* If we contrive to look above the mists and
clouds which there obstruct our view, we shall find it
much brightened in the *distance ;* a very great distance
unquestionably; for it is only at that of five or six centuries that we get sight of Cædmon, and Aldhelm, Bede,
Alcuin, and Alfred. All these, indeed, were still
monks, or educated by monks; but *they* wrote in their
native tongue; and, in the rude ages in which they lived,
were exactly what Chaucer and Wickliffe were, when
the Saxon language had become English ; and what
the illustrious Greek and Roman writers were, in their
respective times and countries of greater civility and
refinement—the arbiters of the language then living.
Neither are these great Anglo-Saxon luminaries to be

* The very few names which might be added, are principally, if
not entirely, those of Metrical Chroniclers, as the monk of Gloucester
was.

viewed as having burst forth from chaotic darkness, as
having had no predecessors, and as having left at their
death, so vast a chasm unoccupied by successors; but
as being the earliest known writers, whose works are
in part come down to us, in that language to which we
must trace back our own.

They had a language to work upon, and an ancient
one; though what it was before they had wrought upon it, we have extremely scanty means, if any at all,
of judging. There can be no doubt that they greatly
improved what they found, and largely contributed in
their days to make their native language the copious
and expressive one which it is allowed to have been.
The period in which they lived extended, from first to
last, nearly through the eighth and ninth centuries.
The improvements they effected were therefore successive. They were all students in monasteries, in
which some of them passed all their days; others went
forth into public and active life. Few of those religious establishments at that time had libraries and
professors. Those which had them were thronged
with youth from all quarters. It is not to be supposed,
that in those days more than in others, any great proportion of students reached considerable eminence in
literature; but they all carried away with them, and
diffused among society, some portion of such acquisitions as they had made. And it was thus that the
learned, in that as in all other ages, without coming in
immediate contact with the vulgar, exercised their
proper influence in providing language for them. Similar influence, which it is not possible to investigate,
had been exercised before, and was exercised after, the

times of those great men, by inferior agents, in darker times; though whatever might have been their literary productions, they have either perished, as though they had never been, or, what comes to the same thing, lie yet unknown and unexplored, the prey of moths and mice. In short, whensoever. there were any writers, they provided words and phrases to be conveyed directly or indirectly to the talkers. When it happened that there were no writers, the most intelligent talkers might afford some little help to those who were less so. In default of both, if ever that happened, as the mere vulgar would never conceive the idea that their diction needed any mending, nor if they did, would know how to set about mending it, it must even remain stationary till some other *classical* authority might arise to give it farther improvement.

On the general fact, hitherto taken for granted, that modern English is the lineal descendant, through many generations, from ancient Anglo-Saxon, few words are necessary, as it is universally admitted. We will only refer to the last chapter of Turner's excellent " History of the Anglo-Saxons," the subject of which is their language. He has adopted a very simple and striking mode of exhibiting the prodigious prevalence of Saxon words in present use, by printing them in a different character from those otherwise derived. Never were the words of a poet more happily exemplified and illustrated:

> Segnius irritant animos demissa per aurem
> Quam quæ sunt oculis subjecta fidelibus.

They exhibit the clearest *demonstration.* He has selected passages from the best authors of different ages,

beginning with Shakspeare, and ending with Samuel
Johnson. We will borrow one of those quotations;
which has the double recommendation of being at
once the shortest and the strongest.

" Then when Mary was come where Jesus was, and
saw him, she fell down at his feet, saying unto him,
Lord, if thou hadst been here my brother had not died.
When Jesus therefore saw her weeping, and the Jews
also weeping which came with her, he groaned in *spirit*
and was *troubled*, and said, where have ye laid him ?
They said unto him, Lord come and see. Jesus wept.
Then said the Jews, behold how he loved him." John
x. 32—36.

With the exception of proper names (which either
retain the same form in all languages, or are varied
only by some slight modification) this passage contains seventy-two words, nouns, pronouns, verbs, and
particles. Of these, all are Saxon, but the two printed
in italics, one of which is of Latin, the other of French
origin. This is, indeed, the English of the early part
of the century before the last. It is above two hundred years old. But it is also the English of the present day. Not one of the words, as they stand in this
passage of our New Testament, is either obsolete, or
in any degree unusual. If the passages had been trans-
lated in our time we should, indeed, very probably
have found it less purely Saxon. The passages quoted
by Mr. Turner from Robertson, Hume, Gibbon, and
Johnson, contain a much greater proportion of words
derived from other languages. But, as the author
well observes, " we must not conclude that the words
which are not Saxon could not be supplied by Saxon

c 3

words. On the contrary, Saxon terms might be sub-stituted for almost all of them." The force of the demonstration therefore remains unimpaired.

But, however certain be the proof that such is the origin of a vast majority of the words and phrases in the formed and polished diction of our most eminent writers in different ages, understood and approved wheresoever our language, in those different ages, has been in use,—will it be contended that the coarse talk of our common people, the vulgar and colloquial tongue of secluded or almost insulated districts, never heard beyond their respective boundaries, or if they should perchance stray abroad, perfectly unintelligible, and received with ridicule and contempt—will it be contended, that this is, to the same extent, derivable from the same source? It is the main object of the following pages, not only to contend, but to prove that it is so. To prove it, as far at least as one of the great branches of the common Saxon stock is concerned.

It has already been laid down as a principle, that the vulgar are in all ages provided with words and phrases by their betters. And, on due consideration of probabilities, it may farther be asserted, that the populace are likely to keep old ones safe and sound long after they have been forgotten by the followers of new fashions. There are several good reasons to expect this; first, because they make few migrations; secondly, because they receive few visits from strangers; very few from those who are likely to have influence on their language by sufficiently intimate connexion; thirdly, because new usages are very scantily imported among them in books. For all these reasons, the progress of change will be very slow among the stationary and unlettered vulgar; among whom many very ancient remnants of genuine old English, or rather of Anglo-Saxon, have remained hitherto unmoved, apparently still immoveable; some in one district, some in another, or in more than one, even perhaps, in many. No where, indeed, is the "well of English * undefiled" to be found; but every where some streamlets flow down from the fountain head, retaining their original purity and flavour, though not relished perhaps by fastidious palates. None can boast that they retain the language of their early forefathers unimpaired, but all may prove that they possess strong traces of it, and even scattered members in their proper forms. It would be absurd, for instance, to say that an East Anglian clown is actually speaking good English, when, to a fine lady, or a well-bred gentleman, he seems to be uttering a barbarous jargon. But it may be safely and justly alleged on his behalf, that he has much better authority for a great deal of what he says, (if he knew where to look for it, and if he could pronounce somewhat better than he does,) than is at all suspected by those who laugh at him, because they have never considered the matter in its proper light.

---

* Indeed, what is to be understood by "English undefiled!" Chaucer, to whom this compliment was paid, wrote a language much mixed and compounded. That of Spenser, who paid it, was still more so, and from the same sources. But what defilements did he suppose it had contracted? It seems to be no more than a poetical flourish; of which an etymologist can certainly make no use.

But it is not enough, thus generally and indefinitely, to acknowledge the Anglo-Saxon as the common mother of all the English that has ever been spoken, in every age of our history, in every part of our country, and in every rank of our countrymen. It is farther conducive to our purpose, limited as it is, to take as clear and as comprehensive a view as may be gained, without spreading into undue prolixity, of the whole posterity of our " Antiqua Mater," and of the foreign alliances and affinities contracted in different generations of it.

The Saxons brought their language into this country exactly in the middle of the fifth century. With the particular state and character of it at that time, it it is impossible that any researches can make us acquainted. No documents of it are now to be found. This we know, that not many years had elapsed, before those fierce invaders, to whom it belonged, throwing off the insidious character of allies, under which they came, had not only occupied the greater part of the country, but had driven out its ancient inhabitants, and replaced them by successive hordes of barbarous invaders from the north-western coasts of Germany.* The whole history of mankind does not afford a stronger, perhaps not so strong, an instance, of the entire conquest and extermination of a whole people by an invading enemy. Of all the proofs of such a conquest, the most cogent and demonstrative is that of language. In our case, the language of the invaders so totally † superseded that of the original inha-

---

* In little more than a century the country was parcelled out under the Heptarchy.

† This has, however, been denied; and some antiquaries of great

bitants, as to have soon become, in body and substance, the language of the nation, retaining no more than a very scanty sprinkling of the old British, and even that, in a great proportion of the instances, fairly disputable.

The language, thus introduced and extensively established, is called, by the learned and laborious Dr. Hickes, in his "Thesaurus Veterum Linguarum Septentrionalium," *pure Saxon.** He proceeds to consider it in a second stage, as intermixed with Danish words, introduced by the inroads of the Danes; and in a

---

eminence, though (with much deference be it said) not of the highest authority in the particular department of etymology, have contended for the Celtic origin of our language. Mr. Whitaker, the learned historian of Manchester, may be mentioned as an instance. But surely, the chapter of Turner's History of the Anglo-Saxons, may alone be accepted as an ample and all-sufficient refutation of that opinion.

* Though these nicely defined distinctions be not generally adopted, they are not without their use in disquisitions on ancient languages, or on ancient acts. In the eager pursuit of a favourite object in the dark, it is quite natural, that those who are most earnestly desirous of discovering it, should persuade themselves that they have caught a light, which others, less sanguine and more cautious, dare not trust. Still they may lead on farther through the gloom than any have gone before. The celebrated author of "Munimenta Antiqua," who (without a quibble on his name) may justly be denominated the Prince of English Antiquaries in an age in which the study of antiquity has been pursued with so much zeal and success, has ventured to discriminate Saxon architecture, as Hickes has divided the language, into three æras, assigning distinctive characteristics to each. It is to be presumed that very few have embraced his whole system. It is certain that a very great number of judicious antiquaries are still of opinion that no certain criteria have yet been established even between Saxon and Norman architecture. Yet how much light has King in his great work thrown on both.

third, as farther compounded with Norman. Now, without any disposition to question the differences, alleged to be observable at different times, which we have fully admitted to be always probable; allowing that those differences are fully proved by the several charters cited by Hickes; not presuming to question the decision of so profound a Saxonist on any philological point; we may still venture, on the fair open ground of historical fact or probability, to doubt the accuracy of these formal divisions ; and, however useful they may be in some views of the subject, to deny their utility in that which we propose to take.

And first, of the term *pure Saxon*. It is not to be conceived that the Anglo-Saxon on its arrival in this country, had any claim to the character, given by the Roman historian to the hardy natives of that country, from a skirt of which it came; that it was " propria, et sincera, et tantum sui similis." There are reasons very strong at least, if not positively demonstrative, that it was not so. There must always have been great affinity among the different languages or dialects (and they seem to have been scarcely more) of common Gothic origin. Our best etymologists, in case of their not * finding an Anglo-Saxon etymon of a modern word, assign one from some other, and perhaps from more than one, of the kindred Gothic tongues already

---

* And sometimes, and even not unfrequently, when they *can* find one. It is by no means uncommon to meet with a choice of derivations, from words iu two or three of the old Northern languages, in addition to the Anglo-Saxon ; words differing from each other, only in a few letters or a single letter perhaps easily commutable, and therefore having all the appearance of mere dialectical varieties.

enumerated. Who can pretend to account for the
*introduction* into this country of words from those languages? What events are recorded in the history of
the Saxons in this country, which can reasonably account for the adoption of words from more than *one*
of those sources, the Danish? And how far even that
may be allowed as an exception, will presently come
under consideration. And yet these nominally aliens
must have got among us, at some time, or in some
manner or other. Otherwise their posterity could not
have existed here, as it assuredly does, and is allowed
to do, at this day. The inference is unavoidable; that
they were mingled with the Saxon (so far as we are
concerned with it) *originally*. Our Saxon Dictionaries, like all other dictionaries of dead languages, have
been compiled from the written documents remaining
of it, in its different stages, whatsoever they may have
been. Those documents are very abundant. Some
have been printed, but many more are still in manuscript, and for the most part, likely so to remain. The
second volume of Hickes's Thesaurus, less bulky, indeed, than the first, but still a ponderous tome, consists entirely of a catalogue of Anglo-Saxon manuscripts, preserved in the libraries of the two Univer-
sities, in those of private Colleges, of Cathedral
Churches, and other repositories. Multitudes of these
have been laboriously explored by the great * Saxon

---

* Members of the University of Oxford, in which Saxon literature
has always been most diligently and successfully cultivated, and is so
still. Our acknowledgment of obligation is not to be confined to
writers of a former age. In particular it would be unjust, not to
comprehend in it, the late translation of the Saxon Chronicle, from

scholars of a former age, and the result of their labours has been a proof that the language was most
copious and various. There can be no doubt that much
additional proof of the same sort would be found, in
the still greater number of manuscripts yet unexa-
mined, and by the discovery * of others (and such no
doubt there are) not yet inserted in catalogues. The
general result of all would probably be, that for those
words which we now derive from the kindred † Gothic

---

a text amended by collation of manuscripts, enriched with learned
notes. And in this work, it would not be less unjust to pass unno-
ticed, the literal translation from the printed copies of those curious
annals, by an East Anglian lady; whose work was printed but not
published, about four or five years ago. Whatever additional value
may be conferred by collation and annotation, the Oxford Professor
could find no room to improve on the characteristic simplicity and
purity of our fair countrywoman's style.

* In like manner, the present bulk of Latin and Greek lexicography might be enlarged and enlightened, by the discovery of those
numerous ancient works, of the best ages, which are known to have
once existed, but are now unknown; many of them, probably, lost in
the dark recesses of vast libraries, yet unexplored. This may be particularly the case with those libraries which have been emphatically and
very aptly called the grave of manuscripts,—the Vatican and Ambro-
sian. The late edition of the supposed lost treatise of Cicero de Re-
publicâ from a manuscript imperfectly discharged, and with some
monkish theology written over it, found by the Abbate Mai in the
Vatican, is a highly curious specimen of the mode in which some of
those treasures have been lost and may be recovered.

† Of the strong traits of family likeness among the various languages or dialects descended from the great Gothic stock, a most
ingenious and convincing illustration is to be found in the fifth volume
of the Archæologia, in Mr. Drake's valuable Paper on the Origin of
the English Language. It is written in refutation of Mr. Whitaker's
notion of a Celtic origin. The learned and sagacious etymologist

tongues, we should find etyma in our own native stores; in other words, the intermixture would be proved to be *original.*

But, before we consider the probability of farther intermixture by the Danish inroads, it is necessary to observe in this place, that Hickes's *pure Saxon* was not only compounded with other Northern languages, but even with those of Greece and Rome. The admixture of Greek and Latin with English, in much later times, is a matter of separate consideration, to which we shall come in the course of our argument. What is now before us is their connexion with Saxon. We have no concern with the truth or error of the opinion of many great etymologists, that whatsoever in the Latin language is not Greek, Etruscan, or of some other very ancient dialect of Italy, is Gothic; deduced, in the course of ages and of intercourse, from some of the Northern tongues, left in some period of indefinite antiquity by Northern barbarians on their inroads into the regions of the South. We are neither concerned to assent nor to deny. We have nothing to do with the formation of the Latin language, or with its early

---

particularly compares two of the Gothic tongues; the Moeso-Gothic and the Anglo-Saxon. He has selected one chapter from the Gospel of Saint John, in the version of Ulphilas, and compared it, verse by verse, and word by word, with the Saxon version; and *through* that, has rendered it, still verbatim, into English; finding throughout, with very few exceptions, words which have been, or now are, in current use, or at least have a clear and undeniable connexion with such words. This surely is even demonstrative. The demonstration might in all probability be strengthened by a collation of the same chapter in the Islandic version. The three ancient Gothic dialects might be brought as near to each other as the two have been.

stages. It is enough for us to account, and we are abundantly able to account, for its having travelled far North in its improved and matured state. Wheresoever the Romans extended their conquests, there they left permanent and indelible traces of their language. Their arts every where followed their arms. Wheresoever they established provinces, and planted colonies, they communicated the blessings of civilization to the vanquished barbarians. That was the æra of the commencement of civil, social, and moral improvement among them. This must amply account for the incorporation of much Latin with Anglo-Saxon before its introduction into this country. In the region from which they came, the Roman power and predominance had been quite sufficiently felt to produce this effect. But farther; when the Saxons had been long established in this country; when they had become considerably humanized; when Christianity had been partially introduced among them by Augustine in the very end of the fifth century; and still more, when an incipient disposition to learning had been encouraged and improved among them by Theodore and Adrian in an advanced period of the seventh; direct intercourse with Rome became frequent. By this, indeed, we may more particularly account for the introduction of theological and ecclesiastical terms; but, upon the whole, through these several inlets a great deal of Latin must have been admitted, before the termination of Hickes's æra of *pure Saxon*. It is easy for any one to convince himself how great the proportion was, by merely running his eye down half a page of Somner, or Lye.

· And, with respect to Greek, still forbearing to bewilder ourselves in the mists of remote antiquity, (not
presuming to entertain the disputable and disputed
point, whether the Pelasgi, being a Scythian tribe, introduced into Greece, in a very early age, elements of
the same original and radical languagewhich spread
itself in other directions into the Northern regions,) we
may rest abundantly persuaded, that in much later
times, a great deal of Greek came to us "North
about." Dr. Wallis well observes, that polysyllabic
words from Greek or Latin would become in a
Northern language monosyllables, according to the
genius of those languages; and by such a change, become much disguised, and as far as possible from at-
testing their origin by their form. It is impossible to
forbear an occasional smile at the grave attempts of
Junius or Casaubon, to prove that some reputed native of a hyperborean region, of most barbarous and
rugged aspect, is in fact,

——nec Sarmata nec Thrax
Mediis sed natus Athenis !

And one may sometimes be tempted to laugh outright
at the endless genealogies of our East Anglian lexicographer, Mr. Lemon, in his most amusing of all dictionaries. We cannot, however, help conceding to
those recondite etymologists, that they produce many
striking, and even convincing resemblances, though
we are unable to assent to all they advance as proof.
But, be this as it may, no doubt can exist, that from
the many Grecian colonies on the coasts of Samo-
thrace, the Hellespont, and the Propontis, their language travelled along the banks of the Danube, and

intermingled itself with the Teutonic, and through
that with other Gothic dialects. This intermixture happened, indeed, in a much later age, but
quite early enough for our purpose. It appears that
the Moeso-Goths, who had their settlements in that
tract of country north of Thrace, and not far from the
mouths of the Danube, in the middle of the fourth
century, used letters nearly, or even exactly, resembling in form, in organic power, or in both, those of
the Greek alphabet. These letters are to be found
(and many words also) in the celebrated translation
of the Scriptures by Ulphilas the Gothic bishop, of
which the inestimable, though scanty, remains exist in
the famous Codex Argenteus at Upsal; and of which
ample specimens are given in the works of Junius,
Skinner, Hickes, &c. Now, whether the Gothic alphabet was borrowed from the Greek, when the Goths
first began to use alphabetic writing, or whether both
were deduced from Cadmean or other common origin,
we have no interest in inquiring. It would be going a
great deal too far back, and out of our way.

·  ·The introduction of Latin and Greek words into the
Anglo-Saxon, before it came into this country, de-
priving it, as far as they go, of the character of native
purity, having been thus, as it seems, reasonably explained; our next point of inquiry must be, the probable effect of the Danish inroads on the language so
compounded, in addition ·to that general intercom-
munity of the Northern dialects, which has already
been remarked. Perhaps too much weight has been
attributed to this. An attentive consideration of dates
may throw light upon the question. There is certainly
no little force in the historical fact that those very

Danes were themselves no other than Saxons. They
were the posterity of those who, after the successive
emigrations of their countrymen into this island, continued to occupy their own country, in the lower part
of the Cimbric Chersonese, on the sea-coast, stretch-
ing in general direction south-westward, thence to the
mouth of the river Elbe, and to a very considerable
extent inland. At an advanced period of the eighth
century they were expelled by the victorious arms of
Charlemagne, and sought new settlements in the higher
parts of the Chersonese; in the neighbouring islands
of the Baltic, now constituting the kingdom of Den-
mark; and in the southern parts of Scandinavia. But,
not long satisfied with the change, they began their
predatory adventures by sea; some came into this
island under the name of Danes; others went, under
that of Normans, into different provinces of France
long before their actual and permanent occupation of
Neustria. In point of language then, they could have
nothing more to contribute to the Saxon, which they
found here, than what they might have acquired either
at home, since their ancestors had migrated hither
about four hundred years before, or during their own
short migration, or that of their immediate ancestors,
northward. That so barbarous a people should have
had enough of the necessary intercourse with others,
to acquire much, is not very probable. Whether, of
what they had so gained, they were likely to communicate enough to make any characteristic change in
the Saxon, to effect a sort of new æra in it, is the precise subject of present inquiry. The Danes made their
first descent on our coasts in A. D. 787, and were very

soon repelled. During the following 230 years, they
made many successive invasions, at different intervals
of time. While they staid, their ravages were most
ferocious and desolating. " Their hand was against
every man, and every man's hand against them." In
every instance, the Saxons got rid of them as soon as
possible, either by force of arms, or by large contributions of money. Whether the time were long or short,
they were objects of too much terror and abhorrence,
to allow the possibility of such coalescence with their
enemies as to produce any considerable intermixture
of language. Time and peaceful intercourse must
have been necessary to effect that. Where colonies
were established, they must have been strong enough
to defend themselves, and have taken care to keep
aloof from the exasperated and desperate natives. At
the end of those 230 years of warfare and mortal
hatred, a Danish dynasty, indeed, mounted the throne
in A. D. 1017; but it became extinct in 1041, and a
Saxon prince succeeded. These twenty-four years
were too few to produce any great effect upon language, even if the two nations, no longer at deadly
feud, lived together in tolerable concord, as subjects
of the same sovereign. It was, moreover, very near
the end of Dr. Hickes's second stage of the Anglo-
Saxon language, and the commencement of the third.
But though it be, for these reasons improbable that
the whole mass and body of the national language
should have been affected by the Danish inroads, yet
there can be no doubt that stray words would be dropped here and there, particularly in those parts of the
island which were most completely overrun and longest

occupied by those fierce barbarians. None were longer or more completely so than our kingdom of East Anglia. The conclusion is that there must be much doubt and difficulty in ascertaining the *importation* of such a number of Danish words as to give any thing of new colour and character to the Saxon language ; that such a distinction is not worth making : certainly not in our view of the subject.

Nor does it seem easier or more important to account for the accession of a sufficient number of words from Normandy, and for the incorporation of them with the language of this country, while it bore the denomination of Saxon, to effect a change in the general character of it. About the same time, at which the Danes invaded this country, their brethren the Normans made equally destructive inroads into different provinces of France, and were either repelled or bought off in much the same manner as they were here. At length, at the very end of the ninth century, the illustrious chieftain Rollo obtained, from the imbecility of Charles the Simple, quiet possession of the rich province of Neustria, thenceforth denominated from its new masters, Normandy. The genius of Rollo appears to have been as great in peace as in war. He was soon firmly established in his new dominion; and wisely availed himself of all the advantages it afforded. His followers, not so numerous as to overpower and supplant the old inhabitants, as the Saxons did here, became amicably incorporated with them. The language, which the Normans carried with them, must have been very nearly the same which the Danes brought hither. But in their case, it was uninterruptedly blended with

that of their new country; and that mixture was what
may properly and definitely be called *Norman French.*
This term appears to have been used with too much
latitude. It is commonly said there is in the English
a great deal of Norman-French. The fact is, that
there is very little of what ought to be called so. It
is plainly and incontestably true, that no inconsiderable part of our language is French, and due attention
will be paid to it in its place. But it was not Norman-
French. Whatsoever could with propriety bear that
name must have been contributed during the Saxon
æra, which is limited in respect of language by
Hickes, and of history by the Saxon Chronicle, to the
accession of Henry II. in 1154. Sufficiently occupied
at home in consolidating and perfecting their new institutions, and securing them against their continental
neighbours, by whom they must have been regarded
with a jealous eye, the Normans, during the greater
part at least of the tenth century, appear to have had
very little intercourse with the Saxons in this country,
to whom they were neither enemies nor allies in their
almost constant harrassing struggles with the Danes.
To the Danish dynasty, which commenced in an early
part of the following century, they were even positively hostile; and afforded protection and support to
the exiled Saxon princes. Here was an opening, indeed, but it was late in the time assigned to the last
stage of the Saxon language; and it must have been
confined to persons of high rank, and their immediate
attendants. When the Confessor returned and mounted
the throne of his ancestors, it is well known that the
intercourse between the two countries became more

open, enlarged, and diversified, and more likely to
have effect upon language. But this state of things
continued but a very short time; only twenty-five
years. When the Norman Conqueror came over, together with the civil and military institutions of his
country, he brought also its language entire; that language, which, during more than two centuries, had
been gradually compounded by an intermixture of
French with the Dano-Saxon, or Saxo-Norman, or by
whatsoever other name it may be more distinctively
called, which had been introduced by Rollo and his
followers. This language (Norman-French) must of
course have contained much which the Saxon of this
country had not. But it is to be questioned much,
whether it were communicated or communicable to
any considerable extent. It was spoken and written
by all the higher orders in society; the court, the
great landholders, the superior clergy, regular and
secular. For the most part, indeed, it was their native
language. Those to whom it was not so, the very few
of the Saxon nobility and clergy who were allowed to
retain their possessions, had a direct interest in making
themselves masters of it. That acquisition was a
fashionable accomplishment. The people at large;
the inferior landholders, who in successive degrees,
held of those who held of the crown; the immediate
cultivators of the soil; the villans, the bordars, the
traders and artisans in cities and towns, and other
wretched prædial slaves to their new feudal lords,
knew enough of their language if they understood
their commands, frequently conveyed, no doubt, by

intimations more significant, than words in an unknown tongue. At any rate they had no inducement to incorporate it with their own, which was treated with insult, contempt, and abhorrence, likely enough to be amply requited. It has been said, indeed, that the Saxon language was intended to have been utterly abolished, as the British had been by the Saxon many centuries before. If such an intention were ever actually entertained, which is much to be doubted, it has been very far indeed from having the same success!

The probable paucity of really Norman-French words, is justified by actual appearances. Etymologists rarely assign such a derivation, in the language at large; and certainly, in our dialect in particular, there are very few. Perhaps, more may be found in the provincial language of the southern counties; but in proportion to the whole they must, at any rate, be inconsiderable. Kelham's Norman dictionary, the most generally acknowledged authority of its kind on this subject, is by no means an ample collection; yet we must suppose the author to have collected all he could find. But they fill only an octavo volume of very moderate bulk, and loosely printed; very different indeed, in that respect from our Saxon tomes— "grandes, Jupiter, atque ponderosos!" The object of the author was to collect the language of the law, while the proceedings of our courts were recorded in the Norman-French language. As there are very few things, indeed, which have not at one time or other been subjects of litigation, it might be reasonably expected that such a compilation would incidentally con-

tain many words of common life. The fact is, however, that the number of *these* is very small, and still
smaller, that of such as are not *also* to be found in
Saxon dictionaries; which were therefore not French
acquisitions, but of the old Gothic stock,* common to
Saxons, Danes, and Normans.

Far more copious was the influx of French
words into our language, which soon after began,
and which may be said to have never ceased, and
scarcely to have been intermitted, from that time
to this. During the reigns of our first three Norman Princes, the Conqueror and his two sons, con-
tinual intercourse, in any degree of intimacy, was
confined to their Duchy of Normandy. The turbu-
lent reign of the usurper Stephen is scarcely worth
mentioning, but that the *end* of it has been fixed as the
termination of our Saxon æra. Here then, the terms
Saxon and Norman-French are to cease. The language of our country assumes the denomination of
*English*. For the French, which from that time was
imported, we may be thought to want an appropriate
epithet instead of *Norman*. *Old French* may perhaps
be allowed to serve tolerably well for lack of a better.
And, if it be not sufficiently definite to express what the

---

* A philological friend of the Author, who, a few summers ago,
passed some months in the province of Normandy, caught among the
peasantry several sounds quite familiar to his ear in Norfolk. Unfortunately, in this instance, he put too much confidence in a memory of
extraordinary powers, and made no memoranda. He has lost all but
one, which of course he offered as a Norman-French etymon. It is,
however, of this old common stock, and occurs in our Saxon dictionaries. *V.* UPADAY.

language was, it may be enough to intimate what it was not. On the accession of Henry the Second, communication with the continent was very much enlarged and diversified. That Prince had lived many years on the continent, and made large acquisitions of territory. By his mother and his wife, he received the accession of the rich provinces of Maine, Anjou, Touraine, and Poitou. Farther additions were made by the marriages of succeeding Princes; until, within 200 years, Edward the Third laid formal claim to the sovereignty of France. During all this time, and beyond it, those contributions from France were perpetually pouring in, which confessedly constitute so large a part of our compound tongue. This was the French of which our great poet, Chaucer, was absurdly accused, by Skinner, of importing "integra vocum plaustra." The accusation was absurd, because Chaucer was certainly, among his contemporaries, a very popular writer, as well as a great favourite at court. And he certainly could not have been so, had he used a multitude of words, which had been used by no preceding writer; which, to a great proportion of his readers, would be quite unintelligible; and, to those who understood them, would most probably savour of affectation. We may be quite sure, that neither he nor any other writer ever brought home new words by the " cart-load," though many before, and many since his time, have taken up such as happened to come in their way, and seemed worth taking; under a general caution, however, to write nothing but what their readers would be likely to understand. It seems strange that Skinner, who has so very ably investi-

gated the etymology of his native language, should
have attended so little to the history of it, as to have
been unaware that Chaucer used no more French
words than his contemporaries. Among these, Sir
John Maundevile might, indeed, have been suspected
of being, like some other travellers, fond of larding
his mother tongue with out-landish words, phrases,
and idioms. But this cannot possibly be suspected in
Wickliffe, who assuredly intended his translation for
popular use and instruction. Going a little farther back
we come to the two monks of Gloucester and of
Bourn. The former, indeed, carries us back about 30
years into the thirteenth century; terminating his
chronicle in A. D. 1270, in all probability but a short
time before his death. He must certainly have been
writing within a century from the accession of Henry
the Second, the date already assigned for the free and
copious admission of French. Robert of Gloucester
is the earliest English writer cited by Dr. Johnson,
in the History of the English Language prefixed to
his Dictionary. He observes upon him, that he " uses
a diction neither Saxon nor English." What is alone
important to our present purpose, is to remark, that,
in this ambiguous diction, be it what it may, there is
a very visible interspersion of French words. His
immediate successor, and in part contemporary,
Robert de Brunne, or Bourn, has more; but, in his
turn, has fewer than Chaucer, and other writers of the
next age. The historian of English Poetry gives
specimens from writers earlier than Robert de Gloucester. He gives as many, probably, as he could find;
at least, as were sufficient to his purpose. And if the

series be not absolutely unbroken, till all that can be
called English is lost in mere Saxon, the proof is satisfactory, that from the first few scattered Norman-
isms in the latest Saxon, French became progressively
more and more discernible, particularly after the
opener and more enlarged communication with France.
Not, indeed, that the effect was immediately discernible. It could not be so.  For a century at least after
the accession of Henry of Anjou, although it was
working its way by oral communication through many
channels into popular use, but little would appear in
books.  When authors submit their works to the *public*, they mean, of course, the *reading* public; a very
confined description of persons in those days.  There
were no such persons in existence as the *general
readers*, of whom we have now such multitudes.  Those
of them who wrote for scholars used the Latin language.  Those who purveyed for the taste of men of
the world wrote in French.  At length, when the
great and the learned condescended to encourage,
cultivate, and improve, their mother-tongue, what had
been long privately accumulating appeared publicly.
Geoffry Chaucer was the first writer of great celebrity
in whom it is to be found; for the plain reason, that
he found it in general use, and knew that it would be
generally understood.

From other European languages we have received
much scantier contributions.  It might seem probable
from some circumstances, that we might have a good
deal of Italian.  The fact is, that we have very little;
for there were strong counteracting causes.  From a
very early age to that of the Reformation religion af-

forded an open and frequent intercourse with Italy. Ecclesiastical persons were very often resorting to the Papal Court. From time to time, Nuncios with numerous trains were sent into this country. The Pope thrust multitudes of Italians into our Bishoprics, Abbacies, and principal parochial benefices. But the Papal yoke had been so intolerable to our ancestors, long before it was shaken off, that the Pope's emissaries, of whatsoever rank, were very unlikely to be allowed to coalesce much with them, or to find them very docile in the adoption of foreign terms. Not to mention, that a great many of them had no opportunity of making the attempt, being entirely non-resident, and having all their revenues sent to Rome or Avignon. Commerce also might seem likely to have considerable influence of the same sort. The Lombards had much of it in their hands, and consequently much of the wealth of the nation, from the days of our early Henries and Edwards for a very considerable series of years. They were, indeed, principally resident in London, and even in one quarter of it, which bears their name to this day, or were scattered in some few other trading towns. But, however occasionally useful they might be, they seem to have been generally looked upon with jealousy and suspicion.

Still fewer Spanish terms are likely to have been incorporated with our language. There was never any open and permanent channel for their admission. Three events in our history may seem to have afforded some opening; the marriage of Edward I. with Eleanor of Castile; that of Henry VIII. with Catharine of Arragon, and that of their daughter Mary with Philip

II. of Spain. All these royal personages were, no doubt, attended by numerous trains, speaking their native language. The Castilian Princess lived about 35 years in this country, but it was at a time when her language, whatever effect it might otherwise have had, was overborne by the tide of French, at that time setting strongly in. The ill-fated and injured Catharine remained here much about the same number of years, at an interval of three hundred from Eleanor. Very soon after came the gloomy and ferocious tyrant Philip, who staid among us but four years, and, during that time was held in utter abhorrence. In fact, in none of these instances was it probable that the foreign language should descend freely from the court among the people. In the last instance, indeed, some stray words seem to have been left, and to have continued for a time. In the comedies of Shakspeare and his contemporaries there are Spanish words and phrases, not so numerous, as frequently occurring. They seem to have been used with a sort of fashionable affectation, and like all other fopperies of that kind, were transient. They are all gone out of use long ago, or if one or two remain it is under some disguise.

Of other modern European languages, the admixture, if there be any, is much less easily detected. Should we have received any small fragments of the ancient languages or dialects of those countries which are now provinces of France, the Provençal, the Langue d'Oc, or the Breton, they are covered and concealed under the general name of French, through which we must have had them. A few scraps of Portugese, if such there be, would easily be taken for

Spanish. Our immediate contact with Portugal, has been comparatively recent, and only maritime and commercial. As for the more northern languages having so very intimate an ancient connexion, their modern derivations are likely to approach so nearly to our own as not to be worth taking, or not to afford any proof that they have been taken.

But the two ancient languages of Greece and Rome must be mentioned again here. Besides the remote and obscure connexion, already noticed, we have numerous derivatives from them, in much later times. In very great measure, they have come to us through the French. This is most observable of Latin words, by far the more numerous of the two. Very little Greek has come to us through that channel. The French scholars (with a very few exceptions) have never had any to share. Some little may have come to us through the Italian. Of these transmissions. proof is exhibited in those variations which are made, more or less, when words migrate from the language to which they belong, into another. The strangers must wear the costume of the country. This is especially observable in words taken into the French from other languages. The French, like the Greeks of old, take nothing as they find it, but shape every thing to their own liking. Even proper names must undergo this transformation, and lose a great deal of their Roman air. If we take the same liberty, it is in a few instances, and we are to blame for following a bad example. Latin words which have come to us through French are instantly discernible. But there are many other words, both Latin and Greek, which have come to us immediately, without passing through any medium. These are principally terms of science (Greek words in particular) which have been introduced since the revival of arts and letters; the number of which has increased, and is still increasing with the advances and improvement of arts and sciences.*

* The coinage of Greek or Greek-like words has been prodigiously abundant in our days. Some very few of them may be allowed to get into general and permanent currency. But the greatest part of them are struck off on adulterated metal and a coarse die; such as cannot possibly pass longer than they can be made to serve the purposes of their fantastical fabricators, or perhaps patent proprietors. It is scarcely possible to take up a newspaper without finding some puffing advertisement, headed with a hard word, meant to be for Greek, but for the most part put together with perfect ignorance, or disregard of the manner in which the Greeks formed their compound words. Should any of these have been admitted, through inadvertence, into a dictionary, it is to be hoped, that on the next revision, what may have privily crept in, will be authoritatively turned out. Fifty years hence, when the shews, or quackeries, or fooleries, which they are now employed to designate, are forgotten, it will be impossible to conjecture what the names ever meant. It would be trifling, as well as tedious, to give instances; and, moreover, might be thought invidious, for one might probably hit upon something very ingenious in itself, and with nothing ridiculous about it, but its nickname. Upon the whole it is seriously to be wished that none of these scaramouch Hellenisms may be allowed to become settled as English denizens. And it seems worthy of observation in this place, that the mighty steam-engine, the most powerful of moving forces constructed by human art, worthy to have been invented and used by Archimedes himself, as the nearest approach ever made to his grand conception of the possibility of moving the earth, does not bear a Greek name. There was no need of it. An apt and adequate denomination was easily found in our own language, by compounding, according to the known usage of it, two plain words, one of them genuine Anglo-Saxon, the other, though remotely Latin, certainly coming from the Norman-French, and naturalized among us many ages ago.

The enumeration may be closed by mentioning collectively, certain sources of communication which might seem likely to be copious, but in fact, have been very scanty. In different and distinct parts of our own island, two languages now exist; and a third existed not very long since, distinct from each other, and from the English. The Cambro-British in the principality of Wales, and the Gaelic in the Highlands of Scotland, are spoken and written at this day by great multitudes unacquainted with any other language. Scarcely more than fifty years are said to have elapsed since the final extinction of the Cornish. Of every one of these, many derivations may, and probably do, exist in the provincial dialects of neighbouring districts. Very few indeed have found their way into the general body of our language. Johnson gives but few; but more than can be unanimously admitted by etymologists, more competent to form a correct judgment, in such cases, than the great lexicographer himself appears to have been. Jamieson, for the reason above suggested, has a larger proportion. What may have caused our ancestors, who made such large importations from beyond sea, to be so inattentive to the produce or the manufacture of their own country? For a considerable time, and to a great degree, it may be accounted for, by supposing that both in the north and in the west, the race, expelled from its own settlements, and that which occupied them, were effectually kept asunder by the joint causes assigned by the Roman historian for a like separation; "montibus et mutuo metu." When fear was removed, it was certainly succeeded, and perhaps in equal force, by mu-

tual hatred. And may we not, in addition to these
visibly operating causes, imagine, that, as in the animal and vegetable kingdoms of nature, certain phy,
sical sympathies and antipathies, serve to perpetuate
the distinctions, and to prevent the utter confusion of
genera and species; so, by some analogous principle,
languages, from different original stocks, are withheld
from intimate intermixture; and that a hybrid language, between Gothic and Celtic, would be as much
a monster, as the rose blossoming on the crab-tree, or
the progeny of the panther and the camel.

Having now finished the proposed general view of
the composition of our multifarious language (which
has run into greater length than was apprehended) we
may consider it summarily under a similitude sufficiently expressive, " fluminis cum pace delabeutis." Of
the fountain head of the noble stream, we may be
contented to remain as perfectly ignorant, as of that
of the Nile. If we cannot be said positively to know,
we are obliged to believe, that it made its first appearance in this country, nearly fourteen hundred
years ago. What it might be before that time, we are
still less able, and not at all concerned to know. We
may, if we will, conceive it to have burst forth,
like Eridanus in the Æneid, from the lower regions. At first, and perhaps for no inconsiderable
length of time, it may be supposed to have been stagnant and marshy; but to have settled itself at length,
in a safe and certain channel, flowing, if not with uniform velocity, yet never again with sluggish and im-
perceptible motion; in different parts of its progress,
augmented by tributary streams. If the exact point

of influx cannot in every, or even in any such instance
be discerned, the effect of the intermixture is soon and
certainly perceived ; first, perhaps, as it were by a difference of colour and flavour, which is said to be perceptible in some natural streams; afterwards by the
visibly increasing mass of the mingled waters, which
are copiously poured along without locks or weirs to
intercept their majestic course, ever increasing in
force, expansion, beauty, and utility, till it hath attained the amplitude in which we now view it.* But
let us not suppose that it has reached a point of perfection, beyond which it will not and cannot proceed.
However enriched, enlarged, and embellished, it is
still, whatever some may appear † to think, progres-

---

* Dr. Johnson's opinion strongly confirms this idea of a continuous current. He observes that "it cannot be expected in the nature
of things gradually changing, that any time can be assigned, when
the Saxon may be said to cease, and the English to commence."—
Hist. of the Eng. Lang. The observation is applicable, in still greater
force, to any subdivisions of the one language or of the other, either
local or chronological.

† That Mr. Pegge should be one of those who *appear* to think so,
is somewhat strange. His words are, "our language now seems to be
at its *height* of purity and energy."—Anec. of the Eng. Lan. 1814.
p. 79. It would have been enough to say that it is now purer and
more energetic than it ever was before. But he may be understood
to mean *final* purity and energy. The expression may have been in-
advertently used. So good a philologist would surely not deny the
possibility of further improvement in both respects. As to purity,
this highly entertaining and instructive writer fully accords with Bp.
Lowth in censuring the multitude of gross anomalies which have become inveterate in our language, and may well be called impurities.
Some of them may have been corrected since the learned prelate

sive in all those respects. Additions are neither so likely, so necessary, nor so desirable as they have been. The stream is neither so rapid, nor so much swelled by contribution from other sources, as it was in some parts of its course; yet still it is as much as ever a stream, and shews no sign of present or probable stagnation. " Labitur et labetur."

Every dictionary may be considered as a view of some portion of this stream, taken at a certain point in its course; or, rather, as a particular representation of whatsoever may, from that point, be seen floating on its surface. The general expectation of those who use dictionaries, either for the purpose of acquiring or improving a knowledge of a living language, is to find in them a faithful account of its present current and authentic form, as settled by the best authorities. At most, there are comparatively very few who care what degree of attention, or whether any at all, is paid to those words and phrases which are gone out of use, or are only locally or partially known, and the compilers of dictionaries, on their part, have been willing to accommodate their works to those expectations; and have, from time to time, given as much as they have thought useful and interesting. Such has been their general character from the Promptuarium Parvulorum, our first printed dictionary by Wynkyn de Worde, A. D. 1516, to an advanced period of the last century.

---

called the public attention to them in his Grammar. Many, however, certainly have not hitherto been, nor is there any present probability that they will be; yet in process of time, they may be corrected.

During that interval many dictionaries have been published of very various merit, some English and Latin some English only; some with the names of their authors, others anonymous. To characterise, or even to enumerate, these would be foreign to the present purpose, if the author felt himself competent to the task. But it would, even in that case, be unnecessary, as sufficient information on the subject may be found, by those who desire it, in Sir John Hawkins's Life of Dr. Johnson. So much was it the general object of all these to " catch the living language as it rose " in common life, that dictionaries of *Hard Words*, as they were called, were from time to time published, as books of science multiplied, and new terms were introduced; which, without such supplementary interpretation, must have been unintelligible to those who were not sufficiently acquainted with the languages from which such terms are derived. Not indeed, that those auxiliary compilations consist entirely of such words. There are many which can scarcely be imagined to have been at any time considered as hard words, or not to have been in common use. Others there are, certainly, very hard, fantastical, or extravagant, " super sesquipedalia," which, if they have ever been used any where else, are only to be found in some forgotten books in which they will never again be sought. These two sorts of dictionary combined, exhibited nothing like a standard of the English Language in any stage of it. The want of it was felt and complained of long before it was supplied. Two great authorities of different ages may be mentioned as having concurred in that complaint. Dryden, in his dedication of Troilus and Cressida to Lord Sunderland, says, " How barbarously we yet write and speak, your lordship knows, and I am sufficiently sensible, in my own English; for I am often put to a stand in considering whether what I write is the idiom of the tongue, or false grammar and nonsense couched under the specious name of Anglicism." Not stooping to so humiliating an avowal, Warburton, towards the end of the preface to his edition of Shakspeare, expresses much the same sense with equal force. " The English tongue is yet destitute of a test or standard to apply to in cases of doubt and difficulty. We have neither Grammar nor Dictionary, neither chart nor compass to guide us through the wide sea of words. Both are to be composed and finished on the authority of our best established writers, their texts being correctly settled, and their phraseology critically examined; and by these aids they may be planned on the best rules of logic and philosophy." These two great men certainly spoke the general sense of scholars in their respective times. The latter of them saw the grievance redressed within eight years after he had complained of it. Johnson's Dictionary of the English Language was published in 1755. Within that short period, one mighty mind atchieved for our native tongue, what had been before accomplished for those of France and Italy by the combined effort of their respective national academies, continued through five or or six times as many years!

It is obvious that such a dictionary as this cannot be figured under the same image and similitude with any which preceded it in this country. It is not a partial delineation of any district or department, but a general chart of the great stream of language through its whole course. To expect that such a work should be at once exhibited in perfection would be absurd. A multitude of lines must remain to be added from time to time to bring it nearer and nearer to correct delineation. Some little of this kind was done by the master hand in subsequent editions. A professed Supplement has been published by Mason—not with all that respect which English scholars in general would think due to Johnson, even should they happen to differ from him. A more copious dictionary has also been published (not surely in a spirit of rivalry) by Ashe. Neither the one nor the other has been admitted to share, with the great work, the honour of being considered as the standard. That character must be continued entire from Johnson's own editions to the enlarged and improved one published a few years ago by Mr. Todd. His valuable and successful labours have been conducted most judiciously in scrupulous conformity with Johnson's plan. He has added a multitude of words and authorities. He has made much addition, improvement, and correction in etymology, in which point the great lexicographer himself seems to have been most deficient. And, if he has done comparatively little in definition, it is because that part of the original work was executed with such consummate skill, that little was left for him to do. Yet, after all, Mr. Todd himself would surely be one of the last to deny, that there is still ample room, not only for more addition, but for farther improvement. ·

Considering the present bulk of that work, and the indefinite enlargement of which it is still capable, and may hereafter receive, indeed must receive before it can be said to give a complete view of the English language; it is obvious that an inquirer, wishing to consult some particular part of the huge chart, may feel bewildered and encumbered, and wish it were divided, in order to be more conveniently consulted. Mr. Archdeacon Nares, in the Preface to his Glossary, published in 1822, aware of this inconvenience, proposes to make the division by " throwing out of Johnson's Dictionary all the words not actually classical, at that time, so as to make it a standard of correct phraseology;"—then to make three more dictionaries, corresponding with three different stages of the language, one or other of which is of course to receive all that is to be " thrown out" of Johnson. Such an arrangement, however, is expressly considered as a thing more specious in theory than likely to be realised in practice. Certainly no such likelihood is conceivable. And with all the deference unquestionably due to the opinion of such a veteran in philology as the Archdeacon of Stafford, it may not be too presumptuous to doubt, whether he has hit upon the happiest principle of division. One primâ facie objection, pervading the whole system, would be this. A word or phrase occurs of which a reader wants explanation. In which of the dictionaries in the series is he to seek it? He must either already know the age of his word or phrase, that is, the *history* of it (which it is the professed design of the arrangement to teach), or he must work his way through them all, if he happens to have them, till he finds what he wants. This utterly does away the benefit of division. Again, is it possible to keep the different æras distinct? Must they not of necessity run one into another. Is it not so in the learned author's own practice. Of the Elizabethan age, or the age of Shakspeare, which he calls his own "link of the philological chain," he has given a very copious (not to say superabundant in point of cited authorities), and certainly a very interesting and entertaining account. But does he keep it distinct? He even expressly apologises for not doing so; and his apology is Spenser's well-known affectation of Chaucer's words. He draws no line, then, on that side. Two of his ages intermix their words. From Shakspeare downwards no line of separation is proposed. If it were, some instance, like that of Spenser, or more than one, would interfere with that also. In fact, in both those intervals, between Chaucer's time and Shakspeare's, and between Shakspeare's and our's, indeed in all times whatsoever, the state of change has been perpetual. These "winged words" scorn to be confined to any one district, and some there are among them, which extend their bold flight over all. But farther, if three æras be fixed upon, why not more, especially on this side of Shakspeare's age? Why not the age of Dryden? It might very properly be denominated from so very distinguished an author in prose as well as in poetry. It was certainly an age of great improvement, though that great ornament of it has been cited to prove, that in his own opinion, enough had not been done. The language of it was assuredly very different from that of Shakspeare's time, or of our's. If, then, a chronological division involves difficulties, apparently insuperable, we may be allowed to inquire farther, whether it may be effected on some other principle; on some property of the words themselves, and not merely on their dates, that the desired improvement in our lexicography may become, if not more likely to be realised in practice, yet more practicable in case it should ever be undertaken, and, if ably executed, more comprehensive.

The words in Todd's edition of Johnson, below the modern "standard of correct phraseology," amounting to a very great multitude, but, according to Mr. Nares's proposal, all to be "thrown out," are, in different degrees, antiquated or obsolete. All such words may be divided into three classes:

1. Words, now no longer in use, but occurring in works of past ages, never likely to be forgotten, or to be held in less estimation than at present. Surely the language of these is genuine English, abounding in nervous, expressive, energetic words, "actually classical" at any time, and at all times,

> "Et maribus Curiis, et decantata Camillis."

A dictionary of "correct phraseology," excluding all these words, would be full as much limited in utility as in bulk. That man's reading must be very narrowly confined, indeed, who did not soon complain of the want of more assistance and information than such a dictionary would afford. All such words being retained, it would be perfectly easy, by affixing to them a cautionary mark, to secure very effectually correctness of phraseology. There would still be many which might be got rid of. All those which are cha-

racterised as low, coarse, burlesque, obscure, obsolete,
&c. All known provincialisms; all which are no better authorised than by writers of inferior note,* of
which not a few have been admitted by Johnson, and
retained by Todd; all those, which though vouched
by first-rate names, occur only in those species of composition in which homely language must be used, for
instance in low comedy, of which we have a great
abundance under high names.

2. Words, which, if not totally and irrecoverably lost, are to be found only where they are not
at all likely to be sought; in books, which still, indeed,
continue to lumber the shelves of old libraries, but by
a sort of tacit common consent, are allowed to lie un-
disturbed; which nobody now opens, or only perhaps
now and then, a dry and determined antiquary, for
some particular purpose, about which nobody else
cares a straw. Such words might be "thrown out"
of every dictionary. There are, or rather have been,
many such in our language. For a very large sample
of them, recourse may be had to Skinner, who has
subjoined to his Etymologicon, under a separate alphabet, between 2,000 and 3,000 of them, which he
considers as having actually perished between the
reign of William the Conqueror and his own time
about the middle of the seventeenth century. No
doubt the number would now be found much increased,
if any body thought it worth while to inquire. To

---

* L'Estrange and Tusser may be mentioned as instances. Both
are often quoted; both were East-Anglians, and understood, and
used their dialect; which their authority, unsupported, cannot possibly convert into standard English.

revert once more to our similitude of the stream, these
were all once freely afloat on the surface, but have
sunk to the bottom, and are not worth the pains of
fishing up again.

3. Words, which, though they may be supposed
obsolete, are in fact still in use, and likely long
to continue so. These have also all been buoyant,
and have not sunk to the bottom; but, at many different
times and places, have been cast on shore; and the inhabitants of the bank, fortunate in finding so valuable
a sort of wreck, have duly estimated and retained the
use of them. This is the great body of Provincial Language, which, when it shall have received the deserved
attention not hitherto bestowed upon it, will yield so
ample a contribution of sound old English, as to form
more than is yet imagined, of the bulk of even a large
dictionary. Many of these words have lurked in such
profound obscurity, as never to have found their way
into a dictionary, or, indeed, into any other book.
Yet not a few can produce vouchers for their legiti-
macy, not less strong than those which have procured
for their more favoured contemporaries in times past
admission into the standard dictionary. From this,
however, they must be positively excluded; and the
few of them which have been introduced, must be
turned out again. They are totally unqualified for
such a station, having no pretension to be considered
as correct phraseology, in the present state of the language, and not being now " actually classical," whatever they may have been reckoned in the days of their
prosperity. To these must be added the many words
under the first of these three classes, which are to be

dislodged from the stations they at present improperly occupy; those of the second class which are recoverable, and worth recovering, if peradventure some few there be; and whatsoever of humble pretension, may still have a valid claim to admission somewhere. All these collectively would form ample materials for a supplementary dictionary.

· On this principle, two dictionaries might be constructed, perfectly separate, but of concurrent authority and utility. One would contain all that is necessary for the various purposes of Science and Literature. The other a complete digest of the vulgar and colloquial tongue. In one or the other, fit reception would be provided for every known word, properly English, with the total exclusion of all cant, slang, and flash; for which the proper place is one, of which the author has often heard, but never saw—the Scoundrel's Dictionary. Some difficulty might occur in drawing the line of separation with accuracy. Doubts might arise, and errors be committed, in determining where to place some, which seem to hover on the border, and in deciding for or against others, which may seem not to belong to either. The necessary care and vigilance, might, however, obviate any important intermixture or omission. The two jointly would give a continuous and consistent history of the English Language from the time at which it could be pronounced to be no longer Saxon. They must be distinguished by two sufficiently characteristic names. They have already insensibly, and for convenience of speaking separately of them, been called Standard and Supplementary. Those two names may perhaps serve as well as any.

Ancient and Modern they certainly must not be called; for each would contain as much archaism as the other. But it will be time enough to think of names, if the scheme be adopted. However that may be, it is submitted with unaffected deference to superior judgment and correction.

Before we proceed to consider more particularly what may hereafter be done in this way for our Provincial English, it will be right to bestow a little attention on what already has been done. The very existence of it seems scarcely to have been recognised till within the last 200 years. Not that such varieties had no earlier existence, but that they had been disregarded. General and local, old and new, coarse and refined, language was mixed together with little or no distinction in our old dictionaries; and certainly our old authors in general were by no means nice in their choice of words. The first recorded instance of any notice vouchsafed to Provincialisms, and that a very slight one, seems to have proceeded from the pen of the learned Sir Thomas Browne. We may be allowed, perhaps, to indulge a little venial vanity on this point. It was our own dialect, which was honoured with this first particular attention. Sir Thomas, who was a native of London, came to settle as a physician at Norwich in the year 1637. No doubt his ear was soon struck with many unwonted sounds. It was, however, some years after that time, that, in one of his miscellaneous Tracts (the eighth, on Languages), he gives a small sample of Norfolk words, twenty-six in number, to illustrate his subject, the Saxon origin of the English language. He does not, however, give either the

derivation or the meaning of any one, but simply cites
them, without order or connexion, as they occurred to
his recollection, and suited his purpose.  Many of
them are still in use; some have become extinct ; two
or three were surely never properly to be called provincial, being used by good authors contemporary with
Sir Thomas himself; and it seems strange he should
not have heard them till he came into Norfolk.  From
the manner in which he must be conceived to have
picked up his words, by occasional and infrequent, not
by common and habitual, conversation with those who
used them, he may perhaps have been led into some
other mistakes.  However that may be, every one of
them is, with due respect, inserted in its proper place
in the Vocabulary.

  Not many years after, the illustrious Ray stooped
from his elevation in science, to make a pretty considerable collection of these poor despised outcasts, as
they were then to be found in the North, the South,
and the East Country.  So far as we are concerned
with them, these also, for the most part, are still in existence.  He has adopted all Sir Thomas Browne's
words, not in his alphabetical arrangement, but by way
of honorary distinction in his Preface : of most of them
he has given etymologies.  So he has of some of his
own ; but by no means of so many as might be wished.
And it is farther to be wished, that he had found
leisure, inclination, and opportunity, to give something
from other districts of the kingdom.  Indeed, his correspondent * Lloyd has contributed some little, which

---

* Ray's correspondences were of course with the most eminent

might be useful, from the counties bordering upon Wales. Ray was the first writer who condescended to treat on this subject directly. Sir Thomas Browne's small fasciculus was only incidentally introduced. " It lay in his way and he found it."

Next in point of time to Ray,* are to be mentioned the collections of provincialisms given in some of the County Histories. But these are very inferior parts of those laborious and voluminous compilations; scarcely, if at all, more than mere appendages, which it was thought fit or necessary to affix ; much like the catalogues of rare plants, &c. accepted and inserted as they were offered, and not deemed to require any industry of research. In some of the later works of that sort, these collections may be somewhat more ample, but no where approaching to complete enumeration. However that may be, they can scarcely be said to be given to the public, being pretty safely locked up from readers in general in those rare and

---

literary, and scientific men of his time. By such men large contributions were made to his collections of words. Truly, this seems very consolatory and encouraging to scholars, though of far inferior note, who, in these days, may seek amusement to themselves, and attempt to communicate it to others, by investigations of the like kind.

* Here is evidently an omission. The Author makes no mention of Major Moor's Suffolk Words. But that it was his intention to have done so appears clearly from a memorandum in pencil on the blank page of his copy. He even refers to the book in more than one place ; and would certainly have noticed it with becoming respect, if his life had been spared to revise his book.—EDIT.

costly works. In our East-Anglian Topography we
have nothing of the kind.*

The Society of Antiquaries has, from time to time,
bestowed its attention on this particular branch of
antiquity. There are some papers in the Archæologia, more considerable in value than in number. Mr.
Drake's convincing comparison of the Mœso-Gothic,
the Anglo-Saxon, and the modern English languages,
in the seventh volume, has already been mentioned.
There is a second paper, from the same able pen, in
which the subject is continued. We must add Dr.
William's words from the West Riding of Yorkshire
in the sixteenth, and Mr. Wilbraham's Cheshire words
in the nineteenth. Perhaps, no other names need be
mentioned. †

In all the works hitherto enumerated, their respective authors appear to suppose that they are communicating information worthy of some serious attention.
A different class is now to be mentioned, in which it
seems to have been the object to raise a laugh at the
expence of the poor rustics, who express themselves
in so ridiculous and barbarous a manner. These
works are more accessible, indeed, or rather were so

* In making this assertion, the Author's memory must evidently
have failed him. In the last edition of Sir John Cullum's History of
Hawsted, there is a list of Suffolk words, certainly not a large one,
but filling two or three quarto pages; and the Author must have
been aware of this, because he quotes it in another part of the
work.—EDIT.

† Here is again an omission of Mr. Brockett's book on the Dialect of Northumberland, to which the same observation will apply,
as to Moor's Suffolk words in a preceding note.—EDIT.

at the times of their publication, mostly pretty late in
the last century, being printed in separate forms, and
at low prices. There was one Timothy Bobbin, as
he called himself, a Lancashire man, who certainly
had no other intention but to make fun. He was a
shrewd vulgar wag, whose waggery is more useful
than he was aware of. He gives some few Saxon derivations, wherever he got them.

The dialects of Exmoor and Sedgmoor in the West,
were also printed in separate forms, and much in the
same ludicrous manner. The Author remembers to
have met with them many years ago, but has not been
able to get them, since he has been led to think of
putting his materials together. One, if not both, has
been printed in the Gentleman's Magazine; but
neither is that within reach. It is no matter; for there
is sufficient reason to believe, that all in either, which
was worth taking, has been taken by Grose. There
may have been some other local collections, of like
character, but of less note.

Grose's Provincial Glossary was first published in
our own memory, and has passed through several
editions. It is avowedly taken from the collections
above mentioned. He seems to have used all he
could find in Ray, a great deal from Exmoor, Sedgmoor, and Tim Bobbin, probably, all he thought
worth having. To these, he is indebted for considerably more than one half. He speaks also in his preface of some topographical works, to which he ac-
knowledges obligation. The remainder he professes to
have collected while he was in country quarters, in
different parts of the kingdom, in the course of his mi-

litary service. What was so collected, could surely
not be very considerable, and would be liable to the
same danger of mistakes, already noticed in the case
of Sir Thomas Browne. He picked up occasionally,
and accidentally, what he did not at all understand.
Upon the whole, his claim to originality can be but
very slender indeed. But he has done very useful
and acceptable service, by putting whatever he got,
and whencesoever got, into a popular and accessible form. He allows the Saxon or Danish origin of
a large part of his words, whatsoever may be the
value of his opinion, but gives the particular derivations of a few only, and for those is principally indebted to Ray. His whole number of words is about
2500.

The only name which now remains to be added is
entitled to peculiar respect. It is that of the late
Samuel Pegge, F. S. A. His valuable collection of
Provincialisms he has thought fit to entitle a Supplement to Grose's Provincial Glossary ; and he has
annexed it to his Anecdotes of the English Language
without a word of introduction or explanation.
Whence he collected his materials, therefore, we
know not. In part, perhaps, from local collections
which had not fallen in Grose's way. But from the
number of words from Derbyshire (his native county),
and from some contiguous districts, it is safely to be
presumed that his matter is, in very great measure,
original. However that may be, in the highly entertaining little work to which his Provincialisms are
annexed, this most ingenious philologist has con-
trived, by a peculiar vein of playful pleasantry, so to

relieve and enliven the inherent dulness and dryness
of his subject, without once losing sight of its real
importance, that though he totally discourages and
defies rivalry, he strongly intimates to all who may
succeed him in the same sort of composition, to do
all they can to prevent their readers from throwing
aside the book in disgust, or dropping it in a fit of
drowsiness; either of which they might be very likely
to do, if the subject were treated with grave and di-
dactic formality. This addition to Grose, contains
above 1000 words. The aggregate is, therefore, at
least 3500.

This, then, is to be considered as the present public stock of Provincialisms. Mr. Todd has largely
availed himself of it, in the very considerable addition of such matter, which he has made to Johnson's
Dictionary. In this point, it was certainly very defec-
tive; and no wonder. The same sources were not
open to the author. He had himself little knowledge
of that local and obscure part of the language; and
he might be very well excused, if he were not anxious
to collect and insert, unless it were directly brought
to his hand, what he might reasonably suppose that
only a small proportion of his readers would value.
But whatever be the paucity or abundance of such
words, in the view we are now taking, they, with
many others, must be dislodged and turned over to
the Supplemental Dictionary. To the present stock
very great additions may be made. And it could not
be insuperably difficult to collect them. Contributions might doubtless be raised from many, or from
all quarters. The habit with which the Author began

to amuse himself so many years ago, is neither a singular, nor probably a very uncommon one. There must
be in every county, philologists with sufficient leisure
and curiosity to have made such collections for their
own amusement; and with as little thought as the
Author entertained till very lately, of laying them before the public; but which would be forth-coming if
they were properly solicited, and to be deposited in
proper hands. Even if not habitually and progressively
collected, a great deal might be got together in a
short time. Every man who passes his life in retirement, and intermixes with his home-bred neighbours,
must become a good deal acquainted with their dialect.
Nay, he must even be constrained in some degree,
occasionally at least, to adopt it himself, or he would
very often speak unintelligibly. Among contributions
thus made, it is indeed likely that many superfluities
would be found, if rigid caution were not used to
avoid every thing that might come under the denomination of mere slang, manifest corruption, or slight
deviation from authentic words. But all such things
might be thrown out once for all, on general revision
and arrangement. The more copious and miscellaneous the immediate communication, the better.
What ample materials might thus be brought to light
for the Supplemental Dictionary may be made the
subject of a little calculation. The joint stock of
Grose and Pegge has been stated at 3500. The
following collection contains at least 2500, alphabeti-
cally arranged, besides what are comprehended under general observations on pronunciation and grammar. Of the 2500 about 600 are to be found among

the 3500, either in the very same form, or with some slight variation, but certainly the same words. Consequently about 1900 East-Anglian terms are produced, which have not before been recorded. If, as we are in pursuit of Saxon antiquity, we follow the Saxon division of the country, and suppose a return made from each of the other ancient kingdoms with nearly the same numerical results, the whole number of words so brought to light would exceed 13,000; a pretty plentiful accession of materials for an additional Dictionary; and no weak proof of the necessity of a division. However, not venturing in such a matter to trust implicitly to an arithmetical calculation, into which many particulars must be taken, which it would be tedious to specify here, and which might materially affect the result; and supposing the grand total to fall considerably short of this last number, we may feel fully confident that we should thus obtain, from every corner of the country, enlarged and diversified proof of the prodigious fecundity of our Antiqua Mater. And the Author feels himself warranted to exhort, in the terms of his motto, all who may be fitly circumstanced and disposed, to contribute their endeavours to "search her out" to as much perfection as possible. With respect to his own contribution to that effect, he is not vain enough to fancy that he is giving an example and mode of what ought to be done, but merely an indication of what may be done; and no one would rejoice more sincerely, to see much more effected, by abler hands in other districts, than he has accomplished on behalf of the East-Angles.

In speaking of this service to the East Angles at large, he may be thought to assume too much. It may be said that this title is too large for his subject. It may be so; but some explanation may be allowed, perhaps some indulgence. The Saxon Kingdom of East Anglia is reckoned to have comprehended the three modern counties of Norfolk, Suffolk, and Cambridge. Now this collection has been almost exclusively made from Norfolk and Suffolk. It is not, indeed, without a slight sprinkling of words from the third county; but they are no more than what the Author might glean during his residence in the University of Cambridge, from College Gips *(ex. gr.)* or the few other natives with whom he might occasionally converse. Such gleanings would be likely to be even more scanty than those of Captain Grose in his country quarters. For this partial application of a general name, a precedent may be found in the venerable example of the greatest of all East Anglian antiquaries, Sir Henry Spelman; whose tract entitled "Icenia' contains no more than short accounts of some of the towns and villages of Norfolk only; though, according to Camden and others, the Iceni were the ancient British inhabitants of the three counties above mentioned, with the addition of Huntingdonshire. If the apology be not satisfactory, all that can be farther said is, that the objection is easily enough removable. The paucity of Cambridgeshire words might be done away, and the deficiencies of words from the other two counties (which no doubt are many, copious as the collection may seem) might be supplied, by communications from various quarters. The Author, indeed, is not so

absurdly sanguine as to expect to be called upon for
an enlarged and improved edition. He means no more
than to hint that, if his work be thought of any value
at all, a Supplement to it, some time hence, might not
be unacceptable; and to give assurance that if any
corrections of what may be found here, or any addition of what is wanting, were transmitted through his
Publisher, they would be received thankfully, and considered attentively; and, when they seem sufficient in
quantity and importance, be printed, with any explanation which may seem necessary, and as much etymology as possible.*

But another objection ought perhaps to be obviated:
The East Anglian dialect is spoken of as *one*. And it
may be asked, are not the dialects of the counties distinguishable from each other? That no shades of difference exist, would, indeed, be too much to assert.
But, if every thing of that sort were collected and
placed in the strongest light, it would not amount to
what is called in Natural History a different specific
character. No more could be made of them all, than
that, in Norfolk and Suffolk at least, (to say nothing,
for the present, of Cambridgeshire,) they are mere
varieties, and even slight ones, of the same species,
and are therefore properly called by the same name.
If the points in which they certainly agree, and those

---

* The Editor has not thought himself at liberty to omit this invitation to other collectors, as it shews so clearly the zeal of the
Author on the subject of his inquiry. But his untimely death has
cut off the hope of any future communications being laid before the
public.

in which they may be said to differ, some of which
will incidentally occur, were minutely discussed, the
discussion would be insufferably tedious and trifling;
but the former would be found so predominant as to
leave no doubt of their constituting what may very
fairly be called one dialectic character. If they ever
were two dialects, they have been long ago completely
blended and identified by contiguity and perpetual intercourse. Some persons, indeed, either for the credit of their county, or for the joke's sake, seem to
shew a nonsensical sort of jealousy in claiming certain
words or phrases as peculiarly their own. If there be
any such they are certainly not worth contending for.
Any one who, on the ground of his own individual experience, is disposed to pronounce this and that Norfolk words, and to assign another and another to Suffolk, is liable to be contradicted by the very next person with whom he may happen to converse on the subject. For this reason, no marks of discrimination have
been affixed to the words of the Vocabulary, though
the Author very well knew in which county almost
every one of them was collected. His valuable co-
operating correspondent in Suffolk furnished him with
near 1200 words. With about 800 of them he was
well acquainted before. The 400, or thereabouts, were
new to him. But, on shewing them to another friend
(a Norfolk man), well acquainted with his mother
tongue, and who had heard and used it in parts of the
county least familiarly known to the Author himself, a
very considerable reduction was made. And the same
intelligent critic made the same remark on Moor's
" Suffolk Words." Many of the remainder, or most,

or even all, might be claimed in like manner should fit
opportunities occur.  In short, it seems as if certain
of our words and phrases were comparatively rare or
frequent in different parts of the two counties, as some
of our indigenous plants are known to be.  Let us
suppose a meeting of two East Anglian clowns, one
from the Northern coast, the other from the banks of
the Stour or the Orwell, there can be no doubt that,
on entering into conversation, each would recognise a
countryman in the other.  Their language would be
mutually intelligible, with the exception, perhaps, of
some few appellations, if any should unluckily come in
the way, expressive of merely local objects, or of some
figurative terms taken from those objects; which
words there had been neither need nor means of
transmitting.  Now, suppose two other clowns by some
chance to join the party, one from Cumberland, the
other from Somersetshire.  Before three sentences
had been uttered, there would be the most complete
confusion.  The strangers from the North and from
the West would be as foreigners to each other, and
both equally to the East Angles.  The commonest
things with which all four were familiarly acquainted,
would be called by such strange names that it would
be impossible to understand what was meant, and they
must soon have recourse to signs, or talk by things,
like the philosophers of Laputa.  But, after all, whatever may be the local and relative frequency or rarity,
or even peculiarity, of some words and phrases in our
own two counties, we shall soon come to stronger
points in which there is perfect concurrence, which
must establish the East Anglian dialect "one and in-

divisible." These will occur in the following Essay; but, before we conclude this, we must attend to another topic, properly connected with the subject of it, and which may by no means be omitted. An apprehension exists, it seems, of present and pressing danger to the permanence, and the very existence, of ours, and of all our popular dialects. They are imagined to be in a state of rapid decline, and to be actually giving way to a more correct diction. This great change is expected from the general disposition to acquire knowledge, and the increased facilities of diffusing it among those who formerly rested humbly content in their ignorance. These alarming indications have really been urged to the Author by some of his literary friends, as inducements to arrange and publish his collection without delay, lest the peculiarities of our mother tongue, if not recorded in time, be irrecoverably lost. Let those judge who are properly circumstanced and most able, how far this mighty change may have proceeded, and be likely still farther to proceed, in country towns; where there are many and various schools, circulating or subscription libraries, book-clubs, reading-rooms, and other appliances and means of literary proficiency, adapted to the different ranks of a numerous population. In villages, the strong holds of provincial language, we are affrighted with no such portentous signs of change. The Author can only say for himself, that he has opportunity almost every day of conversing with the children or grandchildren of those with whom he was wont to talk forty years ago, and that he perceives very little change indeed, and certainly none that can be attributed to such a cause. It is true that, during what were called the *good times*, which opened many sources of expence never thought of before, many more of our rustic youth, of both sexes, were sent from the farm-yard or the dairy to the boarding-school; some of whom, but a few years before, it would have been thought very absurd so to take out of their proper places. It is no less true, that, though the number is now considerably diminished, it still continues greater than it formerly was. But, in the seminaries to which they are for the most part sent, their rough tongues are not likely to be much filed and polished. Even admitting that some of them bring home from school what is called a love of learning, and a taste for reading, it is likely to have very little influence on their talking. Among us rustics, there is, and ever will be, a wide difference between book-learning and common talk. In the comedy of the "Two Gentlemen of Verona," the servant, who has been charged with a verbal message of more than ordinary importance, talks of "speaking it *in print*," that is, in choice terms, such as are used in books, not in his own every day familiar style. The vulgar are much alike in all ages. Shakspeare drew the character of Speed from nature; and just so would a tolerably shrewd country servant speak at this day, on the like occasion. He would, in all probability, use the very same phrase, for we have it. And who has not observed that a rustic, who fancies himself a great scholar, and talks "in print," (suppose the village schoolmaster, the exciseman, or some fortunate adventurer, who, having left his native cottage in early life, has prospered in the world, and returns late to enjoy

his *otium cum dignitate*,) excites so much gaping wonder in his fellows, that they marvel

" That one small head can carry all he knows? "

But still they will laugh in their own sleeves, if not in
his face, that he does not use common words on common occasions.

But this is not all the danger. Should our popular
dialects withstand these partial attacks, will they not
be overwhelmed and borne down by the general onset
of the various plans and unwearied exertions for the
*education of all?* The zealous promoters of new
schemes are in all cases disposed to anticipate the
most prosperous issues. In plans of unquestionable
beneficence, the world will ever applaud their zeal,
and cordially bid them God speed! But should any
thing be included in the expected result neither essential nor subservient to the intended good, of question-
able utility, and moreover, not likely to come to pass;
the most sincere well-wisher may be allowed to depre-
cate it, and to do what he can to allay the apprehension of it. Supposing, then, all the strong, and some
apparently insuperable obstacles overcome, to the universal adoption of one or other of the rival systems of
popular instruction; supposing that, after a competent
time, there be a reading population; the question is,
whether we may reckon also on a population of correct speakers? Does any thing in the nature of former example warrant the expectation? There is one
precedent, indeed, very strongly in point, from which
certainly that conclusion is not to be drawn. In Scotland, from the very time of the Reformation, there
has been parochial provision for the simple schooling

of the poor. And this facility and universality of elementary instruction has assuredly had no fatal, or
even mischievous, effect on the popular language. On
the contrary, were an instance required of remarkable
exemption from the operation of those causes which
are perpetually working change in living languages,
it must be that of the Lowland Scotch. How little
its purity and integrity have been affected is proved in
the Scotch Novels and Romances, which have been so
popular of late years; which we must suppose to give
the language in its actual state ; and of which, fortunately for this proof, as well as for the pleasure of
reading them, so large a proportion is dramatic and
colloquial. With this example before us, what have
we to fear for the safety of our Eastern English? Of
the little change which actually has taken place within the reach of living memory, can we impute any
thing to the puny operation of a cause which has been
partially working during a few years only of that considerable period? or can we apprehend more, when it is
proved that the same cause, in full force, extent, and
activity, has been so inefficient in this respect in the
course of many ages? It may be alledged that a comparison is not fairly made between a national language,
in which a multitude of books have been written, constantly in the hands of those who use the language,
and a provincial dialect altogether oral, which neither
is nor ever was so exemplified and embodied, but lies
thinly scattered in works not at all likely to be read
by the vulgar. It may seem that this gives to the one
a great advantage over the other, in the probability of
permanence or perpetuity. But it is to be remarked,

that there is, on the same side, a power strongly, and perhaps equally, counteracting. It is a fact, too well known to be denied, that the Northern multitudes who migrate Southward, and the still greater multitudes who must stay where they are, take great pains, if not to get rid of their native tongue, at least to polish and *Anglicise* it as much as they can. On the ~~other side~~, the unwritten dialect rests humbly content in its obscurity, equally ~~unaided and unendangered~~ by any such circumstances. This may be thought to bring the two sufficiently to a level, in the one point in which we want to consider them. And the fact seems to be, that both the men of the North and the men of the East, who stay quietly at home, mind their own business, talk as well as they can what their fathers talked before them, and what all their neighbours understand, will preserve it, if not absolutely unvaried, yet certainly from running rapidly to ruin.

And what has been the change among us within our assumed limits? Why, some few words and phrases have become less frequent; some nearly forgotten; some very few, indeed, have perhaps actually disappeared—just as might have happened, nay, actually has happened, in any other equal period. On the other hand, new ones have been introduced. Not, indeed, such as to compensate the loss of good old English. The stock of vulgarisms is, upon the whole, not at all diminished, but by no means improved. Some of our newly introduced terms are expressive of new ideas, bringing their foreign names with them, which are accepted, though with a little attention we might find names full as good in our own language.

A much greater number is adopted without any pretence of necessity at all, through mere wantonness and affectation, superseding even better native words. There is no limit to this apery of what is supposed to be fine and fashionable. It is to be found in the deepest retirement, and in language no less than in dress and manners, in which it may, indeed, be more seriously mischievous. But to whichsoever of those classes such novelties may belong, they are quite sure, when they come among us, to be grossly or ridiculously misapplied, mispronounced, or both. Happily, however, they are held in very different estimation from our old sound native phraseology by those among us who occasionally make awkward attempts to use them. Though they may seem to be sported off very glibly, and with no little self-complacency or vanity, the fancied necessity or propriety of using them is always, while it lasts, a state of uneasy constraint, from which the embarrassed bumkin is glad of an opportunity of escaping —

> " Vaga prosiliet frœnis natura remotis."

Upon the whole, we may rest satisfied that the provincial dialects are in very safe keeping, and very likely so to remain.

The subject may be summed up and illustrated, perhaps somewhat enlivened, by an anecdote. On one of the many hazy days of the ungenial summer of 1823, the Author was attending an ingenious young lady while she took a sketch of some picturesque object in a retired village. A girl came from a cottage with an umbrella in her hand, which she presented, with an air of modest and simple civility, which became her well, but with an address not quite so expressive of rustic simplicity: "Will you allow me, ma'am, to offer you the use of my *numbarel?*" The mixture of rusticity and affected refinement sounded very comically. But it would be very hasty to infer from it that the girl was unlearning her native phraseology. Forty years ago, indeed, a village maiden would not have offered a *numbarel* at all—for the best reason possible, that at that time no such thing had been ever seen or heard of in a cottage, though now there are few without them. But, whatever her civility might have been, she would not have expressed it in such "holiday and lady terms." The fact is, that the girl had, some how or other, picked up this as a polite phrase used by gentlefolks, and proper to be addressed to them. Perhaps it came from some lady's chambermaid who had lately made a visit to her country cousins. Had she been overheard in familiar talk with the other inmates of the cottage, she would doubtless have used such language as her grandmother did. And even had she at the moment been questioned why she offered the umbrella, it is not likely that she was provided with any more specimens of such dainty diction to carry on a dialogue, but that her answer would have been, "Because ta smur of a rain, and ta fare 'lection to rain pouring." Pure East Anglian, such as was spoken not only by this *mauther's* grandmother, but by that grandmother's great grandmother, and is likely to be spoken by the equally remote posterity of the *mauther* herself.

# ESSAY II.

### On the principal characteristics of East Anglian Pronunciation.

Should any reader expect to find under this title, rules by which he may learn to speak East Anglian, he will be disappointed. No such attempt was intended. If the coarse cacophonies of unlettered boors were of any interest to philologists, the attempt to convey them would be nugatory. As all ideas must enter the mind by their proper inlets, those of sounds (whatever some may have seemed to think) cannot be admitted by the eye. Experiments of the kind have indeed been made. The compilers of some Grammars of modern languages have professed to prescribe rules for correct pronunciation. Certainly a learner, destitute of an oral teacher, may get on tolerably well, to some extent, by comparing familiar sounds in his mother tongue, with those at which he is taught to aim, in the language he is endeavouring to acquire. He will at least feel so well satisfied as not to disgust himself, while he has his books before him. But the moment he shuts them, and opens his mouth, he will be likely to disgust those who are natural and competent judges of his success. He may even puzzle them to conceive what words he means to attempt. At any

rate he must very soon come to certain *shibboleths*,
which exist in any language. For instance, whoever
acquired, by the help of printed directions, and comparative sounds, the exact pronunciation of the French
diphthong *eu*, the Italian *uo*, or the Spanish initial *ll* ;
as exemplified in the substantive *fleur*, the adjective
*buono*, and the verb *llamar?* All these are words of
very common occurrence in those languages ; but how
few foreigners are able to pronounce them so as not to
give offence to a Parisian, a Roman, or a Castilian
ear ? Still greater would be the difficulty of managing
the formidable clusters of consonants which abound
in the German, and other northern nations, our own
not excepted. These, however, are very successfully
smoothed down, and uttered " trippingly on the
tongue," by organs properly disciplined and habitu-
ated ; so that the sound seems widely different from
the appearance, and would never have been conveyed
by written rules, to one before unacquainted with it.
But it may be said that the instances produced, are
from the polished enunciation of highly refined languages, and are therefore nothing to us, who are not
concerned about euphonic niceties. On the contrary,
they strengthen our case. If so much difficulty exists
where great pains have been taken, there must be
much more, where none at all have been bestowed.
The writer, whose own ear is familiar with certain
sounds, may suppose that by putting letters together
into combinations which never actually co-existed in
any word, of any language, he is exhibiting such a strict
graphic delineation, as cannnot be mistaken. Whereas, in point of fact, those only who know what he

means, can at all understand him, and even they may
sometimes be totally unable to conceive what he is
aiming at.   After all, supposing the intended information were effectually conveyed, who would care for it?
None but those who already have it.   Or if, by any
strange and inconceivable chance, any stranger should
wish to obtain a correct notion of East Anglian orthoepy, he must e'en come among us, and hear us talk!
And it is fully to be expected that having heard our in-
describably odd splay-mouthed utterance, in which
all the organs of speech, tongue, teeth, and palate,
seem to be running foul of one another in full play, he
would acknowledge, that an idea of such " villainous
compounds " of ill sounds could not have been conveyed by any possible artifice; and that we might as
well attempt to write down in legible and utterable
characters, the cawing of our rooks, or the croaking
of our frogs, if we supposed there were any difference
between their tones, and those of the same animals in
other districts.

But there is another, and a very different view in
which the subject of pronunciation may be considered,
and in which only it will be considered in this work.
Not for the gratification of a curiosity which, in fact,
nobody entertains, but in order to draw from it, certain dialectical characteristics, and to use it as a secondary, or rather concurrent proof of antiquity.  Any
attempt, indeed, to investigate and ascertain accurately the pronunciation of a language, dead many
centuries since, must be vague and unsatisfactory.
But at least some general principles or outlines of pronunciation may reasonably be conceived to have

passed traditionally into a modern derived language, of which an ancient and defunct tongue forms the main substance. And the less change that has been made in the forms of words, the more similarity is likely to remain of their original sounds. Thus, it is generally and probably supposed that more of the genuine pronunciation of Latin exists in the modern Italian, than in any other of the languages of Europe. Into every one of them, indeed, a multitude of Latin words has been transferred, but adapted both in form and sound, to the peculiar structure of each, and by no means constituting the main substance and bulk of it. It may, indeed, be contended, and with much probability, that on the Spanish, almost as fundamentally and substantially Latin as the Italian, the gravity and dignity of the classic language is more likely to be adequately represented than in the exquisitely smoothed and polished tones of the present language of Italy. However that may be, on a perfectly similar principle, the English must be believed to retain a greater number of original Saxon sounds as well as form. Indeed, modern English seems to be even more substantially Saxon, than either Italian or Spanish is Latin. It certainly does not become the Editor to play the critic in either of those languages. With much diffidence he submits his opinion to those who are competent to judge, together with the reasons on which he founds it. We have at least as many nouns and verbs from the Saxon, as either of those languages from the Latin. We have also retained, without borrowing from other languages, the " whole body of numerals, auxiliary verbs, articles, pronouns, adverbs,

conjunctions, and prepositions," which, as Sir Thomas
Browne well observes, " are the distinguishing and
lasting parts of a language." Whereas, on the other
hand, many of these have been borrowed by the
southern from the northern languages. In particular,
they have assumed articles, definite and indefinite, of
which there is neither in their parent tongue. They
have abolished inflexions of case, in substantives and
adjectives, supplying their places by prepositions, and
retaining no other differences of terminations, than
seemed necessary to distinguish gender and number.
They have made much alteration in the structure of
the verb ; adopting a new auxiliary in the active voice,
and introducing compound tenses, which in the Latin
exist in the passive only ; and increasing the number
of those tenses in both. It might have been observed
before, but better now than not at all, that we retain,
with little variation, the Saxon modes of declension
and conjugation.

Allowing to the English Language at large, this
ample claim for Saxonism, we have farther to observe,
that in its provincial dialects, that claim may have
been more or less varied or superseded by local
causes ; principally by a partial commixture of words
from other sources, introduced by vicinity, and probably accompanied by their native pronunciation, or
something like it. Any one of those dialects which
can refer to the Saxon, the greatest number of its
words now actually in use, must be allowed to advance the best proof of antiquity and originality.
And that proof must be allowed to acquire additional
confirmation, if, on comparison of its modes of pro-

ñunciation with the powers of vowels and diphthongs,
a fair presumption can be established of identity, or
near similarity to the Saxon pronunciation. Of those
powers, as they actually existed while the Saxon was
a living language, it would be absurd to pronounce
confidently. We must make our approaches to them
cautiously. We cannot be in much danger if we do
not venture farther than the mere consideration of
greater or less breadth. Of this, perhaps, a pretty
safe criterion may be established thus: It has been
laid down as a principle by etymologists, that in the
derivation of words, and in tracing them from one language into another, all the vowels may be considered
as one letter. A synoptical view of their gradations
and changes may be exhibited by taking them out of
alphabetical order, and ranging them according to
their organic powers. Taking $i$ and $y$ as homotonous
(and they are sufficiently so in Anglo-Saxon and in
modern English, for our present purpose) and placing
them in the middle, the sound will pass one way
through $e$ to $a$, and in the opposite way through $u$ to
$o$; in either case, the vowel becoming broader at each
step.          Thus, $a \ e \ i = y \ u \ o$.
But the two extreme vowels, being themselves also
commutable, the changes might be rather conceived
circular than rectilinear, bringing the extreme points
of the line into contact. If the interchanges of diphthongs cannot be so simply exhibited, neither is there
so much need of it. Their bearings on the vowels,
and on each other, may, without difficulty, be determined by the vowels of which they are respectively
compounded,

Now, it is observable, that in a great multitude of modern English words derived from Anglo-Saxon, the principal vowels or diphthongs have acquired breadth in the course of their descent. Such are *cu*, a cow; *hus*, a house; *brun*, brown, &c.

A very long list might easily be made, in which other vowels or diphthongs, even all of them, are concerned. But to our present argument, these few, in which one of them only is included, may suffice. If it be urged, that we have no means of being sure that these words were pronounced, either with the long or the short sound of the modern English *u*, this cannot be denied. Suppose it then to have had something like the power of the Italian *u*, still it has grown broader by its conversion into our broadest diphthong. But this tendency to greater breadth, observable in the English language in general, in its Saxon derivatives, is by us East Angles absolutely *inverted*. We are perpetually endeavouring to go back again into the original Saxon *narrowness*.

The most general and pervading characteristic of our pronunciation, which may, indeed, be called its essential character, is a narrowness and tenuity, precisely the reverse of the round, sonorous, "mouth-filling" tones of Northern English. The broad and open sounds of vowels, the rich and full tones of diphthongs, are generally thus reduced. Generally—not universally. Some few words become broader in our mouths; not that we so make them fuller and more flowing, but for the most part harsher and coarser. Instances will occur in their proper places. From this prevalent principle of narrowing, it results that, if it be asserted, as doubtless it will, that we speak the worse English, what we do speak must undeniably be more like Saxon in sound as well as in form.

This narrowness of utterance is, in some parts of our country, rendered still more offensive to ears not accustomed to it, by being delivered in a sort of shrill whining recitativo, which may very possibly bring us to a nearer and more correct resemblance to our parent tongue. This may, perhaps, be one of those distinctions without essential difference, already alluded to. It prevails principally, not exclusively, in the county of Suffolk.. So far, however, as to be commonly called in Norfolk, the "Suffolk whine." The voice of the speaker (or singer) is perpetually running up and down, through half an octave, or perhaps a whole one, of sharp notes; with now and then a most querulous cadence. This squeaking tune is very disagreeable to sensitive organs; and often becomes very ludicrous, when something, even of merry import, is uttered with this "dying fall."

It is time to have done with generalising, and to come to particulars.

### Irregular Sounds of Vowels and Diphthongs.

There is a great multitude of English words, even in the mouths of the most correct speakers, in which every one of the vowels and diphthongs stands as a representative of the power of some other. Such anomalies are to be found, more or less, in every language. In our own they are said particularly to abound, to the great annoyance and perplexity of foreigners, in their attempts to acquire it. An ample, if not a complete, enumeration of these disorderly words is to be found in the valuable work by which the present Archdeacon of Stafford announced himself to the public as a philologist above forty years ago.[*] As there are many particular points on which practice is not uniform, should a reader not feel himself disposed to acquiese in every determination of she learned writer, he will be sure to find a great deal of useful and amusing information. The same method is adopted here; only that complete enumeration is not attempted; but a select and competent number of examples given under the different heads. It may well be conceived that such deviations from strict regularity will become more licentious still, in provincial dialects. Those only which are peculiar to us, or which we use in uncommon and unwarranted latitude will be noted here.

### The Vowel A

has regularly four different sounds in English words, which are commonly thus distinguished:

*a*, long,    as in    ale;

short,    as in    hat;

open,    as in    balm;

broad,    as in    call.

1. Ex. Have, and its inflexions has, hast, &c.

Catch—thank—sack—wax.

Gather—radish, &c.

It is not asserted that this pronunciation is peculiar to us, or that it is in toto provincial. No doubt, some such words, though not many, are so pronounced very

---

* Nares' Elements of Orthoepy, 8vo. Payne 1784.

generally; whether ever properly, is no question for
us. Be they many or few, and be the usage right or
wrong, it is certain that, on our principle of *narrowing,*
we greatly increase the number, and therefore the observation is properly made here. The usage prevails
more in some places than in others. In and about the
town of Lynn, for instance, it seems as if the short *a*
were in all cases to be rejected, and short *e* accepted
in its stead. A *bad man,* is there, a *bed men,* &c.
Whatever may be said of such extreme and ridiculous
frittering, the pronunciation is by no means destitute
of ancient authority. In Spenser we find *wex* for *war.*
In many of Percy's Ancient Ballads, the inflexions of
the verb *have,* are printed *hes, hest,* &c. from *heve.* Ial.
*hef,* habeo. In Wickliffe's New Testament is *geder,*
for *gather;* in Chaucer *ketch* for *catch,* and *lest* for
*last.* And if this be not enough, *esh* (our name of the
ash-tree) is the very Anglo-Saxon *esc* * itself; *grass*
is from *gres,* as indeed we very commonly pronounce
it; *black* is from *blec, trap* from *treppe,* and *mantle* from
*mentl.* In which last instance also, we retain the iden-
tical Saxon word.

2. There are some few instances in which the short
*a* is even pared down to short *i.* We say J*i*nuary for
January, and *kin* for *can,* the auxiliary verb. In these
instances it is plain that *a* has passed through *e* to *i;*
for the intermediate form is often used.

3. The long *a* is in some words reduced to long *e.*
Ex. *Credle* for *cradle,* This is among Ray's North
Country words; doubtless ancient, though no precise

* In the Anglo-Saxon it is plain that *sc* was pronounced as it is in
the modern Italian, like our *sh.*

authority is given there, or at present occurs else-where.

4. In words, in which *a* has commonly its *open* sound, we make it intermediate between that and the *long* one; rather broader than the latter but narrower than the former. Here is a difficulty. Certainly no English word contains such a sound. Perhaps the nearest approach to it is the bleat of a very young lamb.

Ex. Calf—dance—staff—glass.

Cask—glance—raft—grasp.

On the true pronunciation of these and similar words there does not seem to be perfect agreement. We, however, have no opinion to give (*V.* Nares) whe-ther they are to have the *open*, or something nearly approaching the *short*, sound of the vowel, or whether some are to follow one rule, some the other; it is very certain that none of them ought to have the narrow, and somewhat lengthened or drawled sound which we give them.

5. When the *a* would be short, if it were not length-ened by the *e* final mute. We are determined to have it short at all events.

Ex. Bare—stare—dare—flare, &c.

Now *bar* and *dar* both occur in old ballads. Besides one of them is positively Danish, *bar*, nudus.

Learners, however, must be cautious here. All words of this form are not to be indiscriminately so docked. For instance, *care*, *snare*, *spare*, and many others. Every body knows how bitterly foreigners complain of the anomalies in English pronunciation, and into what scrapes they often get themselves, by following too implicitly what they suppose to be *rules*. To a like danger would they be exposed, who attempted to speak East Anglian, without a familiar acquaintance with it. It is an undertaking of much nicety.

6. In a few words, short or open *a* is made long.

Ex. Nasty—natural—past—barn.

The Anglo-Saxon *bærn*, horreum, will go some way, if not far enough, to justify us.

7. In a few others, open *a*, either by itself or combined with *r*, has the sound of short *u*.

Ex. Rather—farther.

The latter word, having become *futther*, receives an additional improvement (by the very legitimate change of the cognate mutes *d* and *t*), and becomes *fudder*. In like manner, though in inverted order, a ladder becomes first a *latther*, and then a *lutther*.

8. In some words, in which *a* has commonly the sound of short *o*, the short *a* is used instead of it.

Ex. Squab—waddle—wash—wander.

     Swamp—want—wasp—swan.

Certainly many words of like *form* are regularly pronounced with the short *a* ; as stab, saddle, cash, sand, &c. These have their proper pronunciation among us ; but, as was observed on a former occasion, we extend it unwarrantably. Our countryman Tusser rhymes *want* to *plant* ; but though he may be strongly suspected of having pronounced both the words alike, a rhyme in itself will not prove this point. Our poets too frequently rhyme to the eye instead of the ear ; even the most correct of them occasionally. Pope for instance, rhymes *vice* to *caprice ;* yet surely no one will believe that he pronounced the two syllables alike. Perhaps, however, this license was not known to the simplicity of Tusser's muse. Wickliffe spells the word wash, *waisch*. It must be inferred, that he at least pronounced the word *narrower* than the modern usage. And when we can go fairly back as far as Wickliffe, we are at next door to Saxonism.

9. In some words, in which *a* is followed by *n*, it takes the sound of *o*, as sand, sond; land, lond. This mode of pronunciation is perhaps more generally used in Suffolk.

10. In some words, in which *a* is followed by *r*, the *r* is dropped.

Ex. Harsh—marsh—scarce, &c.

And to warrant us, there is Anglo-Saxon *hasc*, asper, of which word, as has been before observed, the ancient pronunciation was *hask*, as it is with us.

### The Vowel E

has only two sounds regularly,

Long,   as in   equal;
short,   as in   bed.

1. The short *e* is in many words sounded as short *a*.
Ex. Merchant—sermon—settle—when.
    Errand—vermin—temper—then.

In some such words (but not in all our instances) this is neither modern nor provincial; but surely never correct. Ben Jonson has *marchant*. This, by the way, may be right, as it is certainly the French *marchand*. Piers Plowman gives *sahtle* for *settle*. Tusser, Wickliffe, and Chaucer have *than*; and the very first word of the Canterbury Tales is *whanne*.

2. The short *e* sometimes becomes short *i*.

Ex. Yet—men—ever—kettle.

Yes—hen—seldom—tremble.

Neither is this usage our own, but only a great favourite. There is a great abundance of venerably old authority for it. Holinshed and Tusser have *sildom*. Wickliffe has *togidre*, and Tusser *togither*. He also rhymes *bless* with *miss* and *kiss*. Wickliffe has *yit* and *yhis*. Moreover, *yet* is in Anglo-Saxon *git*, *kettle* is *cytil*, *hen* is *hæn*, and *end* is *ænde*.

3. Short *e* is in some words pronounced like short *u*.

Ex. Fellow—mellow—elder—wether.

Yellow—elbow—better—letter.

In these cases it seems to have passed through *i* into *u*. It may be observed (though this is perhaps not exactly the right place) that the same liberty is taken with words in which a diphthong has the sound of short *e*, as in *heifer*, *pheasant*, and *feather*.

4. *E* long is sometimes changed into *i*.

Ex. Glebe—glibe.

### The Vowel I

has two regular sounds;

> Long, as in abide;
> short, as in bid.

The short *i* has among us sometimes the power of short *e*.

Ex. Pit—kiln—silver—stint.

Bid—mill—cistern—sit.

This usage is not very general; more perhaps in Suffolk than in Norfolk. However that may be, it is venerably antique. Tusser uses *kel* for *kiln*. *Hed*, *hefs*, and *melle*, are used by Chaucer. *Selver* occurs in the Percy Ballads ; and *melk, bed*, and *pet*, are actually Anglo-Saxon. In Isl. *print* is *prants*.

### The Vowel O

has also two regular sounds ;

> Long, as in mode ;
> short, as in modern.

1. We substitute the short sound for the long in
Droll—scroll—roll—mole.

2. Short *o* has sometimes the sound of short *a*.

Ex. From—slop—drop—soft.
Hornet—morning—Norfolk.

And we are at no loss for authority. The Anglo-Saxon form of the preposition *from* is *fram ;* and our word *morning* is from the Anglo-Saxon *margene*, Aurora.

3. The long *o* has often a peculiar sound explained hereafter under the diphthong *ou ;* the most convenient place for that explanation, which is extended to two other sounds ; this being the first of the three. The words droll, &c. under Observation 1, are sometimes thus pronounced, and so are

Old—told—sold—scold, &c.

4. It has also in some words, the common *short* sound of the diphthong *oo* (in *foot*), or that of the vowel *u* in *pull*.

Ex. Bone—stone—whole.

5. It has the sound of short *u*, in the imperfect tenses of some verbs ending in *ive*, as strove, drove, (pron. struv, druv,) but not in the substantive *drove*, nor perhaps in any other substantive. It has however the same sound in *hither* and *wither*.

6. The same change is made in words in which *o* has commonly the long sound of *oo*.

Ex. Prove—move.

Both which words are rhymed by Tusser to *love*. It is very fairly to be presumed that he pronounced them as we do, *pruv* and *muv*.

7. The short *o* becomes short *u*, in

Ex. Not—font—front—bomb. •

In Blomfield's History of Norfolk, vol. x. p. 11, 8vo edit. is an extract from a churchwarden's account at East Dereham in 1468, for the expenses of the new *Funte*. That beautiful baptistery is still the *Funte*.

8. *O* has sometimes the sound of long *e*, as *move—meve*.

### The Vowel U

has likewise a short sound, as in *tub*, and a long one, as in *tube*.

1. One of its *irregular* sounds, very frequent and general, is that of short *oo*, as it occurs in the word *bull*. This irregularity is *corrected* by some of our best speakers, to the legitimate short sound of the vowel itself.

Ex. Pull—puss—pulley—pudding.

Full—bush—bushel—bully.

2. We sometimes meet with the very reverse of this usage. The sound of *short oo* is given where it ought *not* to be.

Ex. Punch—bunch—bundle.

3. The short *u*, forming with *n* a negative particle at the beginning of compound words, is invariably pronounced *on*. And so it ought to be, in words of Saxon origin at least, for it is the Saxon particle. We are apt, indeed, to carry it beyond its proper limit;

and where a word of Latin derivation has assumed the equivalent Latin particle *in*, however neatly it may have been fitted and jointed to its word, we tear them asunder, and substitute our own. Thus the words *impossible* and *irregular* are with us, *onpossible* and *onregular*. *Unpossible* is certainly Old English.

4. To the syllable *ur* (and consequently to *ir* and *or*, which have often the same sound) we give a pronunciation certainly our own.

Ex. Third—word—burn—curse.

Bird—curd—dirt—worse.

It is one which can be neither intelligibly described, nor represented by other letters. It must be heard. Of all legitimate English sounds, it seems to come nearest to *open a ;* or rather to the rapid utterance of the *a* in the word *arrow*, supposing it be caught before it light on the *r*. Tusser may be suspected, from a rhyme, to have thus pronounced the word *worse; shert* (pronounced *shart),* for shirt is Old English, but in pronouncing it in our manner, great care must be taken, not to touch the *r*.* As to Gothic authority, the only instance that has been found, exactly in point, is one which cannot be offered without some scruple and hesitation. It is Islandic, *tdd*, stercus.

5. In words of some of these forms, we merely leave out the *r*, and pronounce the *u* short.

---

* *Bahd* has been used to convey our sound of *bird*. Certainly this gets rid of the danger of *r* ; but the *h* must as certainly be understood to lengthen the sound of *a* ; which is quite inconsistent with our snap-short utterance of the syllable. In short it must be heard from the mouth of a correct speaker.

Ex. Worse—purse—curse—nurse—wus—pus, &c.

May we venture to defend ourselves by Anglo-Saxon *pusa*, marsupium?

6. The *u* is sometimes merely turned to *open a*, and the *r* retained.

Ex. Burst—curse—nurse.

We are in some degree kept in countenance by Anglo-Saxon *bærst*, ruptus.

7. The short *u* is sometimes changed into short *e*, as *shut, shet, shutter, shetter*, which is the universal pronunciation in Suffolk, and in the eastern part of Norfolk. Chaucer has *shet*. Wickliffe narrows it still more. And lastly, it is the true Anglo-Saxon *scyttan*, claudere, whence we have,

8. The short *u*, convertible into short *i*.

Ex. Shut.

In Lowland Scotch, the common form of the verb *put* is *pit*.

### *Irregular Sounds of Diphthongs.*

#### *Ai*

1. Followed by *r* is sounded as if there were no *i*.

Ex. Chair—fair—pair—stair.

In Islandic *pair* is *par ;* no doubt the Latin word adopted.

2. It is sometimes pronounced *broad*, as it commonly is in Greek; or as it is in the modern Italian; so as to make the proper sound of each vowel in a diphthong, perceptible to the ear, if, indeed, it be not thought a profanation of the Bella Lingua Toscana, to use any of its fine tones to illustrate those of our tramontane Gothic *linguaggia !* To the *Greek* we cannot be sure that any such affront is offered.

Ex. Plain—gain—pain—fail.

Nail—twain—maid.

Nay, in some few words it is made *a* broad, as *oi*. We do not táke a *bait* but a *boit*.

3. Sometimes it is like *open a*, or *a* followed by *h*.

Ex. May—play—pray—stay.

Mayor * (pronounced as monosyllable). Islandic, *mah*, may.

4. In one instance, at least, *ai* is sounded like *ee*. A chain is a *cheen;* and so it was in Old English.

*Au*

has very generally the sound attributed to the vowel *a*, in observation *A* 4.

Ex. Aunt—paunch—laugh.

Draught—saunter.

*Aw*

is in many words scarcely to be considered as a diphthong. The vowel *a* is pronounced *open*, without any help from *w*, and *w* holding itself ready to begin another syllable, as if another vowel were coming after it, thus, supposing the word *drawer*, divided and pronounced *dra-wer*. In order to pronounce *draw* alone, *er* only is to be cut off, and *w* left with something of its own power. To those who are not used to it, this may be somewhat difficult, if there be no following vowel. It is easy enough to say "stra-w is dear,"

---

* Forty years ago, the Chief Magistrate of the City of Norwich was called the *Mahr;* and probably some elderly and old-fashioned people call him so still. But in the progress of refinement, the pronunciation is in general smoothed and polished; and that ancient city is now (as the borough of Lynn has been time immemorial) governed by a worshipful personage called *The Mare.*

la-w is expensive. But to pronounce straw and law alone, in this manner, nice aim must be taken.*

### Ea

1. Is sometimes like short *i*.

Ex. Head—heaven—teat—each.

Breast—ready—thread—bleach.

In Percy's Ballads *ych* and *stydfast* occur. *Thrid* is Old English. And there is even Saxon authority in Anglo-Saxon *titte*, mamma.

2. It is like short *u* in

Ex. Feather—leather—weather.

Pleasant—measure—pleasure.

In pronouncing the last two words great care must be taken to admit no power of the letter *h*. They must be muzzer and pluzzer.

3. It is sometimes like short *a*

Ex. Earnest—leather—breakfast.

Learn—early—weather.†

Here we have on our side Anglo-Saxon *arlice*, matutinè.

4. Sometimes it is like *long a*.

Ex. Deal—beard—spread—early.†

Earth—hear—bean—search.

This is a well-known Hibernian pronunciation. How Pat came by it, is not for us to inquire or care.

---

* The pronunciation of the word *straw* varies very much. It is sometimes spoken as if it was written *stra*, without the *w*, and has the long sound of *a*, as in *ale*. At other times, as if it were written *strar*, and pronounced like *star*; as are also *saw* and *law*.—EDIT.

† If the same words be found as examples under different observations, it is not to be taken as an oversight. They are pronounced variously.

We have carefully handed it down from our own fore-fathers. Anglo-Saxon *wac*, infirmus, *laf*, reliquiæ, &c.

5. It has the sound of *long e* in some cases in which it ought not to have it.

Ex. Deaf—tread—endeavour.

Spread—dead—instead.

Wickliffe has both *defe* and *dede ;* and the latter is in Percy's Ballads.

6. Frequently (and particularly in Suffolk) it has the sound of short *u.*

Ex. Leather—weather, &c.

### Ee

1. Is sometimes sounded like long *a.*

Ex. Geer—cheer—beer.

Sneer—fleer—peer.

Whether we might be able to defend all these re-puted mispronunciations would only be known by taking more trouble than the most favourable issue would requite, and finding more opportunities than are likely to occur. Two of them, however, may be easily explained if not vindicated. When we call a *Peer* of the realm a *Pair,* as if we thought him equal to two ordinary men, we use the word exactly as we received it with its proper French sound. For a reason exactly similar we call *beer, bear.* It is from the Norman French, *bere ;* and there can be no rea-son to suppose that the vowel *e* in the middle of a word had in that ancient language any other sound than that of *e masculine,* as it is called, in modern French ; and that sound is exactly the long *a* in Eng-lish,

2. It has sometimes the sound of long *i.*

Ex. Freeze—frize.

*Ei and Ey*

1. Have sometimes the sound of *open a.*

Ex. Either—neither—their.

They—grey—neighbour.

This pronunciation is unquestionably ancient. *Either* and *neither* are, in Old English, *ather* and *nather ;* sometimes *other* and *nother* and *norther.* Wickliffe has even *nouther.* *Ather* is in Lowland Scotch. So, probably, by easy analogy is *nather*, though Jamieson has not inserted it. *Their* is in Old English written *ther*, which is but a step to our word *thar.*

2. They have sometimes the sound of the diphthong *ai*, in observation *ai* 2.

Ex. Deign —either—leisure—conceive.

Vein—weigh—neighbour—receipt.

Grey—convey—obey—weigh.

We may place some reliance here on Anglo-Saxon * æyther*, uter.

*Ie*

Has the sound of *short i.*

Ex. Friend—field—yield.

*Frinde* is frequent in Old English ; and Chaucer has *felde*, a step to *fild*, our word.

*Oi and Oy*

Are very commonly narrowed to *long i.*

Ex. Boil—join—poison—destroy.

Point—soil—foil—spoil.

Ancient authority is good and abundant. In Percy's Ballads we have *file* for *foil*, and *spylt* for *spoiled.* Tusser also has the latter. Wickliffe has *destrie* for *destroy* ; and we find Anglo-Saxon *besylan*, maculare.

### Oo

1. Is in some words narrowed to *long u.*

Ex. Fool—spoon—noose—goose—moor.

    Moon—soon—boot—noon.

· We despise the ridicule we have incurred by this paltry sound, which, after all, is by no means peculiar to us. Should these things be ever thoroughly investigated, as they deserve to be, it will be found in other and distant districts; in the County of Devon certainly, and no less certain in Lowland Scotch. It is ancient. *Cule* and *sune* are both in Percy's Ballads; and we find in Somner Anglo-Saxon *stupian,* se inclinare, and *Brid-guma,* sponsus.

2. It is sometimes decked into *short u.*

Ex. Hood—wood—wool—foot.

    Spoon—roof—proof—broom.

This mode of pronouncing the word *spoon* is much rarer than the former, but a *spoonful* is invariably a *spunful.* A *brume* also is a much commoner domestic utensil than a *brum ;* but if it happened to be made of hair, it ought by all means to be called a *harren brum.* As to ancient authority, Tusser uses both *fut* and *wul. Ruff* is Old English. And there are Anglo-Saxon *wul,* lana, and *wuman,* fæmina.

3. It has the sound of *long o* in many more words than are commonly so pronounced, whether properly or improperly.

· Ex. Moor—poor—took.

In fact words of this form are, and ever have been, readily commutable by the help of *e* final, mute. *Toke, none,* and *rome* are, in Old English, very common modes of spelling *took, noon,* and *room.*

### *Ou and Ow.*

In these last of our diphthong sounds we have the greatest difficulty to encounter, whether in vindicating our practice, or in conveying an idea of it to those who never heard it. In truth, we make very strange havoc with them. They have, with us, three different sounds, all equally departing in different ways from euphony, and from approved usage; sounds which cannot be represented, and to which it is not to be conceived that any natural organs can give easy and habitual utterance, if any utterance at all, but those of a native East-Angle, or of an old he-cat.

1. The first is a broad twanging sound somewhat, but not exactly, as if it were written *au-w*. These three letters are not to be considered as a triphthong; the *w* standing independent, and ready, either to apply its force to an initial vowel following, or to rest in itself, if nothing follows, as in observation *aw* 1.

Ex. Ought—low—owe—moult.
Dough—mow—glow—soul, &c.

2. The second is considerably narrower, and may be attempted by endeavouring to sound the *open a* with *w* after it, as above described.

Ex. Power—sour—devour.
Shower—scour—our.

3. The third is narrower still; and may be described as about midway between the legitimate sound of *ou* and that of long *u*. Or. it may be easier to attempt the pronunciation (should any one think of attemping it at all) by lengthening out *long u*, instead of *open u*, as in the former case.

Ex. Cow—sow—plow.
Now—crowd—proud.

For narrowing this diphthong, some how or other, if not precisely that, we may at least have taken a hint from the Anglo-Saxon, in which *cu* is a *cow*, *hus* a *house*, *pund* is a *pound*, and *brun* is *brown*.

4. *Ou* is sometimes reduced to *short u*.

Ex. Could—would—should.

5. Where it has generally that sound before *gh*.

Ex. Tough—rough—enough,

We give it our *third* sound of that diphthong. *Tow* for *tough* is very common. And Chaucer has written *row* for *rough*.

6. Words in which *ou* is commonly sounded like *au*.

Ex. Bought—sought—nought—thought,

are pronounced without the *first* sound of *ou*. In a Churchwarden's account for the year 1468, the word *bought* is written *bowt*. No doubt they pronounced it as they pronounced *bow*. The two diphthongs *au* and *ou* seem to be pretty easily commutable. Sir Thomas More and the poet Skelton both spell the word *naughty*, as we pronounce (and most likely so did they) *noughty*.

7. It is notorious that the diphthongs *ew* and *ow* are very apt to be confounded. The verb *sew*, for instance, is generally pronounced *sow*. Many like instances might be given. The most common if not the only liberties we take are,

     *Yow* (with our first sound) for *ewe*.
     *Douce* for *deuce*.
     *Fow* (with our third sound) for *few*.
     *Enew* for *enow*, pl. n. of *enough*.

*Irregular uses of Consonants.*

## F for V

Ex. Vane—vetch—vagary—vat.
For the substitution in every one of these words, we
have the authority of Chaucer, or of some other ancient writer. We even find Anglo-Saxon *faet*, torcular.

## G final, hard.

If *g* final be followed by an initial vowel or diphthong, or if it terminates a syllable in the body of a
word, and the next syllable begins with a vowel or
diphthong, the *g* is pronounced as if it belonged to
the following word or syllable. This is more general
and constant in Suffolk ; variably, partially, or locally,
used in Norfolk. If any one be curious to form an
exact idea of this harsh and offensive twang, let him
endeavour to pronounce, with strict attention to it,
the phrase, " bringing in, and flinging out."

## L mute.

It is often dropped in words of the following form,
and the *o* is pronounced as in observation *ou*, 1.
Ex. Old—cold—told—sold—hold.
The same usage is also Northern English and Lowland Scotch, and is, indeed, analogous to the general
pronunciation of such words as could, would, &c. In
fact it is Old English.

## R adscititious.

It is added to words ending in certain vowels and
diphthongs, as *aw*, *ow*, and the *open a* final, in the

names of women. " Set the window-*r* open." " Law-*r*
and justice." " Anna-*r* is at home." It is not meant
that this is peculiar to our, or any Provincial Dialect.
But we constantly use it. It is even sometimes heard
from the mouths of persons of education and refinement, whose delicate ears, forsooth, cannot endure a
hiatus, but who thus produce a much worse sound,
in this offensive and absurd use of the canine letter;
indeed, adopt a positive vulgarism. If the hiatus
must, at all risks, be filled up, it is pity some softer
mode of accomplishing it cannot be devised.

### The aspirated Mutes.

We seem to have a general disposition to smooth
them; which is particularly observable when *th* is followed by *r*, the *h* is invariably dropped.

Ex. Throat—thread—threaten—through.

### W and V commutable.

These two letters, by perfectly correct speakers,
are uniformly substituted for each other, with as much
nicety as, in some parts of England, the initial as-
piration is used wheresoever it ought not to be, and
sunk where it is actually necessary. Of this barbarous
violation of euphony, we seem to be quite clear. Nor
is it at all common to be scrupulously exact in the
misapplication of the two cognate letters, now before
us. In general, *w* for *v* is used by rude rustics, and *v*
for *w*, by those whose diction has been polished by a
town breeding. For the liberties we take with these
kindred letters, some excuse may be derived from
comparision of Anglo-Saxon with Islandic words.

Many, which in the former begin with w, have in the latter, an initial v. Vide Somner and Hickes.

To these might be added some very perverse uses of single consonants; but occurring only in particular instances, and reducible to general rules, besides being undeniably exposed to the charge of positive corruption, they will be better enumerated under that name at the end of this essay, as in their proper intermediate place. Too intractable to be brought under these general remarks on pronunciation, they have still less claim to be formally inserted in the vocabulary. In the mean time, then, we will pass on to some observations on

### Syllables.

The system of English accentuation has a direct tendency to produce indistinctness in pronouncing final syllables. Very few indeed, if any, genuine English words are accented there; and we generally take the liberty of adjusting, as much as possible, to our own practice, the accentuation of those which we adopt from other languages. Even in such words, an accent on the last syllable is almost invariably a mere mark of necessary distinction of one word from another, with which it is liable to be confounded. * This general care to avoid touching final syllables may easily be conceived to produce a more particular neglect of them in the illiterate, with whom the language is merely oral, who never think of such a thing as orthography; still more in those who use some provin-

---

* The substantive *accent*, and the verb *accent* may, themselves serve as well as any for instances.

cial form of it.   Whether we excel particularly in this
respect is not our concern to determine.   We are to
contribute what we have, at least what has been noted,
and leave it to comparison with what others may produce.   Certain it is that we utter final syllables in
such a clumsy, careless, and slurring manner, as often
to defy all guess at the letters of which they may consist.   And if at the same time, a little disguise be bestowed on preceding syllables, it becomes very effectual indeed.   Who, for instance, quite unskilled in our
dialect, could construe the words in the first column
below, if he laid his hand over the second?   Still less
would he be likely to interpret, if he heard them properly pronounced.

| | |
|---|---|
| Ashup, eshup, or ushup, | an ash-heap. |
| Muckup, | a muck-heap. |
| Nettus or nuttus, | a neat-house. |
| Duffus or dowus, | a dove-house. |
| Allus, ellus, or ullus, | an ale-house. |
| Wuddus, * | a wood-house. |
| Sidus, | sideways. |
| Bridle, | bridewell, |
| Ollus or allost, | always, |
| Wammle-cheese, | one meal cheese. |

If in these specimens of pronunciation, to which

---

* Of the exactness with which the "unlettered muse" spells by
the ear, a curious proof was exhibited during the ever-memorable con-
tested election for Norfolk in the year 1817.   It was thus the name
of the popular and successful candidate was inscribed on barn-doors,
throughout the county, and on all the dead walls in the city.   "Mag-
num et venerabile nomen!"  though it was thus incidentally made
ridiculous, at the very time when it was receiving additional lustre.

more might be added, we be thought too slovenly, there are others in which we are very elaborately distinct. The termination *ive*, of adjectives, for instance, which, in the English language commonly glides faintly off the tongue, is drawn out to its full length.

Ex. Expensìve—positìve—abusìve—natìve.

Here we are quite ready with our defence. These words are French ; or rather Latin originally, coming to us through French, and therefore accented on the last syllable. So we found, and so we use them.

Nor are words of this form the only ones which we thus use (contrary to the general rule) neat as imported. Enemy' and envy' are instances. And we follow the analogy of the latter word in its adjective envious.

Adjectives in *able*, which have commonly the accent on the antepenultimate of polysyllables, or even farther back, are accented by us on the penultimate, especially when it is intended to give them emphatic force.

Ex. Lamentáble—abomináble, &c.

Here we may plead the same defence.

Adverbs in *ly*, particularly when the sense of them is meant to be emphatical, have the accent on the last syllable, as continually', certainly', &c. This termination is Saxon, and is in fact, a word, *lick*, synonymous with *like*. So those adverbs in strictness are a sort of compound words, and the last syllable is likely to have been pronounced more distinctly than it commonly is in its present form.

Words of exclamation, of whatsoever grammatical rank, are used in the same manner. Mr. Pegge no-

tices this use of Goodness! And we have "Lord ha'
mercy!" and others, seemingly ad libitum.

To that very meagre and insignificant syllable *le*
final, which a Frenchman bites off at once, and an
Englishman scarcely deigns to touch with the tip of
his tongue, we are apt to give very undue prominence,
by pronouncing it *ul*, as *possibul*, &c. For this pronunciation, coarse and awkward as it may seem, we
appeal to Spencer, who writes *bafful* for *baffle*. Indeed, he is himself under authority; for the *le* is no
other than the Saxon termination *ol*, of which very
many instances may be given.

So much then for final syllables. But we are not
satisfied with slurring them over in the manner, of
which a sufficiency of examples has been given. We
clutter and huddle together, the syllable of two or
more words, into a combination of which no constituent part can be recognised. Many instances of this
sort are afforded by connecting together the negative
particle and a verb. Such forms are pretty numerous
in all dialects, and in colloquial use. We have only
to enumerate our own, or a competent number of
them, to which additions might be made.

| | |
|---|---|
| Shant, (a. 4.) | Shall not. |
| Cant, (a. 4.) | Can not. |
| Ont, wont | Will (wull) not. |
| Dint ⎫ | |
| Dent ⎬ | Did not. |
| Dānt ⎭ | |
| Shunt | Should (shuld) not. |
| Wunt | Would (wuld) not. |

| | |
|---|---|
| Mant, (a. 4.) | May not. |
| Warnt | Were not. |
| Eent | Is not. |
| Aint | Am not. |
| Heent | Has (hes) not. |
| Hănt | Had not. |

Of like sort are several combinations of the pronoun *it*, represented by an initial or final *t*.

| | |
|---|---|
| Tut | To it. |
| Dut | Do it. |
| Wut | With (wuth) it. |
| Het | Have it. |
| Tebbin * | It has been. |

Some are combinations of verbs, with other words :

| | |
|---|---|
| Cup | Come up. |
| Gup | Go up. |
| Gout | Go out. |
| Gin | Go in. |
| Giz | Give us. |

Shakspeare uses *dup* for *do ope*. *Doff* and *don* for *do off* and *do on*, are very well known, and certainly Old English.

Perhaps the four following are our own :

K'ye here, or k'ere.
K'ye there.
K'ye hinder, or k'inder.
K'ye thinder.

---

* The pronouns possessive hisn, ourn, yourn, theirn, so very common among cocknies, are little used by us; only, perhaps, by some affected persons who seem to consider them as more than common elegancies. They are certainly condensations of his own, &c.

respectively signifying, "Look ye here, there, or yonder."

But all these are tight compact condensations of two, or, at most, three short words. Some are on a larger scale. An example or two had been preserved, but have unluckily escaped. This loss is the less to be lamented, as Major Moor's Collection of Suffolk Words, supplies a very queer one. A girl was employed to keep cows, a task commonly allotted to boys. She called herself a *galcobaw;* a word which might puzzle the most learned East Anglian philologist. It was found, however, to mean a *girl-cow-boy.* Whether the strange word be in any degree of currency, or whether it was merely hit off by chance, does not appear. It may serve to exemplify the habit of jumbling words together, which is, indeed, pretty much ad libitum. The following may be thought a neat cluster of small samples: "M'aunt bod me g'into th'archard, and call m'uncle into house."

If Ray's interpretation of one of Sir Thos. Browne's words be correct (as it probably is) our ancestors in his time possessed more skill and bestowed more pains on these ingenious fabrications, than we do. The word alluded to is now, indeed, and probably has very long been, totally out of use. But the celebrity of the name (on which alone it rests) must rescue it from oblivion. The same consideration must also save it from being thus swept into a corner among rubbish. It must be inserted and interpreted in its place in the Vocabulary. Therefore, *V.* Samodothee.

We seem now to be naturally and easily led to the subject of

*Corruptions,*

A title under which we must be content to class many perversions and distortions of legitimate words, not reducible to the foregoing, or to any rules; not mere peculiarities of pronunciation, changes of the organic powers of letters, or of the form of syllables; but, more or less, of the very structure of words. Such aberrations are to be found in abundance in every provincial dialect; the same in more than one; in many; in most; or even in all; so as rather to deserve the name of general vulgarisms. They seem to have been too freely admitted into some recent Glossaries. In this a few choice specimens only will be inserted for special reasons. From this opprobrious character it would be trifling to attempt a general vindication of them. Yet, for some may be pleaded, in different degrees of exculpation, their high antiquity, their analogical formation, their occurring in the works of grave authors, or their possible derivation from such sources as make them not less, perhaps even more expressive, than the words of which they seem to be awkward or fantastical representatives.

The following catalogue coincides * in a great measure with that given by Mr. Pegge in his Anecdotes of the English Language. He keeps these words se-

---

* This coincidence may serve to prove, as far as such words can prove, and as far as they are of competent antiquity, the good sympathy and sisterly likeness between the popular language of the East Angles, and that of their near neighbours the East Saxons; for with that ancient nation must Mr. Pegge's favourites and protegés, the cockneys, be numbered.

parate as they are kept here, that they may not en-
cumber those which he means more particularly to
discuss. The whole of his collection is not inserted
here, only as much of it as we can claim. Yet this is
much ampler than his; and it might have been considerably enlarged, had not the rule been rigidly observed, to admit no word which could not be fairly
said to be in current use among us. There would
be no end of noticing every missed aim at a hard
word, which one may have happened once to hear.
Besides, it might be thought uncourteous, as well as
tedious to call Mrs. Malaprop, or Mrs. Slipslop, to
a very strict account for their diction. There is
scarcely a trisyllable in the English language (to go
no farther) of which a travestie might not be exhibited off-hand every day and every where, by those
who are fond of using what they reckon fine words,
without knowing the form or the meaning of them.

There is, indeed, another class of anomalous words,
of more value than these, connected with, but not to
be identified with them. Words so slippery and fuga-
cious as to elude any attempt to form a collection of
them, but which ought to be noticed somewhere, and,
perhaps, no where more opportunely than at this
point. It is observable, most likely in all cases, certainly in ours, that in popular and oral language,
where there is no recorded and acknowledged standard
to which speakers feel themselves obliged to conform,
there exists a strong propensity to what is called the
*coinage* of words. Words are struck off on the spur
of the occasion, on the principle of the figure *onoma-
topoeia*, but sometimes strongly and happily expressive,

such as to remind one of the courteous reply of a polite Frenchman to an Englishman who had apologised for his bad French: "Ce que vous dites, Monsieur, n'est pas François, mais il merite bien l'être;" words suggested to the speaker by anger, grief, disappointment, surprise, or some other vehement and sudden emotion; random and extemporaneous words, never thought of before, never likely to be used again *. These απαξ ειρημενα can have no pretension to appear among words of "good admission." If a single one has found its way into these pages, it is an estray, which was allowed to creep in through inadvertence, and not detected on revision.

To almost every one of Mr. Pegge's words is annexed a short note, explanatory, illustrative, or in some sort exculpatory, and all expressed with his characteristic pleasantry. With not one of these annotations has the Author ventured to make free. Nothing is more dangerous to borrow than a jest; and no mode of borrowing more clearly betrays poverty, or rather beggary. Any *East Angle* who wishes to claim a share in these apologies, as far as they concern him, will do well to have recourse to the book, and may depend on finding much amusement and information. And, in return, if in any case it should happen, that

---

* In other words, on the principle of making the "sound seem an echo to the sense," or rather a *comment* on the sense. This explanation may, perchance, enable some reader, well acquainted with his mother-tongue, but not familiar with the names or powers of the figures of rhetoric, to bear witness to the correctness of this observation.

more light is thrown here on any word than Mr. Pegge
has afforded, the Cockney is heartily welcome to the
benefit of it.  It is intended to give here, as nearly as
possible, a simple nomenclature, and to leave the
words in general to shift for themselves, as best they
may.  Entirely to avoid encumbering the List with
notes, should some lucky formation, some quaint analogy, perhaps some weighty authority, seem to entitle
any word to particular notice, it will be marked with
an asterisk here, and repeated in the Vocabulary, as
the properer place to say whatever can be said on its
behalf.  Some little improvement has been attempted
in arrangement, by throwing the words under different
heads, in order to give a clearer view of them.  Whether this may have been worth the trouble, let the
reader judge.  It will of course be understood, that,
in our use of them, they are subject to the rules of
pronunciation, if they can be so called, which have
been above laid down.

1. To some words is added the letter *d* or *t*, by the
figure called *paragoge:*

| | | |
|---|---|---|
| Attact | for | Attack. |
| Close-t | | Close. |
| Drownd | | Drown. |
| Epitapht | | Epitaph. |
| Gallont | | Gallon. |
| Gownd | | Gown. |
| *Margent | | Margin. |
| Nice-t | | Nice. |
| Paragrapht | | Paragraph. |
| *Regiment | | Regimen. |
| Scholard | | Scholar. |
| Sermont | | Sermon. |

*Simont      for Simon.
Sould      Soul.
Surgeont      Surgeon.
Talont      Talon.
Verment      Vermin.
Wind      Wine.

2. To some a whole syllable is added:

Masoner      for Mason.
Musicianer      Musician.
Physicianer      Physician.
Teamer      Team.

3. Some assume an initial *s*:

Snoose      for Noose.
Snotch      Notch.
Squench      Quench.
Squink      Wink.
Squit      Quit.

4. In some the first syllable is changed:

Bagonet      for Bayonet.
Compacity      Capacity.
Court of Arms      Coat of Arms.
Discommode      Incommode.
Disgest      Digest.
Dismolish      Demolish.
Eminent.      Imminent.
Mislest      Molest.
Perdigious      Prodigious.
Preverse      Perverse.
Star-naked      Stark-naked.
Vocation      Vacation.

5. In some the last syllable:

Agash      for Aghast.

| | | |
|---|---|---|
| Ballat | for | Ballad. |
| Becase | | Because. |
| Bedisle | | Bedizen. |
| Chaply | | Chapel. |
| Chimbly } Chimly } | | Chimney. |
| Clash | | Class. |
| Conquest. | | Concourse. |
| Delightsome | | Delightful. |
| *Disburst | | Disburse. |
| Drugster | | Druggist. |
| Effidge | | Effigy. |
| Fancical | | Fanciful. |
| Flustrate | | Fluster. |
| Furnitude | | Furniture. |
| Jaunders | | Jaundice. |
| Luxurious | | Luxuriant. |
| Moral | | Model. |
| Notage | | Notice. |
| Otherguess | | Otherguise. |
| Portmantle | | Portmanteau. |
| Quite | | Quiet. |
| Refuge | | Refuse. |
| Rheumaties, *s. pl.* | | Rheumatism. |
| Rheumaty pains | | Rheumatic pains. |
| Rinch | | Rinse. |
| Roment | | Romance. |
| *Rubbage | | Rubbish. |
| *Skirmage | | Skirmish. |
| Successfully | | Successively. |
| Timorsome } Timborsome } | | Timorous. |

| | | |
|---|---|---|
| Topsy-tivy | for | Topsy-turvy. |
| Underming<br>Undermind } | | Undermine. |

6. Some are deformed by insertion of superfluous letters:

| | | |
|---|---|---|
| Bacheldor | for | Bachelor. |
| Bing | | Bin. |
| Cavaltry | | Cavalry. |
| Commonality | | Commonalty. |
| Confisticate | | Confiscate. |
| Destolate | | Desolate. |
| Dilantory | | Dilatory. |
| Disposial | | Disposal. |
| Duberous | | Dubious. |
| Enormerous | | Enormous. |
| Flagititious | | Flagitious |
| Frairy | | Fairy. |
| Furbelow | | Furlough. |
| Industerous | | Industrious. |
| Mander | | Manner. |
| Partender | | Partner. |
| Properietor | | Proprietor. |
| Ruinate | | Ruin. |
| Solentary | | Solitary. |
| *Spreckled | | Speckled. |
| Stupenduous | | Stupendous. |
| Stuprify | | Stupify. |
| Sudges | | Suds. |
| Tremenduous | | Tremendous. |

7. Some by omittting necessary letters:

| | | |
|---|---|---|
| Bacca | for | Tobacco. |
| Chai | | Chaise. |

| | |
|---|---|
| *Christan | for Christian. |
| Curosity | Curiosity. |
| Curous | Curious. |
| Debiliate | Debilitate. |
| Fictious | Fictitious. |
| Ingenous | Ingenious. |
| Necessiate | Necessitate. |
| Ruffin | Ruffian. |
| Tedous | Tedious. |
| Vement | Vehement. |
| Versal | Universal. |
| Volumous | Voluminous. |

8. It is easy enough to conceive that Latin words, retained in their own form, as in terms of Law, &c. are very open to corruption :

| | |
|---|---|
| Arcy-farsy | for Vice-versâ. |
| Cavy | Peccavi. |
| Cessarary | Certiorari. |
| Crissy | Crisis. |
| Davy | Affidavit. |
| Diddimous | Dedimus. |
| Hizy-prizy | Nisi prius. |
| Hoxy-croxy | Oxycroceum. |
| Hoizon | Horizon. |
| Nolus-bolus | Nolens volens. |
| Non-plush } *Non-plunge } | Non plus. |
| Primmery } Primminery } | Premunire. |

9. There remains no inconsiderable number in which the distortion or dislocation is too great or too

general to allow them to be otherwise arranged than
in alphabetical order :

| | | |
|---|---|---|
| Acquese | for | Acquiesce. |
| *Artiflexy | | Apoplexy. |
| Bewiddle | | Bewilder. |
| Blather | | Bladder. |
| Brefkas | | Breakfast. |
| Cartrach. | | Cateract. |
| Coalese (diss.) | | Coalesce. |
| Crowner }<br>Cronnier } | | Coroner. |
| Cutriments. | | Accoutrements. |
| Farisee | | Fairy. |
| Farrage | | Fairing. |
| Fidgy | | Effigy. |
| Fisherate | | Officiate. |
| Gash-full }<br>Gashly } | | Ghastly. |
| Hobble | | Hovel. |
| Howsomedever | | Howsoever. |
| *Hume | | Hymn. |
| Inquiration | | Inquiry. |
| Intossicate }<br>Intosticate } | | Intoxicate. |
| *Intrust | | Interest. |
| Jocotious | | Jocose. |
| Juggler's vein | | The jugular vein. |
| Liceness | | License. |
| *Miscomfortune | | Misfortune. |
| *Miscomhap | | Mishap. |
| *Narrow-wriggle | | Earwig. |
| Nechthorn | | Nectarine. |

| | |
|---|---|
| Newelty<br>Neweltry } | for Novelty |
| Nottomy | Anatomy. |
| *Numpost | Imposthume. |
| Obligate | Oblige. |
| Odious | Odorous. |
| Obstropulous | Obstreperous. |
| Oudacious | Audacious. |
| Palaràtoch | Paralytic. |
| Permiscous | Promiscuous. |
| *Plumpendicular | Perpendicular. |
| Porpus | Pauper. |
| Portingal | Portugal. |
| Pumgenet | Pomegranate. |
| Quivy | Equivocate. |
| Rale | Real. |
| Semblitude | Similitude. |
| Sinnable | Syllable. |
| Singafy-fize<br>Sinnify-fize }<br>Singnafy-fize | Signify. |
| Scrummage | Skirmish. |
| Speciously | Especially. |
| *Spettacle | Spectacle. |
| Surficate<br>Snufficate } | Suffocate. |
| Tater }<br>Tate | Potato. |
| Timinate | Intimidate. |
| Trinkle<br>Trittle } | Trickle. |
| Turpentine walk | Serpentine walk. |

| Vamment | for | Vomit. |
| *Viper's dance | | Saint Vitus's dance. |
| Unbombinable | | Abominable. |
| *Upperhand | | Apprehend. |
| *Upperlet | | Epaulet. |
| Wagabone | | Vagabond. |
| *Whosomedever | | Whosoever. |
| Whatsomedever | | Whatsoever. |
| Whensomedever | | Whensoever. |

If any words have been improperly inserted or omitted in this catalogue, placed under wrong heads, repeated in the Vocabulary, or inserted there with less propriety than here; and if any apology be necessary, for errors or oversights so very likely to happen, it is now offered.

# ESSAY III.

*On some peculiarities of East Anglian Grammar.*

The Anglo-Saxon Grammars, of which we now acknowledge the authority, are entirely retrospective. They were not compiled till the language had gone through all its stages; nor, indeed, till it had been many centuries extinct. The English language, in its turn, passed through the greatest part of its progress, without a Grammar. None of any general practical utility has been in existence much above half a century. Dr. Johnson, in discussing the question of Shakspeare's learning, says, he "had only Latin enough to grammaticise his English." In fact, in the Poet's time, it was the only possible way of grammaticising it. His great contemporary and rival, Ben Jonson, indeed, wrote a grammar, but he could not avail himself of it; and it is not easy to conceive who could. The numerous schools founded in the latter half of the sixteenth, and the earlier part of the seventeenth centuries, in which the elements of Latin and Greek were to be taught, were called *Grammar Schools*, and still retain that name. To learn those elements, was to learn *Grammar*, and it could no otherwise be learned.

Our great etymological grammarian Dr. Wallis,

when he enters on his discussion of the Parts of
Speech, excuses himself from giving a formal detail of
them, in confidence that none of his readers can need
such an elementary statement, by their ignorance of
Latin grammar, in which language he wrote. The
same excuse may be made here for a similar reason.
Every reader must be presumed to be competently acquainted with English grammar. Our Provincial formations and constructions agree with it in the main.
We have not wherewithal to construct a particular
East Anglian Grammar, or even an Accidence. Nothing more is intended than to give some account of
certain deviations from general and established usage.
Fastidious critics, who can endure their mother tongue
in that form only which they consider as the most improved and refined, may choose to look upon these as
mere grammatical anomalies. Be it so, if so it seem
good to them. We will not cavil about a term. Thus
much, however, may undeniably be said on behalf of
such local usages. Their regular and unvaried recurrence strongly implies the existence of some rule,
which, though it be no where written, is uniformly
obeyed ; and, like some other causes of infinitely more
moment, operates unseen, to produce constant and visible effects ; while those who contribute habitually to
the production of those effects, are perfectly unconsci-
ous of the cause. In the course of our inquiry, some
of them may, peradventure, be found in the darkness
of remote antiquity, and may add, not inconsiderably,
to the proof afforded by the derivations of our words.
They are said to be characteristic of our dialect. It is

not meant that they are exclusively so. Some of them
may also characterise other dialects. So much the
better. Our proofs of antiquity will be strengthened
by that of common origin. To give them the only sort
of order to which they can be reduced, they will be
placed under the heads of the several parts of speech
in which they are observable.

## The Definite Article.

This little word was of no inconsiderable importance
in our parent language. Besides its necessary pre-
sence to point out any particular object or objects
among many, it was even sometimes prefixed to proper names and abstract nouns, as in Greek, ὁ Ἀλεξαν-
δρος and ἡ Ἀρεζη. It is not our present concern to
ascertain by what rules, and under what circumstances,
it was so used in either of those languages. Our concern is with the omission, not the seeming redundance
of it. Hickes says, that in his Dano-Saxon dialect,
the article "ut plurimum omittitur." Now, as it is
not easy to conceive limits to our oral tradition when
it is once in motion, there can be no violent improbability in supposing that the omissions of this sort, presently to be produced, have been transmitted to us
from the Lord-Danes, who so long domineered in East
Anglia. Such traditional modes of speech may well
be conceived to grow fainter, to waver and vary, yet
still to manifest sufficient traces of their continued existence, though not in full force, even among very remote posterity.

The omission of the article in some instances, in

which it might be used, is very general. Every body talks of going *to town*, or *to church*. The sportsman pursues his game *to covert*, or *to earth*, and finds it above *ground* or under *water;* but these several substantives are used in a general and indefinite sense. The omission of the article to be observed here, is when it properly bears its character of *definite ;* when it should precede substantives in a particular and individual signification ; and that only in the case of nouns of a certain description, and under certain circumstances. The nouns are names of familiar, and for the most part domestic objects; as, house, barn, stable ; parlour, kitchen, chamber ; chair, table, basket ; yard; garden, field ; pond, ditch, river. And farther, the omission is observable only after prepositions signifying motion to or from them. Ex. Walk into house ; go up chamber ; put the apples into basket ; turn the dog into yard ; come out of barn, &c. It is never said that the horse is in stable, that a crow flew over barn, that there are flowers in garden, fish in pond, &c.

It may be farther observed, that when the preposition ends, and its noun begins, with a vowel, some contrivance seems necessary to save our sensitive ears from the pain of a hiatus. To effect this the article is used with an elision of its vowel. Ex. Send him into th' orchard. He is going on to th' ice. Put the bread into th' oven. Though some times the article is omitted even in these embarrassing cases, but not without a similar guard against the hiatus ; as, on t' ice, int' oven. If it be not positively proved, it does not seem safe to deny, that this idiomatical peculiarity is a remnant, vague and obscure as it may be thought, yet still in existence, of an "ut plurimum" characteristic of the Dano-Saxon dialect.

## Nouns.

In a very considerable variety of instances we use the same form to express both the numbers. This is, indeed, by no means a peculiarity of ours, or of any other Provincial dialect. There certainly are some substantives in the English language distinguished by this formation, or rather non-formation of their plurals. But, as it is a subject which does not seem to have been sufficiently considered by any of our grammarians, and is rather a curious one, we may perhaps be allowed to endeavour to throw some light upon it here, without incurring blame for going too far beyond our tether.

Of this identity of the two numbers Dr. Lowth gives only two instances, sheep and deer. He might have given more from the animal kingdom; as plover and grouse among birds; salmon and mackarel among fish. Indeed, the word fish itself is an instance, and several other species of it might be mentioned. He might also have added horse in the military use of it. We could furnish him with another—beast, meaning animals of the beeve kind in a fattening state, or designed for it. Swine too, is pretty generally so used, but very improperly no doubt, as it is essentially a plural word, of which sow is the singular. But whatsoever additional instances might be produced, they could not constitute a rule. The names of animals, wild or tame, terres-

trial, aërial, aquatic, or amphibious, neither are, nor
ever were, in any stage of our language, nor in the
Anglo-Saxon, generally used in the plural number
without variation. Dr. Johnson has not even mentioned this class of plurals.

Lowth, in treating afterwards on the construction of
sentences, lays it down as a rule of English Grammar,
that "nouns of measure, number, and weight, (duration might have been added,) are sometimes found in
a singular form, with numeral adjectives denoting
plurality, as fifty foot, six score," &c. Surely it
is strange that the grammarian should give his express sanction to a violation of that essential principle
of grammar, concord. As this is said only to happen
sometimes, and as the instances which will soon be
produced prove that it happens irregularly or licen-
tiously, it seems safer to refer such instances to the
class of unchanged plurals. And, though it should
be undeniable that plural forms exist of the very same
words in which this identity is *sometimes* observed, by
going a little farther into the subject, it may be shewn
that the difficulty is less of taking the singular form
for the plural, *pro hâc vice*, than of conceiving the barbarous incongruity of singular substantives with plural
adjectives.

In the primitive simplicity of language, it is easy to
suppose that, when a name had been given to any
thing, and it became necessary to speak of more than
one such thing, the idea of plurality was conveyed by
connecting with the name some particle, or other
word of numerical signification; and that, in process
of time and improvement, inflected plurals were intro-

duced by the permanent connection of them. No
actual proof of this, with examples, can reasonably be
demanded. In its nature it can rest on grounds of
probability only. No specimens are producible of
what any language was in its very infancy. That this
observation is applicable to the Anglo Saxon language
is in the very highest degree probable. It is actually
certain that all nouns in it were not so changed. Some
continued, even in its highest state of improvement, to
express under the same form both singularity and plurality, and must therefore have been explained by
some other word or words standing in occasional construction with them. The learned Dr. Hickes makes
six declensions of Anglo-Saxon substantives. They
have been since reduced to three, which seem quite
sufficiently comprehensive. His fourth is one of those
which have been abolished, and thrown in among the
others. It contained the nouns which were the same
in both numbers; and he says the neuter nouns in
general belonged to it. In his Islandic Grammar, he
says that all neuter nouns in that language were the
same in both numbers. Here, then, in two of the
main branches of the great Gothic stock from which
our language springs, we find a general authority for our
economy, in sometimes making one word serve a double purpose. We must rest content that it is general.
It would be waste of time and pains to endeavour to
ascertain whether all the words which we use in this
manner were derived from one or the other of those
ancient tongues; and whether they were of the fourth
declension in the Saxon, or of the neuter gender in
the Islandic. But, if it convey no very valuable in-

formation, it may at least afford some amusement, and perhaps illustration, if we consider somewhat particularly our variable and undefinable copies of our ancient models. We will take the several classes of those nouns as Lowth has arranged them, nouns of measure, number, and weight, taking the liberty to add nouns of duration, which he has not mentioned.

In nouns of measure of *length*, we have mile in the plural, and not furlong or yard; foot and span, but not inch or line. Neither do we so use the superior denominations, league or degree. Perhaps, indeed, it may be safe to assert, in general, that the usage prevails in those words only which have come to us from or through the Gothic.

In measures of capacity, dry or fluid, we have chaldron, last, coom, strike, as plurals; but not bushel or peck. Tun, but not hogshead, barrel, gallon, or quart.

In square or superficial measure, it is usual with us to speak of two rood or twenty perch; but not of ten acre.

In solid measure, we fell so many load of timber, and dig so many floor of earth.

Of nouns of number, million, thousand, hundred, score, dozen, couple, pair, brace, leash, serve both purposes, and seem to constitute the only description of nouns which have been thus used without variation or exception, in old and in modern English, general as well as provincial, and in Anglo-Saxon, so far as it has been traced. And for the practice in this class of nouns, a reason, at least very plausible, may be assigned. The idea of plurality is so necessarily in-

volved in every one of them, that it might not be
thought requisite to invest them with a plural form.
It is not, however, to be understood that these words
have absolutely never distinct plurals. The identity
of the two numbers goes through them all, indeed, but
only when they are preceded by a numeral adjective
strictly so called, a cardinal number; not by a sort of
quasi numeral, as many, several, few. Everybody
says three million, five thousand, &c. but many hun-
dreds, several scores, &c. Indeed, in the former case,
the noun of number coalesces, as it were, with the annexed cardinal, and they become jointly one adjective; in the second, it has its proper character of a
substantive, attended by its adjective. It is like mille
and millia in Latin. The numeral is also properly a
substantive after a preposition, and assumes the plural
termination; as, "lay them in dozens," "count them
by scores," &c. This suggests the mention of a practice among us, totally the reverse of this parsimony of
plurality in nouns of number. We sometimes make
them even a double allowance of it. If we are count-
ing a considerable number of things, by two, three,
&c. we say we count by *twoses*, *threeses*, &c. The
number of such combinations being large, we express
that idea absurdly, and, to confess the truth, barbarously. But I am not aware of any other instance of
this profuse plurality. We certainly never run against
*postesses*, as the cocknies do.

Of nouns of weight, the pound, and all denominations above it, pass unchanged into the plural. Pound,
stone, quarter, todd, wey, hundred weight, and ton,
are equally expressive of one and of many. But not
so are ounce, dram, &c.

On the intermediate word, *pound*, it may be worth while to be somewhat more particular. It is used as a denomination of money, as well as of actual weight. Originally, the two senses were coincident. A pound weight of gold and a money-pound were synonymous. In Saxon times, the pound of gold was divided into sixty shillings, which progressively decreased both in number and value. The shilling was divided into pence, always the same in number, but of course decreasing in value. Neither of these inferior denominations ever followed the example of their principal in the plural number. They have at all times been shillings and pence. Or, if there be any exception, it must be some obscure provincial usage, not yet brought to light. Another inferior denomination was the mark, two-thirds of the pound. This did follow the analogy of its superior, while money accounts were kept in marks, as they now are in pounds. Shakspeare speaks of a "ring worth forty mark." Just so do we say "twenty pound." Pope has repeatedly written "ten pound;" and, to guard against all mistake, has rhymed it. For this word, thus used, we claim not only Anglo-Saxon and continued English, but even Latin authority. Twenty pound is exactly viginti pondo. In Anglo-Saxon, from which we must have had it immediately, it is *pund*. Whether it came to the Saxons from the Romans during their inroads, or to the Romans from the Goths, in a much earlier age, or to both from some other source, is neither ascertainable nor worth ascertaining.

Of nouns of duration, we have positive Anglo-Saxon proof of year in the plural number. In the Saxon

Chronicle we read "twentig geare," which is precisely our twenty year. And we use here the compound words a seven-year (septennium), and a hundred-year (centuria), both unchanged in the plural number. But we never talk of six month, three week, four day, or five hour.

Upon the whole, then, on our own behalf or that of others (to which assistance they are heartily welcome), we seem to have obtained satisfactory general proof of Saxonism in this point. The great irregularity and variableness of the usage, and the impossibility of confining it by anything like a strict rule, we must reverently submit to the unquestionable authority of that "arbitrium loquendi," which gradually erects itself into "jus et norma." Whether, in the present state of our language, any one, who aims at perfect correctness of expression, be justifiable in using any of these archaisms, is a question of criticism in which we have no concern.

We retain the Anglo-Saxon plural termination in *n* or *en*, in such words as *housen, closen, cheesen.* But this ancient formation is not so current and familiar in our dialect as it is in some others, and in old English.

The final syllable *er* of many words, signifying the offices or occupations of men, and nearly resembling the *or* masculine in Latin, and the ηρ and ωρ in Greek, is in the Anglo-Saxon not merely a syllable, but, in fact, an entire word. It is *wer*, a man; the very same as the Latin *vir*. So that a baker is a *bakeman*, a painter a *paint-man*, &c. So firmly established is this ancient traditional termination, that words derived from other tongues, and already complete in their formation, are wont to be lengthened out with this Saxon adjunct, as if it were essential to the conveyance of the full sense of the word; as a masoner, a musicianer, &c. The synonymous word *man*, which is also Saxon, is sometimes employed in the same service, and even in addition to the *er*. But the word thus fabricated is by no means intended as a respectful appellation. . I have often heard of a soldier-man, a lawyer-man, a doctor man, and even (salva sit reverentia!) a parson-man.

The same terminal syllable, *er*, sometimes makes words equivalent to those which are formed in Latin in *anus* or *ensis*, signifying the inhabitants of places. The word *Londoner* is nearly, if not absolutely, the only one which has obtained general currency. The names of very few places admit the termination so easily and fluently. We have no scruples of that sort. Not only are the inhabitants of Norwich called *Norwichers*, and those of the neighbouring villages *Cattoners, Eatoners, Earlhamers*, &c. none of which words is very offensively harsh, but we form similar words at all risks, ad libitum. For instance, an old farmer in West-Norfolk went to Thetford, and took lodgings there to drink the mineral water, with the same hope with which "Dean Spavin, Dean Mangy, and Dr. de Squirt," were sent some years ago from Cambridge to Bath. Returning to see how his household and his cattle fared, he told a neighbour that he must go back again in three days, for he was become quite a *Thetforder*. The formation is still Anglo-Saxon, however offensively to the ear it may sometimes be exemplified by modern East Angles.

## *Adjectives.*

Dr. Wallis has given a small list in *en*, which he calls material, such as golden, wooden, earthen, &c. The whole number amounts to but ten; and he adds, "raro alia." He might have added some which assume only the letter *n*, if the substantive ends in a vowel or diphthong, as *strawn* is used by Bishop Hall; or if it ends in *r*,* as *leathern*. Some might have been noticed with the same termination which cannot be called *material*, as *northern*, &c. The *alia*, not enumerated by the learned grammarian, probably lie scattered in provincial dialects. We can contribute specimens. We make use of *hornen* spoons, *tinnen* pots, and *glassen* bottles. We make wine of *eldern* berries; and have not quite left off the ancient custom of regaling on tansy pudding on *Eastern* Sunday.

Adjectives are often used for the adverbs formed from them; as "to behave rude," "to speak plain." This is readily recognised, however it came to us, as a Greek idiom. Lowth says it is "not according to the genius of the English language." Why not?

The syllable *ful* is added to some adjectives for the purpose of increasing or strengthening their meaning. Ex. "It is a *longful* while since I have seen you"—a *very* long while is meant, longer than if it had been simply called "a long while." It is, in fact, the old English phrase "full long." But by turning this phrase "end for end," as we say, and by making one compound word, we seem to ourselves to express the idea with more neatness and force.

---

* Chaucer, however, has *silveren*.

Of the duplications, and reduplications, and accu-
mulations of comparatives and superlatives, we have
our full share.  We come behind none in this expressive phraseology.  There seems to have been in all
language, more or less, a propensity to hyperbolize in
this matter beyond the strict limits of idiomatical propriety.  In our own it is certainly very conspicuous.
Our principal grammarians seem to have paid little
attention to the subject.  As it was their office to lay
down rules and laws, they may have thought it none
of their concern to enumerate violations of them.
They may have been passed over as vulgarisms and
provincialisms.  Then they come properly within this
our humbler sphere.  Ben Jonson, indeed, offers grave
reasons for some of these.  Of what may be called the
super-superlative, for instance, he says that it is an
English *Atticism;* and very happily illustrates his position, by adding that it is after the *most antientest* of
the Greek writers; who, as the learned Ben might
have recollected, were not *Attics.*  Dr. Johnson observes, that, "in a language subjected so little and so
lately to grammar," such anomalies, even in good
writers, "must frequently occur."  The instances,
which he proceeds to give from some old authors, are
only of adjectives regularly compared by *er* and *est,*
instead of the signs *more* and *most,* which are now
thought more correct in those cases.  This is by no
means viewing the whole of the subject.  Dr. Lowth
mentions "double comparatives and superlatives" in a
note, and passes a general censure on them, with a
single exception, but says nothing explanatory.  Mr.
Pegge, in his Anecdotes of the English Language, is

led by the nature of his subject to do what is much more to the purpose. He gives many instances of these irregularities, with very amusing apologies for the cocknies who use them, in quotations from many eminent writers in prose and verse, and of different ages. Not that he means to vindicate these erroneous practices, but to account for them, and to refer them to their Anglo-Saxon model, not individually, but collectively and analogically. Yet still, much as has been said by that entertaining and instructive writer, it seems as if something farther might be said on the subject, as far at least as double, or more than double, comparatives are concerned; not, indeed, with a view to the vindication of any one of them, but of suggesting some not improbable reason for their origin and formation.

The positive degree is fixed and unchanged. We must take it as we find it. Indeed some grammarians have doubted whether it ought properly to be called a *degree* at all. This, however, is only uselessly disputing about a term. We proceed to the comparative. There we find more, and perhaps progressively more and more, of the quality signified by the positive. There are successive shades of meaning. To express these, the word degree would be very objectionable, as it must produce confusion. Suppose, then, they be called sub-degrees. For example, here is something, no matter what, *positively bad*. On looking farther, we find other things of the same kind, comparatively and progressively *worse, much worse, very much worse*. Why not apply the Saxon comparative termination *er*, and say they are *worse, worser, worserer?*

It is only suggested that these words might thus have arisen. It is not likely they would always be used with exact discriminating precision. But this might be the origin of them, and that is all we want to come at. Supposing them used with due regard to the import of each, we should be able to give in one word, what must otherwise cost two; what has, indeed, been actually expressed in two by many of our best writers. Shakspeare says "more better," "more happier," "more sharper." We might thus get at least an intelligible interpretation of our phrase, "worser and worserer." Sometimes, from inattention to propriety of expression, "worserer and worserer," it would express such a deterioration of what is already bad, as almost to have reached the very extreme point; to have become only not so bad, as that which is absolutely the very worst of all.

From this same progress of comparative meaning, we might get a more plausible account of such words as *better-most, upper-most, inner-most,* &c. All the first parts of these words are of comparative import, whether they be strictly comparative degrees from positive adjectives or not. What have been called the sub-degrees might stand thus:

Better, betterer,         more better;
        better-most,      most better.

The meaning would be so much improved, as to have closely approached, or even actually attained, the extreme point of the good quality.

That point once reached, there can be no farther progress. In the superlative degree, the sub-degrees, which have been mentioned, can have no existence. If

any one be dissatisfied with its full force, as not
amounting to what he wishes to express, no farther intention can be effected, than by doubling the superlative upon itself, as it cannot go backward into the comparative. It cannot be denied that the effect of this
doubling may sometimes be very striking; in some
very few instances, even sublime. But it will warrant
no such low expressions as, "the most wickedest action," the "most worthlessest character," the "most
rascalliest trick," &c. Though truly, should one inad-
vertently blunder into the use of these, or any such
like expressions, he might endeavour to draw some
consolation from knowing that the great Sir Thomas
More has gone as low as "*most basest.*"

If we have a peculiar claim to any of these seemingly
disorderly words, it may be to *lessest* and *worsest*; so
far at least as may be inferred from their not occurring
in the glossaries of other provincial dialects. Dr. Wallis, indeed, contends that *lessest* is the proper Anglo-
Saxon superlative; that *least* is a syncopated form of
it, and ought therefore to be written *lest*. Pennant
has actually adopted this emendation. We use also
*littlest;* which is but an instance of that affectation of
regularity, of which several are given in verbs. *Worsest*
is very properly inserted by Major Moor among his
Suffolk words. This may be accounted for in like
manner as *lessest.* We retain the ancient form, which
by syncope has become *worst.* Our countryman Tusser has *worsest.*

It may deserve to be remarked, that we have a
strong manner of expressing the superlative degree,
by the simple expedient of comparing the positive with

itself. Thus, if any thing be extremely white, we say it is " as white as white;" meaning that it is inexpressibly, or inconceivably white; white as whiteness itself in the abstract. " As old as old," meaning that any attempt to ascertain its age would be fruitless.

Before we quit the consideration of adjectives, some notice must be taken of our great fondness for compound epithets. Though they be generally understood to be the proper ornaments of poetical or highly rhetorical composition, we use them in our most familiar colloquy. It will be readily conceived that the formation of them is somewhat licentious. In fact, they are " graces snatched beyond the reach of art." It is not therefore easy to prescribe rules for the use of them. Some little may, however, be done in this way. For instance, familiar similes are easily convertible, and often converted, into them. If any body, or any thing, be as white as snow, or as black as a coal, it is more poetical to call it snow-white, or coal-black. But we are fond of decorating our plain prose with the same elegance. When we meet with something as dry as a bone bleached in the air; as bitter as gall; as cold as a frog; as slow as a slug; as tired as a dog with his day's hunting; instead of formally detailing our meaning in set terms, we give it, with a more graceful concinnity, in the compound form, bone-dry, gall-bitter, slug-slow, frog-cold, dog-tired. We follow an ancient model. Shakspeare has dog-weary, snail-slow, and key-cold, where he certainly does not mean to make his characters express themselves poetically. One other mode of fabricating these compound terms may be mentioned. It consists in tacking together, off-hand, two or more words, no matter what parts of speech, into one adjective, by means of the terminal syllable *ly*. These bold figures are of course prompted by some vehement emotion. A certain widow Go,* in venting her just wrath on a profligate fellow who had run away and left several illegitimate children to be maintained by the parish, called him, with perfect fluency, "a toss-pot-ly, stuff-gut-ly, smoke-bacco-ly, whore-monger-ly, starve-bastard-ly vagabond." A strong, and certainly an ingenious compression of vituperation. It would not be easy to condense more of it into the same number of words.

### Pronouns.

It is very common to impute to us provincials in general, the use of the letter *a*, as a substitute for the personal pronoun *he*. Shakspeare has put it into the mouth of Mrs. Quickly, and of others of his low characters. But it is not so. It would, indeed, be a very improper and unaccountable representative. An attentive listener, properly qualified with ears, would not catch the power of *a*, or of any modification of it. It is in fact *he*, without the aspirate, and the *e* left alone, pronounced exactly like the French monosyllables, *le*, *de*, &c. Thus it is with us at least, whatever it may be elsewhere.

*What* is very often used for the relatives *who* or *which*. Ex. "The woman *what* came yesterday." "The pigs *what* I bought last Tuesday." *What* is, indeed, very generally used as a sort of relative, but

---

*See Crabbe's Parish Register.

with an antecedent implied, or involved, in it. Ex. "That is what I meant." i. e. " the *thing which.*" But the simple substitution of it for the proper relatives is certainly provincial, if it be not peculiar to us.

Every body occasionally uses the pronoun personal *they* as an indefinite, in such phrases as, " they say," &c. meaning no particular individuals, but that any body, or every body, says so. In short it is equivalent to the French " *On dit.*" But we go farther than this, and speak as if we thought the importation of the foreign *on,* and the conversion of it into the pronoun or pronominal adjective *one,* were quite unnecessary, for that our own Saxon word *they* would have served all purposes quite as well. Instances are very numerous. What Lowth has given may serve as well as any : " One is apt to think," " one sees," " one supposes." In every one of these, and in all like instances, we substitute *they.* And we are not without ancient and venerable authority. In 2 Kings, xix. 35, we read, " When they rose early in the morning, behold they were all dead corpses." The expression is by no means perspicuous. It has even somewhat of an Irish aspect. The word *they* has two different meanings. In the first instance it is *indefinite,* and in French would be, " quand on se levait de grand matin." In the second it is definitely applied to those who had been smitten by the destroying angel.

As we sink all distinction between the nominative and accusative plural of the pronoun of the second person, *ye* and *you,* there seems to be a sort of parity in doing the same thing in that of the first person, and saying both, " Let us go," and " shall us go?" Shak-

speare has used the latter phrase twice at least.  If it
be in familiar and low dialogue, it is more to our purpose.  It was in existence at that time.  We even use
*me* as a nominative case, and are certainly not singular
in so doing.  Ex.  " My wife and me are (perhaps *is*)
going to London to-morrow."  This is, no doubt, a
Gallicism.  *Moi* is so used, and when *je* would be
thought positively improper, which is more than can
be said for our practice.

We entertain so high an opinion of the essential services of the personal pronouns (especially of those of
the third person) as agents or nominative cases of
verbs, that we very commonly obtrude them, even after
the verb is sufficiently provided with one.  Ex.  " Mr.
Smith he came to my house yesterday."   " His family
they are all gone out."   These may be understood as
elliptical expressions ; the words omitted being " as
to " or " with respect to " Mr. Smith and his family.
However this may be, we are not answerable for it.
Shakspeare has it.  Ex.  " The Count he is my husband." All's Well, &c.  " The nobles they are fled."
Richard II.  In fact it is an Anglo-Saxon idiom.
" The Bishop he wrote," is literally taken from a Saxon
document in Hickes ; who seems to consider the usage
as intended to be emphatical.  Certainly it is so, in
many passages of our translation of the Bible, and of
other writings of that age.  But, in the passage quoted
above from Hickes, it seems to be plain narrative.
Certainly we mean no more by it than simple assertion.
Sometimes, indeed, the verb is repeated with the pronominal agent.  Ex.  " Says Mr. Smith, says he."  This

may be emphatical, as far as mere awkward repetition
can make it so.

The demonstrative *them* is very commonly used for
*those*, and in all cases. Ex. " *Them* are the women I
meant." " I saw *them* boys yesterday." *There* is often
annexed, which certainly makes the phrase more
pointedly demonstrative, and perhaps emphatical. Ex.
" Give me *them-there* books.

### Verbs and Participles.

This subject may be most properly begun with the
few remarks we have to make on the verb substantive.

The antiquated form *be* of the present tense indicative, so very common in Old English, and not less so
now, in many dialects, is almost extinct in our's. It
is heard but very rarely indeed, perhaps never, but in
such an exclamation as " Here he be!" On the contrary, it is in very frequent and correct use, as the subjunctive present, after the signs *if* or *though*. This correctness is not a little remarkable in those who use it
habitually, and, being untaught, are unable to give any
reason for their practice.

Our constant use of *war* for *was*, is merely using the
plural form for singular also, and pronouncing it with a
broader vowel. Indeed, *war* appears to have been the
Danish form of *were* or *wer ;* and has therefore been
a very long time in our uninterrupted possession.
Having nothing farther to observe here we may proceed to consider verbs in general.

In the Anglo-Saxon, and in the English, which exactly follows it in this respect, the structure of the
verb is simpler than in any other language. Still, as

no grammar was ever constructed before the language
to which it belongs had reached a state of improvement and refinement, it is not impossible that traces
may occasionally be found of earlier stages, in which
this characteristic simplicity may have been even
greater still. Something like this has already been
observed with reference to our use of certain plural
numbers. On this observation it is intended to found
a conjecture, by no means an assertion, that a particular usage in all verbs, appearing to be grossly ungram-
matical, but to which we are inveterately addicted, is
in fact a stray remnant of very ancient simplicity;
nay, almost of primitive simplicity; if we admit the
literal identity of the original nouns and their verbs
(whichsoever of them might be of prior invention), and
that the only way to distinguish the one from the other
was by position or context.

The indicative mood, present tense, singular number of the English verb, stands thus;

I love—thou lovest—he loveth, or loves.

Now, we so stubbornly maintain that the first and third
persons are of the very same form, " I love, he love,"
that it is not very uncommon to meet with persons of
even rather more than decent education, who are occasionally caught tripping in this point. Of the second
person it is not necessary for us to speak, for we never
use it; though it seems in the Northern dialects to be
no less expressive of easy familiarity than the *tu-toi* of
the French. The proposed conjecture is, that the
sameness of the first and third person is no solecism,
as it may seem to be, but in fact an archaism. Something, it is hoped, may be said in support of this notion.

In the first place, the learned Hickes, in four of the five conjugations in his Islandic Grammar, makes the second and third persons singular alike. In the fifth conjugation, all the three persons singular are so. The example he gives is

  1. ber.        2. ber.        3. ber (porto).

Considering the intimate connexion of the several Gothic languages with each other, this seems to be much to our purpose.

But we may perhaps come nearer still to our point by observing, that in the Anglo-Saxon itself, and in the English after it, the three plural persons are the same in all tenses. What improbability is there, that the same rule prevailed in the singular number, in some early and simpler stage? It is easily conceivable that some light might be thrown on this point in what is·recorded to have been written on the subject of Grammar by Ven. Bede and other Saxon writers. But wherever those ancient tracts are to be found, they are far beyond our reach. Indeed, Wanley's Catalogue, in the second volume of Hickes's Thesaurus, may serve as a guide to them, and, should opportunity occur, they might be consulted. But, in truth, this seems scarcely a "dignus vindice nodus." We may rest well content with probable conjecture.

That conjecture is very considerably strengthened by the certainty that in almost all our many auxiliaries, the first and third persons singular of the present tense are the same. And this suffices us, as we take no cognizance of the second. These auxiliaries are can—may—shall.

Ex. I can—thou canst—he can.

I may—thou mayest—he may.

I shall—thou shalt—he shall.

Let us next endeavour to account for the introduction of the syllable "*eth*" into the third person.

The three persons of the plural number had all anciently that termination.

Ex. We loveth—ye loveth—they loveth.

In process of time this "*ith*" was changed into "*en*."

Ex. We loven—ye loven—they loven;

as in the imperfect tense it had always been

We loveden—ye loveden—they loveden;

and of both these formations instances are to be found in very early English. Long after the language had become English "*en*" was dropped in its turn. Now it is not at all easy to conceive that, whilst "*eth*" was used in the whole plural number, it was also used to distinguish the third from the other persons in the singular. It was more likely to have been transferred to it when a new plural termination came into use. As for the final "*s*" in the third person singular, it is almost a modern innovation; certainly of no considerable standing. If this be no proof, it at least affords some probability, that our very remote ancestors said, as we say, "He love." But, however that might be, some of our nearer forefathers most assuredly did. We find many traces of it in different periods of o. e. Chaucer, in the Wife of Bath's Tale, uses "*chese*" (choose) for "*cheseth*." In the proclamation for apprehending Sir John Oldcastle, in the reign of Henry the Fifth, it is said, "*that he refuse.*" Tusser complains that the corn "shed as it *stand.*" The last authority perhaps, which can be found in point, is that of Pepys, in his Diary. He often writes " *He do*," &c.—Upon the whole, our use of these third persons is not without very respectable countenance and support.

The simple structure of the English verb, exactly following the Saxon, admits of three varieties of inflexion only ; viz. the present and imperfect tenses of the indicative mood and the participle passive. All other modifications of time or action, expressed by inflected tenses in languages more artificially constructed, being conveyed in our's by means of our great abundance of auxiliaries. It has been thought by some that the participle active should be added as a fourth inflexion. But this seems to be a distinction without actual difference, as it is in every instance formed by the addition of " *end*" in Saxon, and of "*ing*" in English, to the present tense.—This is indeed what every body knows ; and it might be impertinent to mention these, and one or two other particulars much of the same kind, did it not seem necessary to introduce them as foundations of what is to follow, and is much more proper to our purpose.

By these three principal parts our grammarians have arranged all our verbs under the two heads of regular and irregular ; an arrangement more comprehensive, as well as more simple, than that of conjugations. We could not have so arranged them, as they are in the Latin and its derivative modern languages, by the penultim. of the infinitive mode, for with us it is invariable ; all infinitives having the adjunct " *an*" in Saxon, and the prefix "*to*" in English. Neither could conjugations be discriminated, as they are in Greek, by

characteristic letters; with us, indeed, the characteristics must have been syllables, not letters. And, in the
original monosyllabic brevity of our simple verbs, the
whole word must have been characteristic, excepting
an initial consonant, or consonants, when there happened to be any. These different forms of our verbs
must have produced a most unreasonable and unma-
nageable multitude of conjugations. But suppose
them made: scarcely in one of these many forms, if in
one, is the change of the present tense into the imperfect and participle effected by any uniform analogy.
Under every one of them exceptions must be made,
and the number of irregulars must still be great. The
difficulty is well cut short by ranging them all at once
as regulars and irregulars.

The character of regularity is allowed by grammarians to those verbs only which form the imperfect
and participle passive by simply adding the syllable
" ed," or, if the present have an " e" final, the letter
" d" only. As

Mend—mended—mended.

Love—loved—loved.

It is not to be understood that all of the same form are
also regular. In the first instance, change but the
initial *m* into *s*, and we steal immediately into irregularity. As

Send—sent—sent

The whole multitude of irregulars has been divided by
Lowth into three classes. It is not necessary for us,
indeed, if it would be possible, to follow him through
this division. Our unconnected remarks upon some of
them, to which we are now coming, may be taken as

they occur with little regard to order: and they may perhaps be best introduced by a general observation, that we manifest a laudable anxiety to bring many of these vagrants into a more orderly state, which, if it be not what the grammarians call regularity, seems to us to be so. Not, indeed, that we attempt it on any consistent and uniform plan. There is one instance in which we perfectly succeed in bringing to order all verbs of one particular form, and that one only. In other instances, either our endeavours or our success are partial. But this only serves to prove the stubborn and inveterate propensity to anomaly, which characterizes the English language: and which cannot be overcome even in those parts of it, in which most pains are taken to that effect. Our first instance shall be an imperfect attempt at perfect regularity. We always say

Sell—selled—selled.
Tell—telled—telled.
Catch—catched—catched.
Teach—teached—teached.
Seek—seeked—seeked.
Work—worked—worked.

Some few occasional attempts of a like sort might perhaps be quoted; but these are well established.

Of verbs in "ow," or "owe," some very few are regular, as          Flow—flowed—flowed,
but the greater number follow the analogy of
Know—knew—known.

To facilitate correctness and uniformity of diction, we contend that all without exceptions should follow it; as          Snow—snew—snown.
Mow—mew—mown.

Row—rew—rown.

Sow—sew—sown.

Here is surely enough of specimens. Of these, the first is o. e. Hollingshed says, "It *snew* during the whole battle." The third is genuine Saxon. King Canute, in the elegant little impromptu * so properly preserved by Bentham and other authors, expresses the pleasure he felt in hearing the monks of Ely sing as he "*rew therby*" in his boat on the river. By the way, the monks, though they were pretty numerous, must have had powerful voices. With respect to the last instance, it coincides in the pronunciation of all the three parts with those of

Sew—sew—sewn.

Ex. "Tom Smith *sew* a furrow, while his wife *sew* a seam."

To the same rule we subject the verb "*hoe*," which we pronounce (according to our rule, q. v.) as if it were written "*how.*"

Hoe—hew—hown.

---

* But not given correctly even by Bentham in the History of Ely, though he had the authentic record of it before him. In the venerable "Liber Eliensis," written considerably within a century after the time of King Cnut, in the year 1107, it stands thus:

"Merie sungen the muneches binnen Ely,
Tha Cnut Ching *reu* ther by
Roweth Cnites noer the lant
And here we these muneches *seeng.*"

It is finished with an "*etc'a,*" and the munkish scribe adds that in his time the whole of it continued to be sung "*in choris.*"—Pity he did not give the whole! This one stanza however affords almost a contemporary authority for our imperfect tense, and for the plural termination in "*eth.*"

, Ex. " When Tom had finished sowing his barley, he *hew* his banes."

We are not much less assiduous and successful in bringing into order verbs which have a long *i*, in the present. Some of them assume a short one in the imperfect; others change it into a broader vowel, *a, o,* or *u*. To the first we give a decided preference, and are desirous of reducing those of the second form to it : as Rise—ris—ride—rid.

Rive—riv—stride—strid.

Smite—smit—drive—driv.

never *drove*, but sometimes *druv*, which is merely a step from *driv*. Shakspeare has *requit* in Tempest, and *betid* in Richard II. and Chaucer has the same.

On the contrary, if the *i* in the present is short, we prefer the broad vowel to the narrow in the imperfect, as bid—bod—give—gov—sit—sot. If it be said that we are somewhat capricious, we despise the censure, for we can prove it Anglo-Saxon. We also use *swum* for *swam*; and Shakspeare has *swum* in Two Gentlemen of Verona.

Among so many well-meant endeavours to regulate and methodize, it is really mortifying to be obliged to cite even one instance of a contrary description; but candour compels us to acknowledge that in the word *give*, mentioned above, we are far from consistent. In fact, we make sad confusion in its imperfect and participle, using indiscriminately for the one or the other *giv, gav, gov, gin, gan, gon,* syncopated from *given, gaven,* or *goven;* or even those words themselves are used in their proper length and barbarism.

Almost all the words in *ing* take *u* in the imperfect, as sing—sung.

We wish to bring the few stragglers under the same rule; as      Ming—mung.

            Ding—dung.

            Bring—brung.

We use *brought*, indeed, for the most part as the participle (with our own pronunciation, of course), but we say just as often *I have brung*, as *I have brought*.

Verbs involving the syllable *eave*, or *ave*, follow very generally the analogy of leave—left.

We manifest here the same love of uniformity; we say      Weave—weft.

            Save—seft.

            Wave—weft.

Dr. Lowth gives a list of verbs ending in *d* or *t*, which have the present, imperfect, and participle all alike; as      Cast—cast—cast

            Shut—shut—shut.

He accounts for this uniformity by supposing the second and third to be contractions, to avoid the harsh forms "*casted*" and *shutted*." We use some few others, without being at all scrupulous about their terminations, for which we have not the same excuse to make, but full as good a one—correct usage.

Come—come—come.  Ex. She come this morning.

Bid—bid—bid.        I was bid to do so.

See—see—see         I see her yesterday.

Run—run—run.      He run for a wager last week.

If we are called upon to account for our diction, we

may shew some cause. In the first instance, the imperfect should probably be written *cum*, as it frequently is in Old English, and by illiterate modern scribes. For the second, we have the authority of Shakspeare, in Romeo and Juliet. For the third, that of Chaucer, who makes *sey*,* or *seie*, the imperfect of *see*, which could only be faintly distinguished in pronunciation from the present, and we make no distinction at all. The fourth must even take its chance.

Some few detached instances of departure from modern formation might have been added, but are not worth formal mention here, as not constituting a rule or analogy ; such as *steal—staul, shriek—shruk.*

It may seem as if some of our verbs had, in process of time, grown up out of the imperfect tenses of others; or rather as if they were those imperfects themselves in some sort emancipated, and, if not become absolutely independent of their principals, at least clearly distinguishable from them in sense. As the vowel of the derived verb is broader or narrower than that of the original, it becomes in one case an intensive or augmentative, and in the other a diminutive. Under those heads, indeed, it will be better to range examples.

The subjunctive form of a verb, without its sign *that*, is as anciently and idiomatically used in East Anglian as in Latin, instead of the infinitive. Ex. " This was what made me I would not act as constable." In precisely the same form is Mrs. Quickly's

---

* By very clear analogy, Chaucer also uses *flee—fleye*, in which we do not follow him.

consolatory advice to Falstaff, when she "bade him he should not think about God."

The omission of the sign *to* before an infinitive, though certainly not peculiar to us, seems to be much more familiarly in use than is common. Ex. " Come and help me dress, reap, or mow."

The sign *to* is omitted also after other verbs than those enumerated by grammarians, *bid*, *dare*, *need*, &c. Ex. " You ought not walk so late a' nights." " Why need you do it?"

### *Participles.*

A little remains to be said on participles in particular.

It is observable that in our participles active the final *g* is always mute; for instance, *taking* is never distinguishable from *taken*. Indeed, by those who do not pique themselves on grammatical accuracy, and spell by the ear, they are very commonly written in the same form. It is not difficult to account for this. We seem to retain the Saxon termination of the participle, which was *and* or *end*, not *ing :* and it is certain that the letter *d* is more easily lost in such a place than *g*.

In participles passive ending in *d* we are extremely apt to substitute *t* for it : as *kilt* for *killed ; spilt*, with the short *i*, from *spill*, and with the long *i* from *spoil*. It may be allowed to be very easy in many cases to confound these two final mutes ; and that, in some such combinations with other letters, it is even difficult to give the *d* its distinct and proper sound in the rapidity of utterance. There must have been an original disposition to this substitution of *t* for *d*. The Low Scotch always has it for *ed*. So have we in some instances, as *raggit* for *ragged*. If this will not serve us a defence, I know not what we can do further than appeal to Irish authority for the first word.

Of our disposition to confound imperfect tenses with passive participles a passing notice has already been taken. But this seems the proper place for our defence. We not only often make one word serve both purposes, when it appears that two have been provided for us; but we sometimes form a participle from the imperfect, as *tooken*, *forsooken*, &c. uncouth words enough, but justifiable by ancient authorities. Our ancestors had formations of the same kind, scarcely less awkward. Chaucer has *clomben*, from *climb*, *clomb*; and *cropen*, from *creep*, *crope*. *Gotten*, from *get*, *got*, is very common in modern English; but *getten*, very common in the north, is at least a more orderly formation from the present tense.

### Prepositions.

We are accustomed to make the preposition *in* serve in our dialect, as it does in the Latin language, to express both motion and rest. In the one language, the difference is marked by the case of the noun which follows; but we can effect it only by a preceding verb. We say indifferently to "go" and to "stay *in* the house." Certainly the substitution of *in* for *into* appears at this time very incorrect; but we have old authority for it in abundance. In Shakspeare we find " Bring *in* grace," (i. e. into favour). All's well, &c· " Go *in* the vault." Rom. and Jul. " Turn this fellow *in* his grace," (i. e. into it). Rich. III.

The preposition *by*, signifying continuance of time, "*by* the space of many years," is common enough in old authors, as far back as Chaucer at least; but Johnson says it is out of use. It is not so with us. Ex. "He took care to do it *by* his life-time."

There is another sense of the same preposition, which Johnson does notice at all, but which is perfectly familiar to us. It is expressive of relation to some person or thing. Ex. "I never heard no harm *by* the man." Here again Shakspeare supports us: "*By* him, or *by* this woman, what know you?" All 's well, &c. This may indeed come under the comprehensive figure ellipsis, the participle "done," or "committed," being understood.

*On* is used for *of*. Ex. "I heard *on* it yesterday." Shakspeare has "out *on*" for "out *of*," in Troilus and Cressida. Whether misled by the ear, or in what other way, may not be worth enquiry, but we carry it a step farther; in which it is pretty certain that we can derive no countenance from Shakspeare, or any one else. We change the *on* into *in*, and always say, "Go out *in* the house." "He is out *in* health;" "out *in* temper;" "out *in* spirits," &c.

*Of*, in its turn, is also substituted for *on*. Ex. "He got up *of* his horse." But there is ample authority for confounding *on* and *of*. If we say, "I told him *on* it," or "I bestowed it *of* him;" the former is very frequent in old English, and Shakspeare must answer for the other.

The preposition *off* is always followed by his humble and kindred attendant *of*. Ex. "He fell *off of* his horse." But here, by the unlucky intimacy of connection between *of* and *on*, we are apt to say *off on*, a combination which may be thought no less whimsically contradictory in terms than *out in*, though neither the one nor the other strikes us with any impropriety.

For the preposition *upon*, when it signifies motion to, we use *onto* (why not as good as *into?*) Ex. " Throw some coals *onto* the fire." In use, this seems distinct from *unto*. Yet it is certainly the same word, and with a better, i. e. the true Anglo-Saxon, pronunciation.

The prepositions *on* and *upon* seem to coincide exactly with *super* in Latin, expressive either of motion or rest; those significations being discriminated in each language respectively, as was just now observed of the preposition *in*. We say in English, " the book stands *on* the shelf," or "set it *on* the shelf." In Latin, "*super* pluteo," or "pluteum." Johnson has not exemplified the latter use of the preposition, though he has given many senses, or rather applications, of both *on* and *upon*. *Into* is now generally, and probably has always in great measure, been used, with respect to *in*, as denoting motion. We use (as has been before observed) *onto*, with the like relation to *on*. So, probably, do other provincials, and on the same warrant of antiquity. The analogy is certainly good.

For *on* and *upon*, as betokening rest, we are much in the habit of using a whimsical sort of compound preposition, *a-top-of*, or *a-top-on*. No doubt it is common enough to say, that a man "is *a-top-of* a tower," or "*of* a tree." But we use it in such phrases as " I see Mr. Smith yesterday *a-top-of* his new horse;" and, " the dog is asleep under (or rather, undernean) the table, and the cat she is playing *a-top-on* 't."

### Negatives and Affirmatives.

We do not accord with the rule, that " two nega-
tives make an affirmative, by destroying each other;"
nor yet, as we learn in our Greek Grammar, that they
make the negation more vehement.  In using two, or
more, we mean to express simple negation.  A cot-
tager, complaining of the failure of his orchard in a
bad season, said, " I have no apples to year, no pears,
no plums, no cherries, no nuts, *no nothing at all.*"  The
vindication of my poor neighbour is easy and ample.
The double, or more than double, negative was in use
in the Saxon language, from which Chaucer had it, as
Dr. Hickes expressly says.  This usage was continued
down to Shakspeare's time undoubtedly, for he abounds
in it.  In fact, the single negative has only been used
since the modern improvement of our language, within
less than two hundred years.  Bentley uses the double
one in the letter on Phalaris, though he would most
likely have " slashed " it, had he found it in Boyle.

# THE

# VOCABULARY

## OF

# EAST ANGLIA.

# ABBREVIATIONS.

---

| | |
|---|---|
| A. S. | Anglo-Saxon. |
| B. A. | Barrett's Alvearie. |
| B. G. | Barn's Glossary. |
| B. JON. | Ben. Jonson. |
| B. TR. | Bible Translation. |
| BR. | Brockett's Glossary. |
| CH. | Chaucer. |
| CR. | Craven Glossary. |
| DICTT. | Dictionaries in general. |
| E. A. | East Anglian. |
| GR. | Grose's Provincial Dict. |
| JAM. | Dr. Jamieson. |
| JEN. | Jennings's Glossary. |
| JUN. | Junius Etymologium. |
| L. SC. | Lowland Scotch. |
| MIN. | Minshew's Dict. |
| M. S. | Moor's Suffolk Words. |
| N. E. | Northern English. |
| N. G. | Nares's Glossary. |
| O. E. | Old English. |
| O. V. | Ortus Vocabulorum. |
| P. B. | Percy's Ballads. |
| PE. | Pegge's Supplement to Grose. |
| P. G. | Percy's Glossary. |
| P. L. | Paston Letters. |
| P. PL. | Piers Plowman. |
| PR. PA. | Promptuarium Parvulorum. |
| q. v. | quod vide. |
| R. N. C. | Ray's North Country Words. |
| R. S. E. C. | ——— South and East Country Words. |
| SC. N. | Scotch Novels. |
| SH. | Shakspeare. |
| SK. | Skinner's Etymol. |
| SP. | Spenser. |
| SOM. | Somner. |
| T. | Tusser. |
| T. B. | Tim Bobbin. |
| T. J. | Todd's Johnson. |
| V. D. | Various Dialects. |
| W. C. | Wilbraham's Chesh. Gloss. |
| W. W. R. | Willan's West Riding Words. Archæol. |
| W. | Wickliffe's Translation of the Gospels. |

# VOCABULARY.

## A.

A. This letter has been used to serve many irregular
purposes; as an awkward contraction of the verb
*have ;* as a still more awkward representative of the
pronoun *he ;* as a substitute for the several prepositions *at, to, in, into, on,* and *of;* as an useless initial augment of a word ; and as a ridiculous ap-
pendage to a verse. Of all these anomalies, an account sufficiently particular is given in Todd's Edition of Johnson's Dictionary. For the origin of
some of them it seems easy to account from careless
and confused pronunciation ; for that of the others,
in great measure, if not entirely, from analogy
with the French preposition *à.* At any rate, we
are not particularly interested about them here
We use them, indeed ; but they are by no means
peculiarly our own, nor used more by us than by
others. If any one of them seem worth notice, it
will be found in its place.

ABOUT, *prep.* near to. This sense is, of course, in the
DICTT.; but there is a particular East Anglian mode
of using the word in conjunction with a pronoun,
which is not common. Ex. " Is the horse worth

forty pounds? Nothing *about* it." "Is he a mile
off? No, nor *about* it." "*About* forty pounds," and
"*about* a mile," are phrases common enough; but
in those now quoted, the prep. *near* would certainly
be used.

A-DAYS, *prep.* a shorter form of the general phrase
"now-a-days." Ex. "Corn sells cheap *a-days*."
" I seldom see Mr. Smith *a-days*."   o. e.

ADDLE, AIDLE, *v.*

1. To grow, to thrive.  Ex. "That crop *addles*."
2. To earn, to profit gradually.  Ex. "I have at last
*addled* up a little money."

A. s. *eadlian*, præmium. R. s. e. c.  T.  w.c.

AFEARD, *adj.* afraid.  In Chaucer's time there was
certainly some difference between the significations
of these two words, though with us they are perfectly synonymous. They occur in the same verse:

" This wif was not aferde ne affraide."—*Cant. Tales.*

The difference seems to result, naturally enough,
from their different derivations. *Afeard* is clearly
of Saxon origin, (from A. s. *ferght*, timor,) and
means, affected by fear, or *in* a fright. *Afraid* is
French, from *effrayer*, to startle or scare; and
therefore signifies put into a fright by some recent
cause. BR. JEN.

AFORE, *prep.* before.  o. e.  JEN.

AGAIN, *prep.*

1. Against.  Ex. " I am not for it, but *again* it."
2. Near to. Ex. " She stood *again* the door." If she
stood very near the door, it would be more correct
to say " close *again*," or " right *again*;" if facing
it, at some little distance, "over *again*."

AGE, *v.* to grow old, to assume the appearance of old age. The very common word *aged* is the regular part. pass. of this verb. It is strictly Saxon, though in that language a compound word is used, and by us the simple A. s. *aldagian*, veterascere.

AGGRAVATE, *v.* to irritate. v. D.

AGONE, *adv.* ago. Our word is the better of the two. It involves the part. pass. and therefore expresses more distinctly time actually past : indeed it is precisely and identically A. s. *agan*, præteritus.

AGREEABLE, *adj.* compliant. Taking this word in its ordinary sense, a man announcing himself to be so, would certainly be thought vain, and perhaps mistaken. In our sense of it there is neither vanity nor possibility of mistake : " I am agreeable," means simply " I agree to your proposal." w. c.

AGUE, *s.* swelling and inflammation from taking cold. An "*ague* in the face" is a very common consequence of facing a Norfolk North-easter.

AGUE-OINTMENT, *s.* an unguent made with the leaves of elder, held to be of sovereign efficacy in curing agues in the face.

AHUH, *adv.* awry, aslant. A. s. *awoh*, tortè.

ALE-STOOL, ALE-STALL, *s.* the stool or stand on which casks of ale or beer are placed in the cellar. A. s. *eale*, cerevisium, and *steal*, subsellium.

ALLEN, *s.* grass-land lately broken up. *Ald-land*. It is synon. with OLLAND, q. v. *Ald* is the A. s. form of *old*. This word is most familiarly used in Suffolk, the other in Norfolk.

ALLEY, *s.* a choice taw, not made of baked clay, as

vulgar marbles are, but of alabaster, or what is
supposed to be so ; and thence its name. BR.

AMPER, *s.* a sort of inflamed swelling. A. s. *ampre,*
varix, SK. JEN. " a small red pimple."

AMPERSAND, *s.* the character &, representing the
conjunction *and. V.* N. G.—*A per se A.* This is
*and per se and;* by a little smoothing and elision
in pronunciation, becoming *Ampersand.* "The expression," says the learned author referred to, " is
not yet forgotten in the nursery." No ; nor far
beyond the nursery. It is remembered and used
in the village-school, in the cottage, the shop, and
the farm-house. This formula of spelling and
putting together was applied to every syllable
consisting of one letter only ; as we all may remember who learned our first elements on the
principles of the old school. Only, indeed, the
dame was wont to express *per se* in her own English, and teach us to say " *A by the self A.*" The
character & is, however, in fact, originally and
properly *Latin,* and is a combination of the two
letters *e* and *t,* which constitute the common conjunction copulative in that language. It has been
adopted and transferred into other languages, for
the same use, with or without the same propriety.
It must be allowed to exhibit stronger traces of its
two constituent letters than the majority of those
Greek abbreviations, tables of which, more or less
copious, are inserted in almost all grammars, and
which are so very embarrassing in ancient MSS.
and early printed editions. A curious and irrefra-
gable proof of the Latinity of this character exists

in the rich library at Holkham, Norfolk. In a
Latin MS. of the Four Gospels, supposed to be of
the tenth century, it is used as a part of many
words, at the end, and even in the body of them.
Instances are, *posset* and *sciretis;* written thus,
*poss&* and *scir&is*. There is a multitude of others.

AN, *conj*.

1. If. Ex. " *An* I do," &c.
2. Than. Ex. " Little more *an* a half." Both o. e.
In this sense it seems a corruption, or licentious
abbreviation.

ANAN! *interj*. How! what say you? It is often contracted to *A'an*, or *N'an*. It may be, as Mr. Brockett
conjectures, the Fr. interrogation *ain*, said by Le
Roux to be "commune aux petites gens, et fort
incivile parmi des personnes polies;" which is precisely the case with our own word. Or perhaps
we may make it more our own by considering it
as an invitation to come near, in order to be better
heard, and deriving it from a. s. *nean*, prope. BR.
W.C. JEN.

ANBERRY, *s*.

1. A small swelling, or pustule, to which horses are
are subject on the softest parts of their bodies. In
books of Farriery, and in the DICTT. the word is
*Ambury*, which may possibly be right; and so, peradventure, may Skinner's elaborate derivation of it.
Still I beg leave to submit a very different one.
2. A small knob, or excrescence, on turnips and other
roots. In both cases, these are very well known
to be caused by the punctures of insects to deposit
their eggs. If, therefore, it be not attributing to
our rude and remote ancestors more accurate ob-

servation of nature than they may be thought
likely to have made, our word may be a derivative
of A. s. *anbryrdan*, compungere.

ANCHOR, *s.* the part of a buckle commonly called
the *chape*, put into a slit in the strap; so called
from some resemblance in shape to an *anchor*. BR.

ANCHOR, *v.* to hold like an anchor. The strong
tenacious spreading roots of trees or vigorous
plants are said to "*anchor* out."

AN-END, *adv.* onward, towards the end. The letter
*a* (becoming *an* before a vowel) is prefixed to the
word *end*, as it is to many others, *along*, *aside*, &c.
When Protheus, in the "Two Gentlemen of Ve-
rona," calls his man Launce "a slave, who still
*an-end* puts him to shame," though he puzzles the
learned commentators, he is familiarly intelligible
to an East Anglian clown, who calls to his companion to "*go an end*," when he wants him to go
forward. It also signifies upright, rearing. W. C.

ANGRY, *adj.* painfully inflamed. Ex. "My corn, or
my kibe, is very *angry* to-night." In the PR. PA.
*anger* is given as a synonym of *anguish*, and rendered into Latin by *angor*.

ANPASTY, *s.* another name for *Ampersand*. It means
*and* past *y*. To be sure it is also on the horn-
book past Z. But that crabbed and impracticable
double letter could not be brought into an euphon-
ous, or even an utterable syllable, to close the word
So the fabricator of it went back, and found the
very next letter suitable to his purpose. In JEN. it is
*Anpassy*; and the author supposes *passy* a corruption of *per se*. No doubt it is very probable; but
we must find a derivation for our own word.

APPLE-JACK, *s.* a homely sort of pastry, made by folding sliced apples with sugar in a coarse crust, and baking them without a pan. It is otherwise called a *flap-jack*, an *apple-hoglin*, a *crab-lanthorn*, and a *turn-over*. q. v.

APPLE-JOHN, JOHN-APPLE, *s.* We retain the name, but whether we mean the same variety of fruit which was so called in Shakspeare's time, it is not possible to ascertain. Probably we do not. In 2d pt. Hen. IV. Prince Hal certainly meant a large round apple, apt to shrivel and wither by long keeping, like his fat companion. This is not particularly characteristic of our *John-apple*.

APRON, *s.* the cawl or omentum of a hog. Its size, position, and the fine vascular and adipose ramifications, which overspread it like lace-work, make the name much more applicable to it, than to the fat skinny covering of the belly of a goose or duck, to which it is commonly applied.

ARGUFY, *v.* to import, to have weight as *argument*. Ex. " What does that *argufy?*" JEN.

ARSLE, *v.*

1. To move backwards. This is the primary signification of the word, which is L. SC. JAM.

2. To be unquiet, to fidget, to move frequently in any direction, particularly on a seat. In this secondary sense the adverb *about* is usually annexed. Belg. *arselem*, retrocedere.

ARSELING POLE, *s.* the pole with which bakers spread the hot embers to all parts of the oven. It is otherwise called a *wrastling-pole*, which seems somewhat better descriptive of its use; for *wrastle* is certainly of kin to *wrest*. The words are the same, varied by a sort of metathesis. The first can only mean, "to throw backwards."

ARSELINS, *adv.* backwards. L. SC. JAM.

ARTICLE, *s.* a poor creature! a wretched animal! Probably the first introducer of this term of extreme contempt meant, that the person to whom it is applicable is as completely insignificant in himself as an article in grammar.

AS, *pron. rel.* who, which. Ex. Those *as* sleep. SH.

AS, *partic. redund.* Ex. "He will come *as* to-morrow." O. E. P. L.

ASOSH, ASHOSH, *ad.* awry, aslant; differently formed from the same etymon as AHUH, q. v. But *ahuh* seems to come nearer to the Saxon original.

A'TOP OF, *prep.* upon. Ex. "I saw Mr. Brown *a'top of* his new horse yesterday."

ATTER, *s.* pus, morbid matter. A. S. *attre*, venenum. L. SC. JAM. GR.

ATTERY, *adj.* purulent. L. SC. JAM.

ATTONCE, ATTONES, *adv.* at once. SP. Ex. "Do it *attonce*."

ATWEEN, *prep.* between. O. E.

AVEL, *s.* the awn or beard of barley. A. S. *awel*, subula. M. S.

AUGHT, *v. imperf.* and *part.* of awe; another form of owe. Ex. "He *aught* me ten pounds."

AVISED, *part.* aware, informed. "Are you *avised* of that?" quoth Dame Quickly to Master Slender's man in the "Merry Wives of Windsor." Just so would a modern East Anglian Dame Quickly say. Fr. *s'aviser*.

AUSIER, *s.* the osier. This word seems to point at

the proper origin of the name. The genus of
plants in question grows for the most part in or
near water. But in all the French Dictionaries
which have come within reach, it occurs only
under the letter O. Surely it must once have been
*eausier*.

AWK, *adj.* inverted, or confused. Bells are "rung
*awk*" to give alarm of fire. This is the only connection in which the word is used among us, without
its adjunct *ward.* L'Estrange (who was a Norfolk
man) uses it, In PR. PA. *awk* is rendered into Latin by *perversi.* Ray says, that *awkward* is opposed
to *toward.* R. S. R. C.

AX, *v.* to ask. V. D. Used by many old authors, and
in fact, original Saxon, A. S. *acsian*, interrogare.

## B.

BAB, *v.* to fish in a simple and inartificial manner, by
throwing into the water a bait on a line, with a
small piece of lead to sink it, lifting it up from time
to time, and dropping it again. Eels are thus
taken in the fens, and crabs on the sea-coast. It
is the same as *bob*, which in T. J. is defined "a term
in angling." Our *babbing* differs from *angling.*
Neither floats, pole, nor hook are necessary to it,
though one or more of them are occasionally used.

BAB, *s.* the bait used for fishing in this manner, which
usually is made of large worms, strung together,
and tied in a bunch.

BABS, *s. p.* small prints to amuse children. Qu.

*babes?* Skinner has *baberies* in the same sense. Our word seems to be contracted. "A penn'orth of *babs*" contains considerable variety of birds, beasts, &c.

BADGET, *s.* a badger.

BADLY, *adv.* in ill health. Sometimes *sadly-badly.* PR. and sometimes *sad-bad.*— BAD, *adv.* JUN. BR.

BAFFLE, *v.*

     1. To gull, to cheat, or make a fool of. In SH. it is applied to the tricks played on Malvolio in " Twelfth Night."

     2. To manage capriciously or wantonly, as in the case of children or cattle. Ex. " He was sadly *baffled* in his bringing up."

     3. To beat and twist irregularly together, as "growing corn or grass is *baffled* by wind and rain."

The derivation offered in T. J. for the word in · the senses there given, seems to suit ours also.

Fr. *en bas fouler.*

BAG, *s.* the dug of a cow.

BAIL, *s.* the handle of a pail, bucket, or kettle. Hence the sailor's term, "to *bale* out." Also the bow of a scythe. Fr. *bailler.*

BAIN, *adj.* pliant, limber. In R. N. C. "willing, forward," which are connected meanings. In W. C. "near, convenient," which brings it to our GAIN, q. v. Isl. *beina,* expedire. BR. W. W. R. W. C.

BALDER, *v.* to use coarse language. A. S. *bald,* audax, comp. deg. *baldor.*

BALDERDASH, *s.* not "frothy and confused" as the DICTT. have it, but filthy or obscene talk.

BALK, *s.* There is some difficulty in determining

on the admission of this word; some of its senses
being recognized by the DICTT. and in general use,
others either peculiar to us, or common to ours
with some other provincial dialects. As there are,
however, connecting links between all the senses,
it seems best to state them all.

1. A ridge of land left unploughed, to serve as a
boundary, either between two contiguous occupations, or two divisions of the same farm, in an
uninclosed cornfield. *V.* MEREBALK. E. S. E. C. T.

2. A ridge so left in the body of the land, at certain
intervals, in a particular mode of ploughing called
*balk-ploughing.* The ridge, JUN. observes, is "*tigni*
*instar.*"

3. A beam in a building, supporting an upper floor
or roof; or, indeed, it may be applied in general
to any piece of timber, squared, and made ready
for that, or any other purpose in building. A. S.
*balc,* lignum. CH. B. G.

4. The failure of an expectation. Metaph. from the
slipping of the plough over the parts which it
seemed to be approaching, but leaves untouched.

5. A simple piece of machinery used in the dairy-
districts of the county of Suffolk, into which the
cow's head is put while she is milked. It allows
her to move her head freely up and down, but
when she attempts to withdraw it, she finds herself *balked,* and that she must stand still till the
dairy-maid dismisses her. M. S.

6. Straight young trees after they are felled; but
before they are hewn, it should seem, for then they
they would become *balks* in the *third* sense. M. S.

BALKER, *s.* a great beam. An augm. of *Balk.* sk. has *bulkar,* which he assigns to Lincolnshire, and derives, perhaps rightly, from Dan. pl. n. of *bielke,* trabs.

BAMBLE, *v.* to shamble, to walk unsteadily and weakly. Is it possible to trace it through the feeble and unsteady gait of young children to Ital. *bambino?*

BAN, *v.* to curse. sh. "fell *banning* hag!" Ex. "Oh! how she did *ban* and blast!"

BANDY, *s.*

1. The curved stick with which the ball is struck at sundry games.

2. Any game so played is called by the general name. Some are distinguished by appropriate additions.

3. A hare, from the curvature of her hind legs.

BANDY-HOSHOE, *s.* a game at ball played with a *bandy* either made of some very tough wood, or shod with metal, or with the point of the horn or the hoof of some animal. The ball is a knob or gnarl from the trunk of a tree, carefully formed into a globular shape. The adverse parties strive to beat it with their *bandies,* through one or other of the goals placed at proper distances. It is probably named from the supposed resemblance of the lower end of the *bandy,* in strength or curvature, to a horse-shoe; or it may be so called from being shod, as it were, with horn or hoof. In particular, the empty hoof of a sheep or calf, which is frequently used, may be well assimilated to a shoe.

BANDY-WICKET, *s.* the game of cricket. Of the several games at ball played with a *bandy,* that in which a ball is aimed by one player at a wicket, defended by the adversary with his *bandy*, must be allowed to be very appropriately called *bandy-wicket*.

BANG, *s.* cheese made, in Suffolk, of milk, several times skimmed; therefore very hard and tough, and with which a hard knock or *bang* might be given. For the same reason it is otherwise called *Suffolk Thump.* Or it may have obtained both those names from another circumstance,—that when it is dry, knock as hard as you will, you can make no impression on it.

BANGING, *adj.* huge; *beating* or excelling in size other things of the same kind. BR.

BANGLED, *part.* when cocked hats were worn, one of the sides was sometimes let down to protect the face of the wearer. The hat was said to be *bangled*. It is even now said of a round hat with a broad and loose brim, such as is worn by Quakers, or of late by dandies. The same name is also applied to the young shoots, or more particularly the broad leaves of plants, when they droop under heavy rain or strong sun-shine. Teut. *abbangen*, dependere. SK.

BARGAIN, *s.* an indefinite number or quantity of any thing; not necessarily conveying the idea of purchase and sale. Ex. "Two good tidy *bargains* of hay from an acre," meaning something less than waggon loads. "A poor *bargain* of wool from three score hoggets." "A sad *bargain* of lazy chaps."

BARGOOD, *s.* yeast; the *good* of the *beer*; the

flower or cream of it. It is sometimes corrupted into *burgood*, and even *bulgood*. But may not *bargood* be from c. br. *bragod* or *bragot*, a sort of country drink in Wales, mentioned by Lloyd in Ray? It was composed of wort and honey.

BARK, *s.* the tartar deposited by bottled wine or other liquor, encrusting the bottle.

BARLEY-BIRD, *s.* the nightingale, which comes to us in the season of sowing barley. To lovers of natural history, it is highly interesting and amusing to mark the coincidences of the arrival or departure of migratory birds with the germination, foliation, inflorescence, or maturation of vegetables. It may even be made useful to some purposes of husbandry. This name of the "sweet bird" of night could have originated only in such a habit of observation. And among whom? Even simple rustics! For neither gentlefolks nor persons of science were ever known to call the nightingale the *Barley-bird.*

BARLEY-MUNG, *s.* barley meal mixed with water or milk, to fatten fowls or pigs.

BARN, *v.* to lay up in a barn. Ex. " I shall stack some of that wheat, and *barn* the rest."

BARNACLES, *s. pl.* spectacles; which, before the invention of springs, were made to keep their proper position before the eyes by simply pinching the nose, like the instrument used by farriers to make a horse stand still, and commonly called *barnacles.* The word was certainly in use 200 years ago.

BARROW-PIG, *s.* the least pig of the litter. The *pitman* has the same meaning, and perhaps is more .

general. In JEN. a *barrow-pig* is a gelded pig. In
T. J. *barrow* is made synonymous with *hog*, and a
passage from one of Milton's controversial tracts is
quoted as authority. But this affords no proof that
Milton thought the two words exactly equivalent.
It might have been quite enough to call his adversary *hog;* but the great poet's virulence and acri-
mony on such occasions are sufficiently notorious ;
and he might mean to apply the most insulting and
degrading term, applicable only to the lowest of
the whole swinish race. However this may be, it
is certainly from A. s. *berg*, porcus.

BARSELE, BARKSELE, *s.* the season of stripping
bark.

BARLEY-SELE, *s.* the season of sowing barley. A. s.
*sæl*, opportunitas.

BARTH. *s.* a shelter for cattle, &c. Seamen give the
name of *berth* to a snug place for themselves, their
vessel, or their cargo. Between the sound of the
two words there is little or nothing to choose in the
mouth of an East-Angle. *Barth*, however, is the
right word; it is from *bar*, implying separation, or
inclosure.

BARTON, *s.* Spelman's account of this word is short
and perfectly clear. It was the demesne land of the
lord of a manor; not let out on lease, either of
years or lives, but held by the lord, in his own
hands, for the sustenance of his household. The
signification of the word has been reduced from a
part of a manor to a part of a farm; to a farm-yard,
a rick-yard, or even a poultry-yard. In this sense
it occurs in some DICTT. and is said to be still in use

in the Northern and Western counties. On the other hand, it has been extended from being the appellative of the Lord's own occupation to be the proper name of a whole manor, or even of a parish, containing more than one manor. There are parishes of this name in Norfolk, Suffolk, and Cambridgeshire. It cannot be improper to record here one East-Anglian instance (and there may be more) of the modern existence of the word, nearly, if not precisely, in its original and peculiar sense. Behind the episcopal palace and gardens at Ely, and separated from them only by a public highway, is a farm called *Barton*, which has been so called as far back as can be traced by records. There is no village, hamlet, or messuage upon it, nor any record or tradition of them, but the lands only, and the buildings necessary to the cultivation of them. From this proximity, there is full reason to conclude that this was the demesne land, on the produce of which the households of the ancient Bishops were maintained, while that system prevailed. Since it ceased, the land has been held, and is still held, of the See, under its original name, by a series of leases for four lives.

BASKING, *s.*

1. A drenching in a heavy shower.

2. A sound drubbing.

In the first sense, it is commonly said that a man gets a wet jacket; in the second, that his jacket has been well laced, or trimmed. Our word may therefore be very well derived from O. Fr. *basque*, a shirt, or flap of a doublet.

BATCH, *s.* a bout; as of drinking, card-playing, &c.

Properly it means a quantity of bread, or other things, baked at the same time. This is a dictionary sense. Our large metaphorical sense is probably not peculiar to us.

BATTEN, *s.* a rail from three to six inches in breadth, one or more in thickness, and of indefinite length. Dr. Johnson says it is a word used only by workmen. With us it is used by anybody.

BATTEN-FENCE, *s.* a fence made by two or three *battens*, one above another, nailed to posts at proper distances.

BATTLINGS, *s. pl.* toppings and loppings of trees. An unhewn rail is also called a *battling*. This and the foregoing are from A. S. *bat*, fustis.

BAUBERY, BOBBERY, *s.* a squabble, a brawl. Fr. *baube.*

BAVIN, *s.* a light, loose faggot. SH. speaks of

> —— " Rash, *bavin* wits,
> Soon kindled, and soon burnt." HEN. IV.

Neither Johnson nor his last Editor makes any thing of the derivation. *V.* GAVIN and GAVEL.

BAVISH, *v.* to drive away. Corruption of *banish.*

BAWND, *part.* swollen. Not in present use; at least, not known to be so. Isl. *bon*, tumidus. Sir Thomas Browne. R. N C.

BAY, *s.*

1. The space in a building between two main beams. We speak of a barn, or a cartlodge, of so many *bays.* Sometimes, but not so correctly, the whole space between the threshing-floor and the end of the barn is so called. SH. applies the word to a house. In " Measure for Measure" the clown talks of houses being let at so much a *bay.*

2. The nest of a squirrel.

BAY-DUCK, *s.* the shell-duck; from its bright colour,
like that of a *bay* horse.

BEAKER, *s.* a drinking-glass. The definition of
this word in T. J. is at least vague: "a vessel for
drink, a flaggon." That given by Dr. Johnson
himself seems purely fanciful: "a cup with a spout
in the form of a bird's *beak*." In our use it is
simply and solely a glass for the table. The *hicher*
of Scotland, and of the Northern Borders, according to JAM. and BR. is a wooden dish, or bowl, of
greater capacity, and used for other purposes.
The latter, indeed, gives *beaker* also, very indefinitely, as "a tumbler, or any thing large." Ours
is a definite and invariable sense, and likely to be
the true one. Our homely ancestors quaffed their
ale from wooden cups, which retain their name,
now they have outgrown it by the general substitution of glass for wood. The word would be better spelled *becher*, or *beker*, from A. S. *bece*, fagus.

BEAR, *v.* Phr. "to *bear* a bob;" to make one among
many; to lend a helping hand, at the risque, as it
should seem, of receiving a bob, or blow. Originally, perhaps, it meant joining a party in some
sport; the antient *quintaine*, for instance, in which
the players were very likely to have a bob to *bear*,
and a pretty severe one too. Or it might originate
in the steeple. Among their terms of art, ringers
have several sorts of bob, all of course, involving
the idea of a blow.

BEARN, *s.* a barn. In this instance we retain the
exact A. S. *bærn*, horreum.

BEAST, *s.* an animal of the beeve kind in a fatting
state. This word, like sheep, is the same in the
plural as in the singular number. A farmer has
so many sheep, so many *beast*, steers, buds, wennels,
&c.

BEASTLINGS, *s. pl.* the first milk drawn after the
cow has calved. GR. V. D. Proper food for the
*little beast.* A beastling pudding is thought superior
to one made of common milk. BR.

BEAT, *v.* to repair, to supply the gradual waste of
any thing. We seem to apply it only to mending
the broken meshes of a net. To "*beet* the fire"
means in the North to supply it with fuel. This
may be the better speaking. A. S. *betan*, restau-
rare. BR. W. C.

BECK, *s.* a brook or rivulet. A. S. *bece*, rivulus. GR.
V. D. O. E.

BED, *s.*
1. the uterus of an animal.
2. A fleshy piece of beef cut from the upper part
of the leg and bottom of the belly.
The first sense is illustrated at least by A. S. name
for the womb *cylde-hama*, q. d. the child's *home*.

BED-FAGGOT, *s.* a contemptuous name for a *bed-
fellow*, as it were, a wretched substitute, no better
than a faggot in the muster of a regiment.

BEE-BREAD, *s.* a brownish opake substance, with
which some of the cells in a honey-comb are filled,
for the food of the insect in its larva state. Jamieson says it goes to the formation of bees. That
eminent lexicographer may be excused for being
no entomologist. A. S. *beo-bread*, favus.

BEE-DROVE, *s.* a great confluence of men, or of any

other creatures; as it were, a swarm of them. But *drove* is a strangely absurd synonym for swarm. It may be remarked, however, that Cowley uses the word *drove* for a flight of birds.

BEGGAR'S VELVET, *s.* the lightest particles of down shaken from a feather-bed, and left by a sluttish housemaid to collect under the bed till it covers the floor for want of due sweeping, and she gets a scolding from her dame.

BEGGARY, *s.* the copious and various growth of weeds in the " field of the slothful ;" the " urenda filix" of neglected lands; the very best are apt to be overrun with *beggary* for lack of sufficient ploughing, hoeing, and hand-weeding.

BEGONE, *part.* decayed, worn out. GR. Norf. & Suff. Sufficiently recognized in the o. E. word *woe-begone*, q. d. wasted with misery.

BEING, *s.* an abode, particularly a lodging. A. S. *byan*, habitare.

BEING, *part.* We have a particular use of this word, much like the construction of the ablative absolute in Latin, when the substantive is represented by a clause of the sentence. Ex. " I could not meet you yesterday, *being* I was ill a-bed."

BELIKE, *adv.*

1. Likely ; L. SC.
2. As it is said.

To speak accurately, this word, in the first sense, must lead in the sentence, and be followed by the potential form of a verb. Ex. " *Belike* we may have snow to-night." In the second sense it must follow, and the verb must be indicative. Ex. " I hear Mr. A. is to be married to Miss B." " Aye, so *belike*."

BELLIBORION, *s.* a variety of apple. It is certainly
a fine sonorous corruption of Fr. *belle et bonne.*

BELSIZE, *adj.* bulky, of goodly size.

BELL-SOLLER, *s.* the loft on which ringers stand.
Chaucer has *solere,* apparently in a like sense.

BEN-JOLTRAM, *s.* brown bread soaked in skimmed
milk; the plough-boy's usual breakfast, served in
a capacious wooden bowl. It may, perhaps, be
mere farm-house slang. Yet, as there must be
some ground even for the most licentious and arbitrary fabrications, we may be allowed to imagine
one in this case; and it might not be altogether
absurd to conjecture, that in the first part of this
strange word an obscure allusion is intended to
*Benjamin's* seven-fold mess; and that the latter
part was meant to express the *joltering* (q. d. *jolt-
ing*) of the flatulent mixture in the stomach of the
young rustic, when he resumes his labour in the
field, after swallowing it.

BENTS, *s. pl.* dry stalks of grass remaining in pastures after summer feeding. BENNET. JUN. Teut.
*bintz,* juncus. SK.

BESS O' BEDLAM, *s.* a sort of vagrant very common in this country thirty or forty years ago; but
now very nearly, if not quite, extinct; either from
the greater efficiency of the Vagrant Laws, the
stricter administration of them, or the diminished
credulity of the public. They were wont to announce themselves as inmates of Bedlam, allowed
in some lucid interval to range the country, and
return at a stated time to their confinement. They
talked in a wild incoherent manner, were great

annoyances to every body, objects of great terror
to many, and, from the general wish to be rid of
them as soon as possible, were likely to collect
considerable contributions. They were in existence in Shakspeare's time, who speaks of "Bedlam
beggars with their roaring voices." The name is
not yet obsolete. Any female maniac, or any
whose dress, manners, and language, are wild, disorderly, and incoherent, is still called a *Bess o'
Bedlam*. *V.* Tom o' Bedlam.

BESTOW, *v.*

1. To deliver a woman. To " put her to bed " has the
same import.
2. To lay up, to put out of the way. It is equivalent
to the seaman's phrase, " to *stow* away." O. E. B. TR.
" to *bestow* my goods."

BETWIXT and BETWEEN, *adv.* exactly in the
middle point.

BEVIL, *s.* a slope, or declivity. Ex. " The road is
laid on a *bevil*, i. e. highest in the middle." The
word occurs in DICTT. as only used in architecture.

BEVILING, *adj.* having such a declivity.

BEZZLE, *v.* when the edge of a tool is blunted or
turned in the process of whetting or grinding, it is
said to be *bezzled*.

BIBBLE, *v.* to eat like a duck, gathering its food from
water, and taking up both together. A dim of *bib*,
and that doubtless from Lat. *bibo*. It means, also,
to tipple. JEN. *Bib* is O. E. " a wine-bibber."

BIDE-OWE, *v.* interpreted by Ray (Pr. to N. C.)
"*poenas dare*." It may be so. It is impossible to
assent or gainsay, as it is totally extinct. It is one
of Sir Thomas Browne's words.

BIGG, *s.* a species of barley; called also *barley-big.*
It is *hordeum hexastichon,* Lin. It is a good deal
cultivated in the fenny districts of Norfolk, and·the
Isle of Ely. It yields and grinds well, but will·not
malt. The Scotch *big,* according to JAM. is *hord.
tetrastichon,* Lin. Isl. *bigg,* hordeum.·

BIGHES, *s. pl.* jewels, female ornaments. O. E. We
use it in a figurative sense. Ex. " She is all in·her
*bighes* to-day," q. d. best humour, best graces,·&c.

BILLY-WIX,·*s.* an owl.

BING, *s.* a bin for corn, flour, wine, &c. The proper
word. Dan. *bing,* cumulus.

BIRD OF THE EYE, *s.* the pupil, or rather, perhaps,
the little refracted image on the retina, or that of
a very near spectator reflected from the cornea.
In many languages there seems to be some delicate
or endearing term of this kind. The Greeks call it
κορα, or παρθενος, the girl or virgin ; and our·an-
cestors talked of the " baby in the eye." In Latin
it is *pupilla.* R. S. E. C.

BIRTLE, *adj.* brittle. These metathetical changes
are, perhaps, scarcely worth notice.

BISHOP, *v.* to confirm. Chiefly used in the part. pass.
and so it was in the Saxon. A. S. *biscopod,* confir-
matus.

BISHOP-BARNABEE, *s.* the pretty insect more
generally called the Lady-bird, or May-bug, *Coc-
cinella septem punctata,* Lin. It is one of those few
highly favoured among God's harmless creatures,
which superstition protects from wanton injury.
Some obscurity seems to hang over this popular
name of it. It has certainly no more relation to the

companion of St. Paul than to drunken Barnaby; though some seem to have supposed it has. It is sometimes called *Bishop Benebee*, which may possibly have been intended to mean the *blessed bee*; sometimes *Bishop Benetree*, of which it seems not possible to make any thing. The name has most probably been derived from the *Barn-Bishop*; whether in scorn of that silly and profane mockery, or in pious commemoration of it, must depend on the time of its adoption, before or since the Reformation; and it is not worth inquiring. The two words are transposed, and *bee* annexed, as being perhaps thought more seemly in such a connexion than fly, bug, or beetle. The dignified ecclesiastics in ancient times wore brilliant mixtures of colours in their habits. Bishops had scarlet and black, as this insect has on its wing-covers. Some remains of the finery of the gravest personages still exist in our academical robes of ceremony. There is something inconsistent with the popish episcopal character in the childish rhyme with which *Bishop Barnabee* is thrown up and dismissed when he happens to light on any one's hand. Unluckily the words are not recollected, nor at present recoverable. But the purport of them is to admonish him to fly home, and take care of his wife and children, for that his house is on fire. Perhaps, indeed, the rhyme has been fabricated long since the name, by some one who did not think of such niceties.

BITCH, *s.* a trull; the female companion of a vagrant. Ray has a "*tinker's bitch*." Our tinkers do not keep *bitches* but trulls. The fiddling vagabond, with us, is the only one who has such an establish‑ ment; and we found upon it an extremely coarse and offensive comparison, "as drunk as a fiddler's *bitch.*"

BLACK‑SAP, *s.* the jaundice in a very advanced state.

BLAME, *v.* a very decent and commendable evasion of the horrible word *damn.* Ex. "*Blame* me," or "I will be *blamed,* if," &c. It is to be observed, however, that the use of it is altogether selfish; confined to the first person singular. Nobody ever heard so mild an imprecation as "*blame* you for a rascal," or, "John Smith be *blamed* for a fool."

BLAR, BLARE, *v.* It may seem an unnecessary ex‑ actness to point out any difference in the appli‑ cation of these words. Correct speakers, how‑ ever, with very nice ears, will apply them differ‑ ently, according to the sharpness or flatness of the tone. It is enough to say that calves, sheep, asses, and children, all *blar,* or *blare* in their several natu‑ ral modes. BR. Belg. *blaren,* mugire.

BLAUNCH, *s.* a blain.

BLAUTHY, *adj.* bloated. From *blow* came *blowth,* a word used in o. e. for bloom. From *blaw,* another form of the same verb (still used in L. SC.) would come *blawth,* and thence our adjective.

BLEE, *s.* general resemblance, not "colour and complexion," as the DICTT. give it; and as might seem to result from its derivation. Mr. Nares asserts that it was obsolete in the reign of Queen Elizabeth. If so, we have a very extraordinary instance of the renascence of a word; for it is in use among us every day in the sense here given to it. Ex. " That boy has a strong *blee* of his father." BR. in the sense of complexion. CH. P. G.

BLEEK, *adj.*

1. Pale, sickly.

2. Sheepish. A. s. *blæce*, pallor.

BLIND, *adj.* abortive. When blossoms fade away without forming the fruit, we say they are *blind*. It seems to be particularly said of strawberries, and other small summer fruits. The process of vegetation is stopped. It should rather be considered as a participle from the Saxon verb *blinan;* an English verb *bline* would come quite regularly; the part. pass. of which would be *blined.* A. s. *blinan*, cessare.

BLIND-SIM, BLIND-HOB, *s.* the game of blindman's buff. The unfortunate wight whose lot it is to be hood-winked, and who is thumped and punched by the other players, bears the contemptuous name of a coarse clown; to make fun for the company, as in a pantomime.

BLINKED-BEER, *s.* Skinner, and after him others, say that sour beer is so called. It may be so, but not by us. The beer which we called *blinked*, has no acidity, but an ill flavour peculiar to itself; said to be occasioned by too long delay of fermentation, until the wort is too cool to ferment with proper activity. Others account for it from insufficient stirring of the mash, so as not to wet all the malt. In either case carelessness or laziness is implied. Either reason, therefore, agrees better with Skinner's etymology than our own, according to which the liquor is intended to be sour. *Blinked-beer* will of course have a great tendency to turn sour; but certainly in our usage is *blinked* before it is sour. A. S. *blinan*, cessare. In L. SC. beer is said to be *blinked* when it is *turned*—become subacid.

BLOB, *s.* a small lump of any thing thick, viscid, or. dirty, as of tallow, dregs of ink, &c. JAM. says, it is "any thing tumid, and circular." An augmentative, or intensive of *bleb*, by means of the broader vowel. It affords some expressive compounds. An ugly fellow has *blob-lips* or a *blob-nose*; and if what ought to be pointed is blunt and round at the end, as a pen, a pencil, an awl, or a nail, it is said to be *blob-ended*.

BLOCK-HORSE, *s.* a strong wooden frame with four handles, commonly called a hand-barrow, for the purpose of carrying blocks.

BLOOD-FALLEN, *part.* chill-blained.

BLOOD-OLPH. *s.* the bull-finch. The first part of the name is from the colour of its breast and belly. We have neither *alp* nor *nope*; but our name is probably a variation of the former. We call the *Green-finch* the *Green-olph.* q. v.

BLORE, *v.* to bellow like a bull. Intens. of *blare.*

BLOUZE, *s.*

1. A woman with hair or head-dress loose and disordered, or decorated with vulgar finery. Whether she be "ruddy and fat-faced," or at all "like a blossom," is nothing to us, though she is so represented in T. J.

2. A woman's bonnet; most properly that sort which is otherwise called a *slouch.* But it seems to be

applied to bonnets of all shapes, fashions, and dimensions, from the bee-hive to the crow's nest. Ex. "I will just slip on my *blouze*, and go with you directly."

BLOUZY, *adj.* tricked out in flaring finery, loosely and carelessly disposed. It is not at all necessary that the fair one should be "sun-burnt and high-coloured," the only characteristics mentioned in T. J. Our senses both of subst. and adj. sufficiently illustrate the passages cited.

BLOW, *s.* blossoms. The DICTT. give the verb, but not the subst. We use the word collectively. Ex. " There is a fine *blow* of apples this year." BR.

BLOWN-HERRING, *s.* a herring slightly cured for speedy use, and home consumption. Those which are intended for exportation, or long keeping, undergo the operation of three successive fires, each kept up for about twenty-four hours. Intervals of two or three days are allowed between the smokings, in which the fat of the fish is drained away. The *blown* fish are smoked but once. That process has the effect of plumping them, without discharging the fat, somewhat like the baking or roasting of apples. In this state of superior richness and flavour, they will not bear long keeping. On some parts of our coasts a blown-herring is called a *tow-bowen*. Why? They are also called *bloaters*, but we do not acknowledge the word.

BLUBBER, *s.* a bubble, from *blob*. L. SC.

BLUBBER-GRASS, *s.* different species of bromus, from their soft inflated glumes; in particular mollis, which infests barren pastures.

BLUTHER, *s.*

,1. To blot in writing.

2. To disfigure the face with weeping.

Sui.—G. *plattra, incuriose scribere.* L. SC. JAM.

BOAR-THISTLE, *s.* the *Carduus lanceolatus,* Lin.

BOARD-CLOTH, *s.* a table-cloth. In o. E. the table was called the *board,* not only poetically, as it still is, but in common use. So it was in Saxon. A. S. *bord,* mensa. L. SC.

BOB, *v.* to cheat. O. E. " the gold and jewels that I *bobb'd* him of."

BOBBISH, *adj.* pretty good, somewhat clever. JEN.

BOBBISHLY, *adv.* pretty well, rather cleverly. These words doubtless belong to the verb *bob,* of which several ludicrous senses are to be found in DICTT. O. FR. *bobe,* a joke or trick.

BODE, *v.* to board. Ex. " He *bodes* and lodges there." A. S. *beod,* mensa.

BODE-CLOTH, *s.* a table-cloth.

BODGE, *v.*

1. To patch clumsily; the same as *botch.*

2. To *boggle,* to fail. SH.

BODILY, *adv.* entirely; in the whole mass; all at once. A wind-mill, a hay-barn, or other edifice constructed in frame-work, without foundation, may be removed *bodily.*

BOGG, *adj.* sturdy, self-sufficient, petulant. R. S. E. C. Two etyma may be proposed. A. S. *boga,* arcus. "Qui *semper arcum tendit,*" is always ready for attack or defence. Skinner spells it *bug,* which he makes syn. with *big,* and derives from A. S. *buc,* or Dan. *bug,* veuter, as it were confidently strutting, "*protenso sesquipede.*"

BOIST, *s.* a swelling. The adjective *boistous*, regularly formed from this word, is used both by Wickliffe and Chaucer, in the modern sense of *boisterous*.
This seems to be one of the very few words of the
ancient British language, which are be found in
our's, at least in the eastern dialects of it.

BOKE, *s.* bulk. Ex. " there is more *boke* than corn
in that goaf." It is in R. N. C. Pegge spells it *booke*,
and assigns it to us. *Bulk, bolk, boke, booke* run easily
enough into each other. BR. CR. It is surely *bolk*.

BOKE, *v.* to nauseate, to be ready to vomit. L. SC.
*bolk.* A. s. *bealcan*, ructare. It is, in fact, intens.
of *belch*. W. W. R. BR.

BOKE-OUT, *v.* to swell out, to gain bulk and prominence. W. C. " to thrust or poke out."

BOLT, *v.* to swallow food without chewing. A sense
not given in DICTT. but connected with others by
the idea of haste.

BOMBAZE, *v.* to confound, bewilder, perplex; as
if a veil were thrown before the eyes, to hinder one
from seeing what he is about. Ex. " I am right
on *bombazed*," i. e. by the communication of some
unexpected news, or the proposal of some puzzling
question. It is certainly connected with the word
*bombazine*, but not in its modern sense. Anciently
it meant a fine web of cotton. This may be enough
to prove our word o. E.

BONE-DRY, *adj.* perfectly dry; as dry as a bone
long bleached in the weather.

BONE-LAZY, BONE-SORE, BONE-TIRED, *adj.*
so lazy, sore, or tired, that the laziness, the sore-
ness, or the fatigue, seem to have penetrated the
very bones. These compound epithets are cer-

tainly very expressive. The only objection to
which they can be liable, seems to be, that they
" may be thought by some too poetical for common familiar language.

BONNY, *adj.* brisk, cheerful, in good health, and spirits. So the word is not, as Dr. Johnson supposes,
confined to the L. sc. We do not indeed include
in it the idea of " comeliness."

BOOBY-HUTCH, *s.* a clumsy and ill-contrived covered
carriage, or seat.

BOP, *v.* to dip, or duck suddenly. There are several
other words of like formation, in more or less
general use, for sudden, quick, and short motion,
and formed to be expressive of it; such are *bob,
pop, dop, dob.* The *dob-chick* must have been so
called from its instantaneous disappearance.

BORH, BOR, *s.* a term of very familiar address, generally understood to be a coarse pronunciation of
the word *boy.* A different account of it is proposed
with some confidence. If boy is actually sometimes
pronounced as if it were spelled *baw,* it is the sole
instance of our so perverting the power of the
diphthong *oy;* we either pronounce it as others
do, or we narrow it to long *i;* we never call joy
*jaw,* nor a toy a *taw;* we do not talk of *emplawing*
or *destrawing,* but of *emplying* or *destrying.* This
one seeming instance of such perversion is therefore likely to have arisen from our not under-
standing the term we use; besides, it may be
remarked, that this word is applied indiscriminately
to persons of both sexes and of all ages; and though
it may be common for elderly people to address as

*boys* those who are much their juniors, or if they have been long intimate, to call each other in jocular familiarity old boys; or if old men, affecting juvenile airs, be so called, yet it would surely be too absurd for old women to give to each other the appellation of *boy*. Now among so many traces as we have of Saxon antiquity, so many instances of Saxon words traditionally retained in their original form and use, it cannot be extravagant to conjecture that the word is, in fact, *bor*, and directly refers to the well-known frame of Saxon society, in which those who constituted every little community, or township (*borg*), were mutually and formally bound by law to and for each other, under a petty local magistrate, or conservator of the peace, called the *borsholder*, *i. e.* the *bor's older*, or *elder*. This official title still exists in some districts. The word under our consideration would thus signify townsman, neighbour, sworn friend, &c., much in the same way as our seamen call each other messmate, and our soldiers comrade. It is to be observed that it is actually a part of the word neighbour (A. s. *neah*, prope, and *borh*); and why may it not exist in the simple as well as in a compound form? If this explanation be admitted, one old woman may, without absurdity, say to another (as often happens), " Co' *bor*, let's go a sticking in the 'Squire's plantations." And the other may answer, " Aye, *bor*, so we will."

BOSH, *s.* To " cut a *bosh*," is something stronger than the more usual expression to " cut a dash ;" something more shewy and expansive. " Bosen out," is rendered by the Latin *tumidus* in PR. PA. Fr. *bosse.*

BOSS, *s.* a hod for mortar, carried on the shoulders like a hump.

BOSSOCH, *v.* to toss and tumble clumsily, as it were, to throw all the limbs together into one heap.

BOTTLE, *s.*

1. "A quantity of hay or grass bundled up." JOHNS. This is very indistinct. "A truss of hay." NARES. This is positively wrong. By a "bottle of hay" is now understood such a moderate bundle as may serve for one feed, twisted somewhat into the shape of a bottle. It had probably always the same meaning. In Shakspeare's time it certainly had. When *Bottom*, in Mids. Night's Dr. (the passage cited both in T. J. and N. G.), expresses his anxious craving for a "bottle of hay," he plainly means enough to make a meal on. To wish for a whole *truss* would be as extravagant and unnatural, as for a hungry man to wish for a quarter of mutton for his dinner. Mr. N. is again mistaken in supposing this phrase to be no longer in use but in the proverbial saying of "looking for a needle in a bottle of hay," which he conceives that few people understand. East-Angles all understand it perfectly, and use the word *bottle* currently.

2. We have also, or had within living memory, *barley-bottles.* These were little bundles of barley in the straw, given to farm-horses. This wasteful mode of giving feeds of corn, is probably now quite disused. Oats are now produced where formerly no spring-corn but barley was cultivated, and are

the universal food of horses. In some years of very high price barley has been substituted, because a less quantity is thought to suffice. But then it was cut in the straw, given in that form, and eaten up clean. After all it is possible that *barley-bottles* may still be given by some very old fashioned farmers, who so much venerate the wisdom of their great-grandfathers, as to abhor and abjure all innovations upon their practice, good or bad.

3. The dug of a cow is called her *bottle,* as well as her *bag.*

BOTTLE-BIRD, *s.* an apple rolled up and baked in a crust, so called from its fancied resemblance to birds nestling in those bottle-shaped receptacles, placed for that purpose under the eaves of some old buildings.

BOTTLE-BUMP, *s.* the bittern, anciently called bittour, or buttour. Of this the first part of our word is manifestly a corruption; the last syllable was formed from the dull hollow sound uttered by the bird. SK. has *butter-bump;* so have we by way of variety. In poetry this bird has been called " booming bittern." *Bump* is much more expressive of its sound.

BOTTLE-NOSE, *s.* the common porpoise. It is so called by the sailors and fishermen at Cromer, and probably every where else on our coasts.

BOUDS, *s. pl.* weovils in malt. T. R. S. E. C.

BOUDY, *adj.* applied to malt infested with those insects which give a nauseous taste to the beer brewed from it.

BOUGE, *s.* Phr. " To make a bouge ;" to commit a gross blunder; to get a heavy fall by taking, an awkward false step.

BOUGE, *v.* to bulge or swell out. Fr. *bouge.* SK.

BOUT-HAMMER, *s.* the heavy two-handed hammer used by blacksmiths. This word is not in the DICTT. however common here and perhaps elsewhere.

BOWRY, *s.* a bower or arbour. The word was anciently written *bowre,* and signified a room, particularly a woman's apartment; and being liable to become a diphthong in poetry (as *showre* does in the very first verse of the Canterbury Tales), has been made permanently so with us in plain prose and common talk. It is from A. S. *bure,* conclave.

BRACKLY, *adj.* brittle. Particularly applied to standing corn, some ears of which are so quickly ripened as to snap off short. M. S.

BRAID, *v.* A culinary term; to beat and blend soft substances or mixtures; particularly to press them with a spoon through a colander or sieve. It may possibly be another form of *bray,* to pound in a mortar, but as it means no more than the gentle pressure of what gives little or no resistance, it seems better connected with BRED. q. v.

BRAKES, *s. pl.* fern. We use it in this sense only, which Dr. Johns. says is the original sense; giving no etymon to prove it is so. Perhaps, what is hinted, not formally offered, by SK. may serve our purpose, " quia fragilis est." The *ptesis aquilina,* Lin. which covers many acres of our sterile sandy districts, and which we almost exclusively call

*brakes* (only occasionally including some other
ferns), is not very remarkable for its fragility; but
it may certainly be called fragile in comparison
with the "thorns and briars," placed in the DICTT.
among other senses of the word *brake*. Those
senses are numerous, and not a little confused.
Archdeacon Nares has reckoned up no fewer than
eight. We are concerned only with our own.
*Bracken* is exactly equivalent to *brakes*, being the
A. S. plural of *brake* or *brak*.

BRAIN-PAN, *s.* the scull. It may seem intended
for a ludicrous figurative expression; but is the
very word used by our Saxon ancestors to express
the cranium. A. S. *panne*, cranium.

BRAMISH, *v.* to flourish, gesticulate, and assume affected airs.

BRAND, *s.* the smut in wheat, making it look as if a
hot iron had passed over it.

BRAND-NEW, *adj.* new worked off, newly branded.
There is *fire-new* in CH.; and, to increase the force
of the expression, we sometimes combine the two
phrases, and call a thing *brand-fire-new*.

BRANDY, *adj.* affected with smut. A. S. *bren*, urere.

BRANK, *s.* buck-wheat; *polygonum fagopyrum,* Lin.
T. R. S. E. C.

BRASH, *s.* an acid and watery rising from the stomach into the mouth. BR.

BRASHY, *adj.* applied to land, overgrown with faint
grass, rushes, or twigs. Teut. *braasch*, fragilis.

BRATTLE, *v.* to lop the branches of trees after they
are felled.

BRATTLINGS, *s. pl.* loppings from felled trees.

BRAVELY, *adv.* very much recovered from sickness.

BRAWN, *s.* a boar. To call the living animal by the name of his flesh when cut up and cured, was an ancient usage. We read of beefs, muttons, and veals, in the accounts of ancient feasts in the Northumberland Household-book, and other such documents. Prince Hal. calls Falstaff "that old *Brawn.*" BR.

BRECK, *s.* a large division of an open corn-field, q. d. *break.* Ray calls it land ploughed the first year after it has lain fallow. It is certainly not so restricted by us. R. S. E. C.

BRED, *s.* a board to press curd for cheese, somewhat less in circumference than the vat. A. S. *bredan,* stringere. The same name seems to have been applied in O. E. to small boards used for other purposes; the pax-bred for instance. The pax was a representation of the crucifixion, presented in the ceremony of the mass to be kissed by the faithful. A silver plate was probably used, when it could be afforded, and in default of it, a board. Elisha Coles calls it the pax-*bread,* and expresses it in Latin by *panis osculatorius,* unfortunately confounding the wood with the consecrated wafer. *V.* C. HAW. and N. G.

BRED-SORE, BREEDER, *s.* a whitlow, or any sore coming without wound, or other visible cause.

BRIEF, *s.* a general name for any written or printed petition, or begging paper, of whatsoever description.

BRIG, *s.* a bridge ; pure Saxon. A. S. *brigge,* pons. BR.

BRIM, *s.*

1. Commonly, but erroneously, supposed to be another name for a boar. We say, indeed, the "sow goes to brim;" but we never call the boar a *brim.* In Cheshire, the sow is said to be *brimming,* which is exactly the A. s. *bremend,* fervens. w. c.

2. A strumpet; abbreviation of *brimstone.*

The same etymon may serve both. A. s. *brymende,* fervens, or *brync,* ardor.

BRINK-WARE, *s.* small faggots to repair the banks of rivers. They are generally made of white thorn for its strength and durability.

BROACHES, BRAUCHES, *s. pl.* rods of sallow, hazle, or other tough and pliant wood split, sharpened at each end, and bent in the middle like an old fashioned hair pin; used by thatchers to pierce and fix their work. A fell of such wood is divided into hurdle-wood and *broach*-wood; the stouter and the slenderer. Fr. *broche.*

BROAD, *s.* a lake formed by the expansion of a river in a flat country; as *Braydon Broad,* between Norwich and Yarmouth, and several others in that part of the county of Norfolk; *Oulton Broad,* &c. in the hundred of Lothingland, in Suffolk.

BROAD-BEST, *s.* the best suit of apparel. Perhaps because·understood to be made of broad cloth.

BROAK, BROCK, *v.* to belch. A. s. *broccetan,* ructare.

BROCK, *s.* a badger; but only used in a dirty comparison. "He stinks like a *brock.*" The animal is generally called *badger,* or else by his proper name. Sui.-G. *brokug,* versicolor.

BRUCKLED, BRUCKET, *adj.* grimy, speckled and ingrained with dirt. Ex. " that child's hands are all over *bruckled.*" Sometimes it is used in a figurative sense ; not meaning that the thing to which it is applied actually wants washing, but that it looks as if it did. " A *brucket* complexion," cannot be better described. Archdeacon Nares having read 1 a " *bruckled* child," but never heard the word in use, supposes it to mean *breeched* ; laughably enough to us, who often see *bruckled* children, with or without breeches.

BRUFF, *adj.* hearty, jolly, healthy, in good case. Should it be spelt *brough?* Ex. " How are you?" " Pretty *bruff.*"

BRUMP, *v.* to lop trees in the night.

BRUMP, *s.* as large a portion of such plunder as can be carried away at once.

BRUN, *s.* bran ; but that is assuredly the corrupt word, and ours is the pure one. It designates the brown part of the grist, from which the white flour has been separated. A. s. *brun,* fuscus.

BRUSTLE, *s.* a bristle. A very easy change ; but there is Teut. *burstael,* seta.

BUCK, *s.* that part of a cart or waggon, which may very properly be called its belly. A. s. *bucc,* venter. R. S. E. C.

BUCK, *v.* to spring or bound with agility, like a buck.

BUCKER, *s.*

1. A horse's hind leg.

2. A bent piece of wood somewhat like it in shape ; particularly that on which a slaughtered animal is hung up, more generally called a *gambrel,* which,

it may be observed, has a very similar connexion with Ital. *gamba*, a leg.

In both senses it is sometimes pronounced Bucket ; a change exactly like that of BADGER to BADGET. q. v.

BUCKER-HAM, *s.* the hock joint of a horse. Teut. *buchen*, flectere.

BUCK-HEAD, BUCK-STALL, *v.* to cut down a quickset hedge to the height of two or three feet, with a view of renovating its growth. The two words are used indiscriminately. *Buck-stall* may have been retained from some supposed resemblance the hedge so reduced bore to a sort of net so called, with which deer were anciently intercepted and caught in a forest. But what connexion can this mischievous practice in husbandry have with a buck's-head. Perhaps from the jagged and forky ends which may be thought to resemble the branches of antlers. Old trees, having their "high tops dry with bald antiquity," are also said to be buck-headed; seemingly from the same resemblance.

BUD, *s.* a calf of which the horns are beginning to shoot. But the name is equally applied to those of the same age, of the polled breed. R. S. E. C.

BUDDLE, *s.* a noxious weed among corn. *Chrysanthemum segetum*, Lin. T. *Boddle.*

BUFFER, *s.* a fool, a buffoon. Fr. *bouffard.* L. SC.

BUFFET-STOOL, *s.* a four-legged stool set on a frame like a table. It is the poor man's side-board, table, or stool, as occasion requires. PR. PA. *buffet-stole.*

BUFFLE, *v.*

1. To handle clumsily, as if the fingers were stuffed or blown up.
2. To speak thick and inarticulately, as if the mouth were stuffed.

Fr. *bouffu*.

BUFFLE-HEADED, *adj.* stupid and confused.

BULK, *v.* to throb.

BULKING, *s.* a throbbing in the flesh.

BULL-FEIST, *s.* the common puff-ball ; *Lycoperdon bovista*, Lin. It is called crepitus lupi, by Parkinson, and *bofist* by Bauhin, whence came the words lycoperdon and bovista. Our provincial name is certainly from *bull*, and A. s. *feist* or *fist*, flatus ventris. In some counties it is called *puck-fist*, which attributes the same flatulence to the jolly goblin Robin Goodfellow.

BULLOCK. *v.*

1. To bully.
2. To bellow or lament vociferously. Ex. " sobbing and bullocking." Here the termination *ock* has certainly the force of an intensive or frequentative.

BULL'S-NOON, *s.* midnight. The inhabitants of dairy counties can feelingly vouch for the propriety of this term. Their repose is often broken in the dead of night by the loud bellowing of the lord of the herd, who, rising vigorous from his evening rumination, rushes forth on his adventures, as if it were broad noon-day, and *blores* with increased rage and disappointment when he comes to a fence which he cannot break through.

BULLY-MUNG, *s.* According to т. a mixture of the meal of oats, pease, and vetches. sк. makes

buck-wheat the main ingredient. With us, it means
any coarse thick mixture for homely food. The
derivation doubtfully proposed by sk. is probably
right. A. s. *bilig*, ater, and *mengean*, miscere.

BULLY-RAG, BULARAG, *v.* to revile in vulgar
and opprobrious terms. *V. Rag.* BR. W. W. R.
JEN. Isl. *bol*, divæ, and *ragian*, deferre. LYE.

BULVER, *v.* to increase in bulk by being rolled over
and over, like snow. The word is often applied to
hay or corn collecting into increasing heaps. Fr.
*bouleverser.*

BUMBASTE, *v.* to beat or baste severely, particularly to inflict school discipline.

BUMBLE, *v.* to muffle. Ex. "The bells were *bum-
bled* at his burial."

BUMBLES, *s. pl.* Coverings for the eyes of a horse,
obstructing his vision more effectually than common blinkers.

BUMBLE-BEE, *s.* a better name than the common
one, *humtle-bee*, and more delicate than the L. sc.
*bum-bee.* It is to be wished it were fairly derivable
from the βομβεῦσα μελισσα of Theocritus. Remotely
and circuitously it may. Teut. *bommen*, sonare.

BUMBLE-FOOTED, *adj.* having a thick lumpish foot
which moves, as if it were made whole, without ar-
ticulations.

BUMBY, *s.* any collection of stagnant filth, into
which the drain from some dirty place runs. It
may suffice to hint a probable derivation, by observing that there is commonly a *bumby* behind the
little concealed retreat at the corner of the garden.
R. S. E. C.

BUMP, *s.* a small round swelling from a blow. Isl. *bomps*, ictus. sh. Romeo and Juliet.

BUMP, *v.*

1. To administer summary justice, or injustice, in some cases of youthful delinquency, not by the birch, which is the master's exclusive right, but by bringing the same part to which it is usually applied, in rude contact with a post or a tree. This process, if incautiously, or too severely conducted, is likely enough to produce *bumps*, in the sense above given. Sometimes, if there be accomplices in the offence, and neither tree nor post be conveniently at hand, both *hammer* and *block*, as they are called, are human. In perambulating the bounds of parishes, it is customary to *bump* the junior members of the procession against a boundary post or tree, to fix the place more firmly in the memory. br.

2. To ride, without rising in the stirrups, on a rough trotting horse.

BUMPTIOUS, *adj.* apt to take unintended affronts, and resenting them petulantly and arrogantly. Apparently it is from *bump* in its derivative sense, *swollen*.

BUND-WEED, BUNDS, *s.* different species of wild centaureæ, particularly *nigra*, Lin. which much infests grass land; and some species of scabiosa (*succisa*, Lin. for instance). It is quasi *bum weed*, from the roundness and plumpness of the parts of fructification in the plants above-mentioned, certainly more applicable to them than to *senecio jacobæa*, or *polygonum convolvolus*, to which it is

applied by Dr. Jamieson. Dan. *bund*, pars ima.
L. SC.

BUNDLE, *s.* an opprobrious term applied to females,
equivalent to baggage, which perhaps means strictly,
a follower of the camp. *Bunch* is used in the same
sense.

BUNGAY-PLAY, *s.* A simple straight forward way
of playing the game at whist, by leading all winning
cards in succession, without any plan to make the
best of the hand. Perhaps it was applied before
the invention of whist, to an unskilful manner of
playing old games, as primero, gleek, &c. At any
rate we are not to understand, that, in this name,
an indiscriminate, and therefore an unjust, censure
is cast upon all the good people of Bungay for their
unskilfulness. In o. e. *bungar* was synonymous
with *bungler,* So this injurious term was, in fact,
*bungar-play* or *bunglar's play*, and should now be
called *bungle-play* or *bungler's play*. After all, let
East Anglian lovers of the old rubber console themselves for being out of fashion, and confirm their
antiquated preference by the certainty that what
they call *bungay-play* is the very essence of the
new-fangled Shorts. It is not Whist.

BUNG-TAIL, *s.* the tail of a draught-horse, docked
and pared down to the shape and size of a *bung*.
This cruel mutilation was practised not many years
ago, in particular on horses of the justly-celebrated
Suffolk breed. It is even at present rather to be
hoped, than positively asserted, that those noble
and valuable animals are never tortured into that
frightful state of deformity.

BUNKS, *s. pl.* the wild succory, *cichoreum intybus.* Lin.
One of the many fancied improvements in husbandry, brought into culture some years ago by
certain distinguished agriculturists, but now found
nowhere but where it ought to be, by the highway
side, and of Nature's planting.

BUNNY, *s.* a small swelling caused by a fall or blow.
Perhaps a diminutive of *bump.* The Nurse in Romeo and Juliet tells of her child getting a *bump*
in her forehead by falling down. From her account
of the size of it, a modern East Anglian nurse
would certainly call it a *bunny.* One would be glad
to derive it from the Greek βουνος, a hillock. It
may be so, through the Gothic. Sir T. Browne.

BUNTING, BUNTY, *adj.* miserably mean and shabby.
Obviously connected with BUNTER, a coarse word
expressing the lowest point of degradation of the
fair sex.

BURBLES, *s. pl.* small vesicular tingling pimples;
such as are caused by the stinging of nettles, or of
some minute insects. Minsh. calls them *barbles.*
Qu. because they have been produced by punctur-
ing the skin with little *barbed* points?

BURN, *v.* Phr. "To burn daylight."
1. Literally, to light candles before they are wanted.
2. Metaph. to waste time and neglect business. It
occurs twice in SH. in this sense, in Romeo and
Juliet, and Merry Wives of Windsor.

BURR, *s.* a mistiness over and around the moon,
which dims her light, as if she were passing
through a slightly-intercepting medium.

BURTHEN, *v.* to charge closely and pressingly.
Ex. "I *burthened* him with it as strong as I could,
but he would not confess." Certainly very expressive. "I left that load upon his conscience, to
*bear* it as he can!" It is o. E. used by Bp. Latimer.

BUSK, *v.* particularly applied to domestic fowls ex-
posing themselves to the sun on a hot day, lying
in the most dusty place they can find, and scratch-
ing up the dust among their feathers, to rid themselves, as it is said, of the vermin with which they
are infested. This seems to have some connexion,
though not very near, with the sense of *busk* in
northern English and Lowland Scotch, which is to
dress. This refreshing exercise is, however, not
confined to tame fowls. Perhaps all the feathered
tribes practise it. Spots are often found where a
covey of partridges has been *busking*. After all, it
may be only a somewhat corrupt form of *bask*.

BUSK, *s.* a piece of wood, whalebone, or other material placed in front of women's stays. Nares supposes the name obsolete. Johnson goes as far back
as Donne for it. Much as our rustic lasses have
departed from their former simplicity of costume,
they still wear *busks*, and call them by that ancient
name. Fr. *busque*.

BUTTER-FINGERED, *adj.* " apt to let things fall,"
says PE.; rather to let them slip through the fingers
as if they were greasy; also unable to handle hot
substances; as if the surface of the fingers were
melted, and so lost the power of retention.

BUTTER-TEETH, *s. pl.* broad and yellow teeth.

BUTTLE, *s.* another name for the *bottle-bump, butter-bump,* or *bittern.*

BUTTON, *s.* a very small cake. " A gingerbread *but-ton.*"

## C.

CADDOW, *s.* a jackdaw. It has been supposed to be so called as being a *caw-daw;* but its voice can scarcely be called a *caw.* It is a harsh sound between screaming and chattering. Another conjecture is *cade-daw.* This seems more likely, for it is sometimes kept in a tame state, and plays many amusing tricks; but its saucy, thievish, and mischievous disposition must make it a very troublesome fondling. *Ka* is the L. SC. word which seems rather to lead to Teut. *kae,* or A. S. *ceo,* cornix.

CAIL, *v.*

1. To throw weakly and wide of the mark. A boy throws a stone, a *mauther cails* it.
2. To move with a wavering and irregular gait.
3. To gambol and throw out the heels like a skittish colt, " kicking and *cailing.*"

In its primary sense it may be derived from a very common missile; Fr. *caillou.*

CALIMANCO-CAT, *s.* that variety which is commonly called the tortoise-shell or Spanish cat, remarkable for its fine and shining fur. Pussy is likely to have first obtained this name at Norwich. The glossiness of her skin was supposed to resemble one of the principal ancient manufactures of that industrious city. The surface of *calimanco* shines somewhat like satin.

CALL, *v.* to use abusive language; to call names, not particularizing any. Ex. "How she did *call* me!" JEN. becall. BR. call.

CALL, *s.* need, occasion. Ex. "There was no *call* for your doing so;" i. e. you were not called upon.

CALLOW, *s.* the stratum of vegetable earth lying above gravel, sand, limestone, &c. which must be removed in order to reach them. The process is called *uncallowing*. There may seem to be a confusion or inversion of terms and senses, but still it may have come from A. s. *calu*, calvus.

CALM, *s.* the concreted scum of bottled liquors.

CALMY, *adj.* mothery.

CAMBUCK, *s.* the dry stalk of dead plants, as of hemlock, or other umbelliferæ; Ex. "As dry as a *cambuck*." A. s. *cammoc*, peucedanum.

CAMP, *v.*

1. To play at the game so called.
2. To kick in general.

CAMP, *s.* an ancient athletic game at ball, now almost superseded by cricket, a less hardy and dangerous sport. Yet *camping*, though not so general, is still a favourite exercise in some districts of both our counties. The late Right honourable William Wyndham, scarcely more celebrated as a statesman and a philosopher, than as a patron of the "Sports and Pastimes of the English People," on a principle truly patriotic, though it might sometimes incur ridicule, gave great encouragement to this sport during his residences in the country, and

had many matches in the neighbourhood of his venerable seat at Felbrigg. He was wont to say,
that it combined all athletic excellence; that to
excel in it, a man must be a good boxer, runner,
and wrestler; in short, a sort of *pancratiast*. Certainly, no kind of manly exercise can display to so
much advantage the powers, proportions, and atti-
tudes of a fine muscular frame. The late Lord
Rochford was also a great patron of this sport in
the neighbourhood of his seat at Easton in Suffolk.
Perhaps some varieties in the mode of playing it
always existed; and certainly it is now degenerated,
and some meaner exercises unworthily usurp its
name. Of the sport itself, however, two varieties
are at present expressly recognized; *rough-play*,
and *civil-play*. In the latter, there is no boxing.
But the following is a general description of it as it
was of old, and in some places still continues. Two
goals are pitched at the distance of 120 yards from
each other. In a line with each are ranged the
combatants; for such they truly are. The number on each side is equal; not always the same,
but very commonly twelve. They ought to be uniformly dressed in light flannel jackets, distinguished
by colours. The ball is deposited exactly in the
mid-way. The sign or word is given by an um-
pire. The two sides, as they are called, rush forward. The sturdiest and most active of each encounter those of the other. The contest for the
ball begins, and never ends without black eyes and
bloody noses, broken heads or shins, and some serious mischiefs. If the ball can be carried, kicked,

or thrown to one of the goals, in spite of all the resistance of the other party, it is reckoned for one
towards the game; which has sometimes been
known to last two or three hours. But the exertion
and fatigue of this is excessive. So the victory is
not always decided by number of points, but the
game is placed against time, as the phrase is. It is
common to limit it to half an hour; and most *cam-
pers,* now-a-days, οιοι νον βροτοι εισιν, have in that
time got enough of so hardy a contest. The spirit
of emulation prevails, not only between the adverse
sides, but among individuals on the same side, who
shall excel his fellows. The prizes are commonly
hats, gloves, shoes, or small sums of money. And
the rustic pancratiast who bears off the first, is not
less conspicuous in the little circle in which he is
known, than the Grecian victor decorated with his
chaplet of olive or of pine. This ancient game deserves the more attention from us, because, if it
was not peculiar to the East Angles and East Saxons, it has probably been always a particular favourite with them. Ray says that in his time, it
prevailed most in Norfolk, Suffolk, and Essex. To
Sir Thomas Browne, who came among us from
another kingdom of the Octarchy, it was new; and
he puts the word *camp* (or as he spells it *kamp*)
into his small collection of Norfolk words. Strutt
gives no account of it in his " Sports and Pastimes
of the English People." All this may serve as some
sort of apology for the length of this article. Ray
is certainly right in deriving the word, not from
Latin but from Saxon. Undoubtedly we had it

from the Saxons, whencesoever they might get it.
A. s. *campion*, præliari.

CAMPING-LAND, *s.* a piece of ground set apart for
the exercise of *camping*. Land was given for this
purpose with all legal formalities. There is a field,
abutting on the church-yard at Swaffham, in Norfolk, which, according to the Continuator of Blomfield's History, was given by will by a Rector, in
the year 1472. From that time to this, it has been
called by this name, and the youth of that popu-
lous parish have enjoyed the right of performing
their exercises in it. Cricket is now the game.
In the little parish of East Bilney is a small strip of
land, or as we call it a *spong*, near the church,
which is called the *camping-land*. And, though
that use of it has long ago ceased, the old inhabitants well remember the time when the lads
of the village regularly repaired thither, after evening service on Sundays, to play foot-ball and other
games. In the late Sir John Cullum's " History
of Hawstead, in Suffolk," the *camping-pightle* is
mentioned under the date 1466. A large piece of
pasture land at Stowmarket is still called the *camping-land*. Other instances might be mentioned in
other parishes in both counties. Tusser, who was
a farmer in both, in the reign of Queen Elizabeth,
speaks of *camping* with much commendation, as
very beneficial to the turf.

CAMPING-BALL, *s.* a ball particularly adapted to
the sport of *camping*. It is to be feared that the
same name is sometimes most abusively misapplied
to the common light *foot-ball*, and that kicking

that ball, and occasionally the shins or breech of an adversary, is called *camping*—a great insult and indignity to that ancient and noble exercise.

CANCH, *s.*

1. A small quantity of corn in the straw put into a corner of the barn or an out-house.

2. A short turn or spell at a job of hoeing, ditching, &c.

3. A trench, cut sloping to a very narrow bottom, or an angle.

Teut. *kante*, angulus.

CANKERFRETT, *s.* verdegrise. The rust of copper or brass. When the tinning is worn off from kitchen utensils, they are said to be *canker-fretted*. It is not used for the rust of any other metals.

CANKER-ROSE, *s.* the common red field poppy, otherwise called *copper-rose* and *head-ache*.

CANKER-WEED, *s.* the *senecio jacobæa*, Lin. together with some neighbouring species, as *tenuifolius* and *sylvaticus;* which were some years ago so abundant in some parts of Suffolk, on commons and waste lands, as to be collected and burned for potash.

CANT, *v.*

1. To set up on edge.

2. To throw upwards with a jerk.

As the course of a missile so thrown may be considered as rather angular than parabolical, it may belong to Teut. *kante*, angulus. BR. " to up-set."

CANT, *s.* a jerk. Ex. " He gave it a *cant*," into the window, or over the wall.

CANT-RAIL, *s.* a triangular rail; of which two are cut from a square piece of timber sawn diagonally.

CAP, *s.* a challenge to competition; victory over a competitor. The latter is the strictly proper sense, for it must be deduced from A. s. *cop,* apex. Or perhaps Isl. *kappe,* athleta.

CAP, *v.* to challenge; to overcome. Something is proposed or done by somebody, which another is to imitate or excel if he can. *Cap* is properly to cover. School-boys *cap verses,* i. e. quote them in succession by a certain rule, and lay them, as it were, one over another. The boy who can go no higher is *cap'd* by his competitor. In puritanical times of old *capping of texts* was a favourite, and doubtless very edifying, sort of pious pastime. With us at large, the word is used on a great variety of profane occasions. An idle boy leaps a ditch, or climbs a tree, and if his play-fellow cannot equal or out-do him, it is a *cap;* he has *cap'd* him. BR.

CAPER-PLANT, *s.* a very common garden weed; the *euphorbia lathyris,* Lin. It is thus called, from a fancied resemblance, surely a very imperfect one, of its capsules to capers, the flower-buds of a very different plant. The substitution is known to have been once at least tried by a remarkably frugal housewife. Fortunately, the first acrimonious taste warned the family to reject the noxious sauce, and they escaped with a little excoriation of lips and tongue.

CAPS, *s. pl.* all sorts of fungi. *V.* TOAD's CAP.

CAPPERED, *part.* usually applied to cream, wrinkled on the surface by standing in a brisk current of air; sometimes to the surface of land suddenly dried after rain. It is rather a curious word. It is almost impossible not to derive it from Lat. *capero*. Yet a word, in such a case, is very unlikely to have been taken immediately from Latin, and there appears to be no Saxon word through which it might have been transmitted. There may have been one, however, though none appears by which this may have come orally down to us; for it is not likely that it has ever been written, much less printed.

CAR, *s.* a wood or grove on a moist soil, generally of alders.

CASE, *s.* cause. We whimsically transpose these two words: Ex. "He did it without any *case* whatsomever." "Oh, if that be the *cause*, indeed!" we say *becase* for *because*.

CASE-worm, *s.* the caddis.

CAST, *part.* warped; thrown on one side as it were, from a straight form.

CASUALTY, *s.* the flesh of an animal that dies by chance. Ex. "Gipsies feed on *casualties*." "This mutton is so pale and flabby, it looks like a *casualty*." "He gave a bullock to the poor at Christmas, little better than a *casualty*." But to be correct, pronounce it *cazzlety*.

CAST, *v.* yield, produce. Ex. "How did your wheat *cast*?" In Suffolk, the question would be, "How did it rise?"

CAT, *s.* a mass of coarse meal, clay, and some other ingredients, with a large proportion of salt, placed in dove-cotes to prevent the pigeons from leaving them, and to allure others to come. Called also a *salt-cat;* meaning, no doubt, a salt-*cate.*

CATCH-LAND, *s.* border-land, of which the tithe was disputable, and taken by the first of the claim-ants who could *catch* it. These matters are now put on a surer footing, in this country at least, if not every where. Tithe so taken, was called *catch-tithe.*

CATCH-ROGUE, *s.* one whose office it is to appre-hend offenders. A constable or bailiff. Is it pos-sible that what has so very much the air of a mere cant word, should be a corruption, handed down through so many ages, of N. Fr. *cacherau,* a bailiff?

CAT'S-TAIL, *s. Hippuris vulgaris,* Lin. Here we correct the great naturalist. This plant is surely much more like the tail of a *cat* than of a horse.

CAVE, *v.* to fall into a hollow below. If a stratum of gravel, limestone, sand, &c. have been incau-tiously excavated, or even a grave or a ditch in a loose soil, it *caves in.*

CAVING, *s.* the chaff and broken ears of corn, swept from the threshing floor.

CAUK, *s.* calcareous earth in general; any sort of limestone. It ought to be spelled *calc.* Johnson calls it a " coarse *talky* spar," and quotes Wood-ward. Talc and spar, according to the present mineralogical nomenclature, do not seem to be of frequent occurrence in East Anglia; but of *cauk, calc* (at least what we call so), we have a very great abundance. Indeed, it is the substratum of a very wide extent of our country, as geologists tell us.

In very many parts are quarries of it: some of great size, and have been worked many centuries. It is of various qualities, from a loose friable marle, to a close grained building stone. It has been proved to be very firm and durable in many modern buildings, where due care has been taken to lay it as it was in its native bed. Otherwise, it soon scales off in laminæ, or even splits through its whole substance. But the great proof of its durability is afforded in the ruined walls of some of our monastic buildings (of which it forms a considerable part), where it has been exposed near three centuries to the action of the elements; and whence much of it has been taken in a sound state to be used in new erections.

CAUNSEY, *s.* a causey, a raised and paved way. The letter *n* may be supposed to have been corruptly intruded. Yet merely the substitution of one liquid letter for another, will bring it to N. Fr. *calsey.*

CAUSE, *s.* case, q. v.

CESS, *s.* a layer or stratum; when successive quantities of things of the same kind are regularly placed one over another. SH. 2 Hen. IV. " out of all *cess.*" On that authority the word is given here; but it certainly ought to be spelled *sess,* as no more probable derivation can be assigned than, Fr. *assesser,* to regulate.

CHADS, *s. pl.* dry husky fragments among food. In L. SC. " gravelly stones in rivers."
Teut. *schadde,* gleba.

CHADDY, *adj.* full of *chads.* Ex. ".The bread is

*chaddy.*" It has been made of meal not properly
sifted to get out husks, fragments of straw, or
gritty particles of the mill-stone.

CHAITS, *s. pl.* fragments or leavings on plates or
trenchers, or of the food of animals, as turnip-
chaits. The same word, no doubt, with *chits,* crumbs
of bread. L. so. or scraps of offal (whence chitter-
lings, dim.) To which may be added *chats,* as *ash-
chats, sycamore-chats, maple-chats* (what are otherwise called the *kegs* of those several trees); *black-
thorn-chats* are the young shoots or suckers of the
black-thorn on rough borders, where they are occasionally cut and faggotted, but the roots left in
the ground. All different forms of the same word,
and of connected meaning.

CHALDER, *v.* to crumble and fall away, as the surface of cawk, gravel, &c. by the action of moist air.
Otherwise *cholder* and *cholter.*

CHALM, *v.* to chew or nibble into small pieces.
Books and papers are too often *chalmed* by mice, if
they can get at them. The letter *l* is dropped in
pronunciation. It seems connected with *champ.*

CHAMBLE, *v.* to chew minutely. Dim. of champ.

CHAMBLINGS, *s. pl.* husks of corn, or other very
small scraps of what has been gnawed by vermin.

CHAP, *s.* a fellow, with whom one does not care to
have dealings. An abbreviation of *chapman.* It
is not wonderful that allusions to dealing or trading
should abound in the vulgar tongue of "la nation
boutiquiere," as we have been called by our envious neighbours and rivals; but if such terms are
expressive of contempt, we may be pretty sure

they had their origin when our ancestors were a proud military nation. In Romeo and Juliet, the nurse calls Mercutio " a saucy merchant." This sounds very oddly in our ears; now, merchant is a term of respect. A modern nurse would have called the gay banterer "a saucy *chap*." There is, however, the same allusion to trading. It is from Sui.-G. *kaeps*, homo servilis conditionis. L. LC. V. D.

CHATTER-PIE, *s.* a mag-pie, q. V.

CHECK, *v.* to taunt, to reproach. Ex. " He *checked* him by the favours he had done him." " She *check'd* him by his cousin Tom," who, perhaps, had the ill fortune to be pilloried, or transported, or was a fellow of infamous character. P. B.

CHEESE-RACK, *s.* a rack to dry cheese on. L. SC.

CHICK, *s.* a flaw, as in earthenware. Fr. *chiche.*

CHICK, *v.*

1. To begin to germinate; as seeds in the earth, leaves from their buds, or barley on the couch in the malt-house. PR. PA. " Chip," BR.

2. To crack, chap, chop, as the skin in frosty weather. At least as good, some may perhaps think a better, word.

CHICKEN'S-MEAT, *s.*

1. The herb chick-weed. *Alsine media*, Lin.

2. Also dross corn, only fit to feed fowls.

A. S. *cicene-mete*, alsine.

CHILD-AGE, *s.* childhood. Intended as a term of contradistinction to old age.

CHILDERMAS-DAY, *s.* That day of the week in every year, on which the anniversary of the Holy Innocents falls. Any of which days is most inau-

spicious for the commencement of any undertaking.
In the Spectator, No. 7, we learn that the same
notion of the weekly recurrence of this unlucky
day was entertained at that time. The word itself
is genuine Saxon. BR. A. s. *childe-masse-dæg.*

CHILL, *v.* to take off extreme coldness from any sort
of beverage by placing it near the fire in frosty
weather. Ex. " Do you like your beer *chilled?* "
It has certainly the appearance of conveying a
sense directly the reverse of that which the word
usually bears; but possibly in strictness it may
not. What was before cold, may be understood
to be thus made only *chill.*

CHIMDY, CHIMBLY, CHIMLEY, *s.* a chimney.
The third form, which is also L. SC. and Lanc. is
merely a substitution of one liquid for another. BR.

CHINE, *s.* the part of a cask into which the head is
fixed. CH. *Chimb,* JEN. Belg. *kime.* ID.

CHINE-HOOP, *s.* the extreme hoop which keeps the
ends of the staves together, and is commonly of
iron.

CHINGLE, *s.* loose gravel, small stones, &c. L. SC.

CHINGLY, *adj.* abounding in small stones, &c. commonly applied to a newly repaired road. The
loose pebbly beach is called the chingle, or shingle.

CHINK, *s.* a sprain on the back or loins, seeming to
imply a slight separation of the vertebræ.

CHINK, *v.*

1. To cause such an injury. Ex. " The fall *chinked*
his back."

2. To cut into minute pieces.

The word in all these senses is often corruptly pronounced *jink*. And so it is in the sense of sound⤴ from collision. Thus, we talk of the *jinking* of money.

CHIP UP, *v.* to recover gradually from a state of weakness. In L. sc. it means to germinate; a connected sense. JAM. derives it from Belg. *kippen*, ova excludere.

CHIPPER, *v.* to chirp. Ours is a metathesis of that word, or rather of *chirrup*.

CHITTY, CHITTY-FACED, *adj.* baby-faced; from *chit*, and that from O. Fr. *chicke*.

CHIVY, *v.* to chace, to run and career gaily, like boys in their sports. An obvious allusion to the old national ballad.

CHIZZLY, *adj.* harsh and dry under the teeth. Teut. *kiesele*, gluma.

CHOBBINS, *s. pl.* unripened grains, not coming out of the husks under the flail, but beaten off by it, quasi *choppings*.

CHOBBY, *adj.* abounding in chobbins.

CHOLICKY, *adj.* choleric. It is generally supposed to be a corruption; but it is not so; we have ancient authority. In SH. Troilus and Cressida, Ajax tells the trumpeter, to " outswell the *cholic* of puffed Aquilo." Though the speech is meant to be bombastic, it would be too extravagantly so, to compare the roaring of Aquilo to a violent fit of the gripes. His rage is certainly meant. *Cholic* is synonymous with *choler*, and better derived from Greek than French. Besides, the intestinal *colic* must be spelled without *h*.

CHOMP, *v*. to chew loudly and greedily. Intens. of *champ*.

CHOO! *interj*. used to drive away pigs, or to set dogs upon them. Cotgr. says "*chou* is a voice where-with we drive away pullein." And why not pigs? O. Fr. *chou*.

CHOP-LOGGER-HEAD, *s*. an intense blockhead. One who has a head, to all appearance thick and stout enough to bear a blow of a hatchet.

CHOUT, *s*. a jolly frolic; a rustic merry-making.

CHOVY, *s*. a small coleopterous insect, which invades gardens and orchards in hot summers, in our sandy districts, and the immediate neighbourhoods of them, in such swarms as to be nearly equal to a plague of locusts; devouring every green thing before them. It is common to drive ducks into a garden, or swine into an orchard, and shake the insects from the trees to be devoured. But their numbers, constantly renewed, are often found insuperable. PE.

CHRISTIAN, *s*. a term of distinction, not from Deist, or Atheist, Jew, Turk, or Infidel; but from brute beast. Of a very docile horse, sagacious dog, or even learned pig, it is common to express admiration, by exclaiming, "He act just for all the world like a Christian!" and we have ancient authority for it. In SH. 2 Hen. IV. the word is used in the same meaning by a prince, "He had him from me *Christian*, and see if the fat villain hath not transformed him *ape*."

CHRISTMAS, *s*. the evergreens with which our

churches and houses are still decorated at the season of *Christmas.*

CHUBBY, *adj.* surly.

CHUFFY, *adj.* in our usage, has no reference to " clownishness or surliness," which is given to it in all the DICTT. It merely means fat and fleshy, particularly in the cheeks. It seems to agree sufficiently with Shakspeare's use of the substantive *chuff,* which we have not. But our own word, though certainly an adjective, is sometimes used substantively, as a familiar and ludicrous name of the *musculi glatæi.* Fr. *jouffu.*

CHUMP, *s.* a small thick log of wood.

CHURCHING, *s.* the church service. To one of the offices in particular, this name is given in the Book of Common Prayer. But we say in general, "We have *churching* twice on a Sunday."

CHURCH-MAN, *s.* an officiating minister. He is a good, bad, or indifferent *church-man,* as he acquits himself in the desk and pulpit.

CHURCH-CLERK, *s.* the parish-clerk. Long in use.

CLACK-BOX, *s.* the mouth which contains a nimble tongue.

CLAGGY, *adj.* clogged with moisture, as roads and foot-paths are after moderate rain. BR. A. S. *clæg,* terra samia.

CLAG-LOCKS, *s. pl.* locks of wool matted together by the natural moisture of the animal, or wet and dirt.

CLAM, *s.*

1. Clamminess. Ex. " The meat has been kept too long, and has got a *clam,*" begins to decay.

2. A slut, so excessively dirty that her skin looks *clammy*.

CLAM, *v*.

1. To stick together by some viscid matter.

2. To emaciate, to starve with hunger. The juices of the body being supposed to be thickened and gradually dried up.

A. s. *clæmian*, oblimare.

CLAMP, *s*.

1. An extempore and imperfect sort of brick-kiln, in which bricks are burned when there is not earth enough near the spot to answer the expense of erecting a regular kiln.

2. A mound of earth lined with straw to keep potatoes through the winter.

In both these senses, the idea of confinement or *close covering* is so necessarily implied, as to point out the derivation from A. s. *clam*, plasma.

CLAMPER, *v*. to make a noisy trampling in walking, as men do whose shoe soles are guarded with iron, women in iron pattens, &c. Teut. *klampern*, metallum tundere. L. sc.

CLAP-DISH, *s*. an ancient utensil mentioned in many passages of old plays, quoted by Steevens in his commentary on SH. Measure for Measure, where in the text, it is called a *clack-dish*. It was a dish, or rather box, with a moveable lid, carried by the beggars at that time, to attract notice by the noise it made, and to bring people to their doors. The thing has been many years out of use, and its name survives only in a ludicrous comparison. Of a great prater it is said, that "his tongue moves like a beggar's *clap-dish*."

CLARET, *s*. any sort of foreign red wine. It is possible that this name, now become ridiculous, may have continued in provincial use from the time when Gascon wines only were imported into this country. There seems to be no other way of accounting for its present existence.

CLART, *v*. to dawb with syrup, juice of fruit, or the like. L. SC. BR.

CLARTY, *adj*. dawbed with syrup, &c. sticking to the fingers. Teut. *kladde*, sordes. L. SC. BR.

CLAUMB, CLOMB, *v*. to clamber in a heavy and awkward manner. Intens. of *climb*.

CLAUNCH, *v*. to walk in a lounging manner, as if the feet were dragged along in the dirt, to save the trouble of lifting them up. Ex. " Yinder go black Betty, *claunching* along in her creepers."

CLAY-SALVE, *s*. common cerate; from its colour.

CLEAD, *v*. to clothe. Dan. *klede*, pannus.

CLEADING, *s*. clothing. O. E.

CLEAS, CLEYES, *s*. claws; as of a lobster or crab. Ex. " Crack the *cleas* in the hinge of the door." A. s. *clea*, ungula. *Cleyes*, O. E.

CLEAT, *v*. to strengthen with thin plates of metal. Shoe-heels are often *cleated* with iron; and kitchen utensils worn thin, with copper.

CLEAT, *s*. a thin metallic plate. Jockies and horse-dealers call the light shoe of a running-horse, a *clate*. BR. A. s. *cleot*, lamina.

CLEPE, *v*. to call. The word is used by our boys at play, who *clepe* (or, as they commonly pronounce

it, *clip*) sides, or opposite parties at ball, &c    A. s.
*cleopan*, vocare.    o. E.

CLEVER, *adj.* dextrous, adroit. Ray says, "neat,
elegant." In either sense it is so very common
and general, and appears so to have been for many
years, that it seems difficult to conceive how Sir
Thomas Browne should have been struck with it
as a provincialism; and still more, how Ray, long
afterwards, should have let it pass as such, without
any remark. If not when Sir Thomas wrote his
tract, certainly long before the second edition of
R. s. E. C. published by the author, it had been
used by Butler, L'Estrange, and South. In
L'Estrange, indeed, it might be positively provincial; in Butler, low, ludicrous, or even burlesque;
in South, too familiar and undignified for the pulpit; but in neither, provincial. But what shall we
say of Addison, who had also used it? In T. J.
it is said to be low, and scarcely ever used but in
burlesque, and in conversation. A colloquial and
familiar term it certainly is; but assuredly not
provincial, nor even low. Sir Thomas Browne is
the only guarantee of its insertion here. And if it
must be ours, let it by all means be taken with our
own rustic pronunciation, *claver.*

CLICKET, *v.* to chatter. Dim. of *clack.* T.

CLICKET, *adj.* voluble. Fr. *cliqueter.*

CLIM, *s.* a sort of imp which inhabits the chimneys of
nurseries, and is sometimes called down to take
away naughty children. He may perhaps have
taken the name of " *Clym* of the Clough," the companion of Robin Hood, as the great Duke of Marl-

borough was for many years, and perhaps still is, the scarebabe in Flanders, under the name of Malbrouk.

CLIMP, *v.*

1. To touch a polished surface with dirty or greasy fingers, and leave marks upon it. A bald head kept very smooth and glossy, may serve as an instance of such a surface; and in a compound Saxon word we find our verb in immediate connexion with it at least, if its sense is not strictly proved by that connexion.

2. It is a sort of cant term for steal.

Isl. *clim*, unguis.

CLINK, *s.* a smart slap; from the sound. Teut. *klinche*, colaphus. L. sc.

CLINKS, *s. pl.* long nails used for fixing irons on gates, &c. where they are wanted to take strong hold. Perhaps so called because strong blows are required to drive them, and they *clink* under the hammer.

CLINKERS, *s. pl.* bricks of a smaller size than usual, burned very hard, and set up on edge to pave stables, or other places where there is trampling of heavy cattle. When thrown together they do not rattle like common bricks, but make a *clinking*, like the collision of metallic substances; whence their name. JEN.

CLIP, *v.* to shear wool. BR.

CLIP, CLIPPING, *s.*

1. The act of shearing.

2. The produce of it. "Farmer A. had but a very moderate *clip* this year." BR.

CLIPPER, *s.* a shearer of sheep. The word *clip,* and all words connected with it, are thus appropriated by us. The great annual meeting at Holkham was more fluently and familiarly called, the Holkham *clip* or *clipping,* than the sheep-shearing. The word shear is peculiarly applied to the reaping of wheat, or other grain severed with the sickle. The DICTT. do not give our sense of *clip.*

CLIVER, *s.* a chopping-knife; better than cleaver. A. s. *clifan,* findere.

CLOD, *v.* to clothe. *Clothe, clode, clod,* which verb certainly existed in the Saxon; for we find A. s. *cloded,* vestitus.

CLODDING, *s.* clothing. A pauper solicits *clodding* for her children; the overseer tells her they were *clodden* but a little while ago. Affording us another good participle of the verb *clod.*

CLODGER, *s.* the cover of a book. As from the Fr. *cosier* (a *cobler*) comes *codger,* so will *clodger,* by a very good analogy, come from Fr. *closier.*

CLOD-HOPPER, *s.* a working farmer, or labourer in husbandry. In T. J. we are told that this is the modern vulgarism for *clod-pole.* Vulgarisms both, undoubtedly; but they can never be synonymous and commutable till head and heels meet. Indeed, none but a very accomplished tumbler can be at the same time a *clod-pole* and a *clod-hopper.* The meaning of each word is quite obvious, and perfectly distinct.

CLOGSOME, *adj.* heavy, dull, tiresome.

CLOG-WHEAT, *s.* a bearded species, or variety of wheat, which in Mark-lane is called rivets.

CLOTCH, *v.* to tread heavily, and move awkwardly.

CLOUGH, *s.* (pron. *clou*). This is an original Anglo-Saxon word, not in use as an appellative noun, or in its simple form, but as a compound proper name; and that only in one instance. But on that very account it deserves notice. It is interpreted by Sumner " fissura ad clivum montis." In the instance about to be produced, there is certainly no mountain, the declivity is very gentle, but the fissure distinct enough. In the ancient town of Lynn, there is a certain narrow lane, happily too obscure and insignificant to have suffered by that mischievous spirit of innovation which has abolished so many ancient, descriptive, and even historical names, in old towns improved under Paving Acts. The lane in question bears at this day an appellation which might have been given to it before the Norman Conquest, on the supposition that it was in existence as a lane at that time. Whether it was so or not, the *Clough*, from which it is called, certainly existed then, or it could not be so denominated now. This venerable name is now affixed in due form on a painted board, to a corner house. At the farther end of the lane is a narrow water-course, with its grassy and weedy sides sloping down to a considerable depth, and giving the idea of a fissure rather than a drain. This small current flows, before it leaves its lane, into a wider channel, called by another Saxon name, Fleet (A. s. *Fleot*), which empties itself into the Ouse on the other side of the town, after passing under three bridges. From Mr. Brockett's copious

and curious Glossary of North Country Words,
1825, it appears that this word is still in use in its
simple and appellative form, and is defined, "a
ravine between two precipitous banks, having a
run of water at bottom." The coincidence is exact
with our single instance.

CLOUT, *s.*

1. A heavy cuff. Ex. "I gave him a good *clout* on
the scull."

2. An iron plate on a shoe. *V.* CLEAT.

Teut. *klotsen*, pulsare. L. SC.

CLOW, *s.* the clove pink. Fr. *clour* de girofle.

CLUE, *s.* three skeins of hempen thread.

CLUMPERS, *s. pl.* very thick and heavy shoes.
Wooden shoes are called by the same name in Hol-
land. Belg. *klomper.*

CLUNCH, *s.* close-grained hard limestone, fit to be
used in building, but soft when first taken from the
quarry.

CLUNCHY, *adj.* short, thick, and clumsy.

CLUNG, *part.* tough, juiceless. SH. Macbeth, has the
verb *cling*, "till famine *cling* thee," i. e. dry up all
thy juices. It is also applied to land which is tough
to work. A. S. *clingan*, marcescere.

CLUTCH, *s.* a brood of chickens, &c. R. N. C. *clotch;*
but ours seems better. As it is applied to the little
animals only in their tenderest state, when first
hatched, it may express the possibility of grasping
or *clutch*ing many or all of them in the broad hand
of the stout wench who generally takes care of
them.

CLUTTER, *s.* confusion, disorder. In our use of the
word, there is no idea of "noise, clamour or bustle,"

which the DICTT. give, and which seem to confound it with *clatter*. Ex. " The room is in a *clutter*," if the tables and chairs stand in disorder. The
box, drawer, or shelf is " in a *clutter*," when the
papers, linen, or whatever else it contains, are con-
fusedly intermingled.

CLUTTER-UP, *v.* to throw into confusion and disorder. Possibly it may have some connexion with
*litter*. Certainly it has in sense.

COAL-HOD, *s.* an utensil of metal or wood, to hold
the coals to be thrown on the fire; otherwise called
the *coal-scuttle*, *shoot*, or *shoe;* all which names are
more or less allusive to its form. T.J. has only
*coal-box* in this sense, which has no such allusion.
Indeed the shape of a box would be a very inconvenient one, and must always require the help of a
shovel. *V.* HOD.

COARSE, *adj.* opposed to fine, as applied to weather.
Ex. " It is a *coarse* morning."

COB, *s.*
1. A sea-gull.
2. The stony kernel of fruit.

COBLE, *s.* a fishing-boat; as Mr. Brockett well describes it, sharp in the bow, with square stern and
flat bottom. By Mr. Todd's leave, a *cobble* and a
*coble* are two very different things. Of the latter
his derivation is certainly right. A. s. *cuople*, na-
vicula.

COBBLE, *s.*
1. The round stones with which most country towns
are paved.
2. The stone of fruit.
3. Any small, hard, pebbly substance.

COB-IRONS, *s. pl.*

1. The andirons on which wood is burned on the hearth. R. S. E. C. P. L.

2. The irons hung upon the bars of the kitchen-range on which the spit is supported.

COCK-BRUMBLE, *s.* the hawk's bill bramble, as it is otherwise called, from its curved spines. *Rubus fruticosus*, Lin.

COCK-EYE, *s.* a squinting eye; which must be set or *cocked*, like the lock of a gun, before aim can be taken at an object.

COCK-FARTHING, *s.* a term of endearment used to a little boy.

COCK'S-EGG, *s.* an abortive egg, without a yolk. This must be like "lucus a non lucendo."

COCK'S-TREAD, *s.* the filmy rudiments of the embryo chick, floating in the albumen of an egg not quite new-laid.

COFIN, *s.* a coffin. B. A. *cophin,* as if from Latin *cophinus.* A. S. *cofa,* fovea.

COFRE, *s.* a chest to keep clothes. Fr. *cofre.* CH.

COIT, *v.* to toss up the head. Of a proud and affected minx, it is said she "*coits* up her head above her betters." BR. gives *coit* to toss, in general.

COIT, *s.* a toss of the head. Fr. *coite,* a canopy.

COLD-CHILL, *s.* a ridiculous pleonasm, meaning an ague-fit, or the first access of a fever.

COLDER, *s.* broken ears of corn mixed with short fragments of straw, beaten off by the flail.

COLLAR, *v.* to sully with soot or coal-dust. W. C. *colly.*

COLLAR, COLLAR-COAL, *s.* black smut from the chimney or bars. We distinctly pronounce it thus. SH. has it *colly*, in the phrase, "*collied* night ;" but there is some authority in O. E. (not duly noted) for *collor*. At any rate it is from A. S. *col*, carbo.

COLLAR-BALL, *s.* a light ball with which children play. There is some allusion, perhaps, to its usual dirtiness.

COLLAR-BEAM, *s.* the highest and shortest beam in a building, which is thought perhaps to hold together and secure the roof, as the garments are held by the *collar*. It seems a better word than its synonym WIND-BEAM, q. v.

COLLOGUE, *v.* to confer together for some mischievous purpose. It has nothing to do with " flattering and cajoling," as in T. J. It has been called a corruption of *colleague ;* but it is not. It has a proper meaning of its own ; and a derivation too, coming directly or indirectly from Lat. *colloquor.* BR. JEN.

COLT, *s.* any person in a parochial, or other office, who attends a public meeting for the first time, is called a " *colt*," and must be " *shod* ;" that is, must pay a forfeit n liquor for the benefit of the company. Ex " We shall have a good frolic to day ; we have four *colts* to shoe."

COME, *v.*

1. To become. Ex. " What is *come* of her ? " It is the original and simple, and why not the proper form ? It is O. E of 400 years standing, occurring in P. L. The prefix *be* is so vaguely and variably

used in a multitude of words, that grammarians are unable to give a satisfactory account of it.

2. Imperf. t. of *come.* Ex. "He *come* yesterday." It is o. e. in p. g. and ch. Perhaps it should be spelled, as it is by some illiterate scribes, *cum.*

3. Intruded into several words, awkwardly and vulgarly, perhaps, but not without meaning. Ex. " To-morrow-come-se'nnight," " Tuesday-come-fortnight," Meaning, no doubt, when to-morrow se'nnight, or Tuesday fortnight shall come; or, let them come, and then the thing will happen. A more facetious phrase is, " to-morrow-come-never." Ad Græcas calendas. To this may also be referred, *miscomfortune* and *miscomhap;* words very injuriously reputed corruptions.

COME-BACK, *s.* a guinea-fowl. Its harsh cry is supposed to resemble the pronunciation of those two words.

COME OUT! A word of command to a dog, when he barks and seems disposed to bite. "Come in" is of course very often what is actually meant. It is, therefore, as Mr. Wilbraham observes, " an odd expression." It may perhaps be interpreted, "come out of the mischief you are in," w. c.

COMMANDEMENT, *s.* commonly reputed a *corruption,* but certainly not so. It is exactly as we received it from the French.

COMPANY-KEEPER, *s.* a lover.

COMPASS, *s.* an outline; as of carpenters' work, of laying out ground, &c. with a sweep, approaching to a circular form, In St. Paul's voyage, Acts, ch. xxviii. the pilot "fetched a *compass.*" A bow-

window was anciently called a *compass-window.*
sh. Troilus and Cressida.

COMPASSING, *adj.* in a roundish or circular form.

CONDITION, *s.* temper. Ex. " An ill-conditioned
fellow!" It is a very old sense. sh. Hen. V. "My
*condition* is not smooth "

CONEY-LAND, *s.* land so light and sandy as to be fit
for nothing but the breeding and feeding of rabbits. A common jest is, that it may be ploughed
with two rabbits and a knife.

COOK-EEL, *s.* a sort of cross bun, made and eaten in
Norfolk during Lent. They are sold cheap, and
may be from Fr. *coquille.*

COOMS, *s. pl.* the high ridges in ill-kept roads, between the ruts and the horse-path.

COP, *v.* to throw something upwards, in order to
reach a mark at some moderate distance. ch.
uses *coppe* for top. w. c. *cob.* a. s. *copa,* apex.

COOP! *interj.* a common word of invitation to domestic
poultry, not to come into the coop to be fatted, but
to peck up the food thrown down for them. It is,
perhaps, an abbreviation of the words *come up. Cup*
is often so used. Coop in the same sense is in Jen.

COPE, *s.* a large quantity or great number. There
certainly must have been such a substantive as
*cope* in the Anglo-Saxon language, though it does
not appear in the dictt. in its simple form. But,
from its compounds or derivatives, it seems rather
to have signified value than abundance. Those
two ideas, however, are commonly so associated as
to warrant the Saxon derivation of our word;
though its remote origin must, no doubt, have been
Lat. *copia.*

COPE, *v.* to fasten up. The use of this word is confined to warreners, who are said to " cope" their fer-
rets, when they sew or tie up their mouths, to prevent them from biting rabbits, when they are used
to drive them from their holes.

COP-HALFPENNY, *s.* the game more generally
called *chuck-farthing*.

COPPER-ROSE,*s.* the wild red poppy. Fr. *couperosé*.

COPPLE-CROWN, *s.* a tuft of feathers on the head
of a fowl, not such as can be depressed at pleasure,
like the crests of many birds, but permanently
erect. It is sometimes called a *topple-crown*, which
is strictly synonymous. *Cop is top.*

COPPLING, *adv.* unsteady, in danger of falling. Ex.
" It stands *coppling,* as if it stood upon its head."
B. JONS. Alchemist, says, "it stands *a-cop.*"

COP-WEB, *s.* a cob-web. Nearer to Saxon. A.S. *at-
ter-coppa*, aranea ; q. d. poison-top.

COP-WEB-WEATHER, *s.* misty weather,

CORF, *s.* a floating cage or basket to keep lobsters ;
used on the Suffolk coast. In M. S. it is *cawf.* In
the Northern Coal Counties the stout basket used
in the mines is called and written *corf.* BR. derives
it from Lat. *corbis.* Perhaps, however pronounced,
it should be written *coph* or *coff*, from Lat. *cophinus.*

CORN, *s.* a particle, a very minute portion, as it were
a grain; B. JONS. has, "a *corn* of salt." A pepper-
*corn* is very commonly used, but certainly not with
propriety. We also apply it to salt, and to many
other things. A smoker is pressed by his companions, at the "heel of the evening," to lengthen
their placid enjoyment of the pipe, with "Come!

put in nine *corns* more." A barley-*corn* is our least measure of length; the third part of an inch. In L. SC. the word is *curn*.

CORNER, *s.* a point in a rubber at whist. We say, we play sixpences or a shilling *a corner*, not sixpenny or shilling points.

CORNY, *adj.*
1. Abounding in corn. Ex. " These sheaves are heavy and *corny*."
2. Tasting well of malt. Ex. " The ale is *corny*." CH.
3. Tipsey. BR.

COSH, *s.* the glume of corn, particularly wheat. " White wheat in a red *cosh*," is a favorite variety. Fr. *cacher*.

COSSET, *v.* to fondle. Fr. *corset*.

COSSET, *s.* a pet, something fondly caressed.

COSSET-LAMB, *s.* a lamb reared without the ewe. R. S. E. C.

COSTLY, *adj.* costive. This may be thought to have deserved a place among obvious corruptions, if it deserved any at all. But let us look a little closer. The DICTT. derive their word from Fr. *constipé*. Perhaps justly; it has the Fr. adjective termination *if* or *ive*. But our word, by its Saxon termination *ly*, seems to claim descent from another etymon, at least equally significant. A. S. *costian*, tentare. *V.* FRUGAL.

COTHE, *v.* to faint.

COTHISH, COTHY, *adj.* faint, sickly, ailing. There can surely be no doubt of the identity of these words: the former is Sir Thomas Browne's, the latter the modern form. Yet in the Pref. to R. N. C. it is in-

terpreted *morose*, without a word of explanation or
proof. It never could have been used in that sense:
Its derivation is so very obvious, that it is wonderful
it escaped Ray. It is amply justified by modern
and very frequent use. A dog is said to be *cothy*
when he is meek and delicate. A. s. *cothe*, morbus.

COTTERLIN, *s.* *V.* Cosset. o. fr. *cadeler.*

COUCH, COUCH-HANDED, *adj.* left-handed. Fr.
*gauche.*

COUNT, *v.* to guess, to suppose, to opine. Ex. "I
*count* you farm 300 acres." It is not to be understood that any trouble has been taken to compute.

COUSIN, *s.* nephew or niece. o. e. In sh. Pandarus
calls Cressida his *cousin*, who was, however, his
*niece.*

COUSIN BETTY, COUSIN TOM, *s.* a bedlamite, or
rather an impudent vagrant pretending to be such.
*V.* Bess O'Bedlam. They were wont to enter
the sitting room of a family, having first ascertained
that there was nobody in it but women and children, with whom they claimed kindred. Whence
their names, which, like many others, have outlived
their meaning, and are now used like their syno-
nyms before noticed.

COWL, *s.* the top of a malt-kiln, moved by the wind;
from some resemblance it may have to a monk's
hood. pr. says, that in the North it is absurdly
called a *cow.* Neither br. nor w. c. notice it.

COWLICK, *s.* a twist or wreathing in the hair of the
forehead, which, in a calf, might be supposed to
have been licked by the cow out of its natural position. w. c. br.

COW-MUMBLE, *s.* a wild plant, more commonly called *cow-parsnip*. *Heracleum sphondyleum*, Lin.

COWSLOP, *s.* a cowslip, O. E.  PR. PA.

COW-TONGUED, *adj.* having a tongue, smooth one way and rough the other, like that of a cow. Expressively applied to one who gives fair or foul language, as may best suit his purpose.

COY, *s.*

1. A decoy for ducks.

2. A coop for lobsters. *V.* CORF; certainly a better word than this, which may be a corruption of it. The poor animals are nòt *decoyed* into their fatal prison.

COY-DUCK, *s.* a duck trained to entice others into the tunnel in a decoy.

COXY-ROXY, *adj.* merrily and fantastically tipsy. JAM. gives *coxy,* coxcombical.

CRA, *s.* a crow. O. E.  A. S. *crawe,* corvus.

CRAB-LANTHORN, *s.* a sort of pastry. *V.* APPLE-JACK.

CRACK, CRAKE, *v.* to brag. L. SC.  V. D.

CRACK, *s.*

1. Something to boast of. Ex. " She is the *crack* of the village."

2. A very short time. Ex. " It was done in a *crack*."

CRACK, *adj.* boasted. Ex. " A *crack* team." Isl. *krekia,* jactare.

CRACKLING, CRACKLE, *s.* the outside fat and skin of roasted pork, so called from its crackling between the teeth.

CRAG, *s.* the craw. Ex. "He has stuffed his *crag* well." Teut. *kraeghe,* guttur. L. SC. the neck.

CRAG, *s.* a deposit of fossil sea-shells, found in large quantities in an extensive district of the county of Suffolk, and used with much advantage as manure on the neighbouring light lands.

CRAMPLE, *v.* to move with pain and stiffness, as if affected by cramps.

CRAMPLE-HAM'D, *adj.* stiffened in the lower joints.

CRAWLY-MAWLY, *adv.* in a weakly and ailing state. In R. S. E. C. it is explained by " indifferently well." It does not mean well in any degree, though it may imply some little amendment in health. It seems to have been fabricated from the words *crawl* and *mawl*, and to mean sorely *mauled*, and scarcely able to *crawl*.

CREEPERS, *s. pl.*
  1. Low pattens mounted on short iron stumps, instead of rings.
  2. Grapnels to bring up any thing from the bottom of a well or pond.

CREEP-HEDGE, *s.* one who prowls and sneaks about, like small wild animals, through hedges.

CREVET, *s.* a cruet. A mere variation.

CRIBLE, *s.* a finer sort of bran. When the broad bran has been separated from the meal, a second sifting through a finer sieve, brings off *crible.* Fr. *cribler.* R. S. E. C.

CRICKLE, CRUCKLE, *v.* to bend under a weight, to sink down through pain or weakness. Dimin. of *crouch,* which Dr. Johnson derives from Fr. *crochu.* His late editor prefers another, which is certainly very suitable to the first of our two words.

BR. gives *crinkle* in the same sense. Teut. *kriechen*, reptare.

CRIMBLE, *v.* to creep about privily, to sneak, to wind along unperceived. A. s. *crymbig*, tortilis.

CRINCH, *v.* to crush with the teeth some harsh and brittle substance, as unripe fruit. In Suffolk more frequently pronounced *cranch*. Fr. *grincer*. L. sc,

CRINCHLING, *s.* a small apple.

CRINKLE, CRUNKLE, *v.* to wrinkle, twist, plait, or rumple irregularly. Dan. *kronkelin*, torquere. BR.

CRISH, CRUSH, *s.* cartilage, or soft bones of young animals, easily crushed by the teeth,

CROCK, *s.* smut, dust of soot or coal. w. w. R. BR.

CROCK, *v.* to defile with smut,

CROCKY, *adj.* smutty. A. s. *crocca*, fuligo.

CROME, *s.* a crook; a staff with a hook at the end of it, to pull down the boughs of a tree, to draw weeds out of ditches, and for a variety of other useful purposes. T. had a *dung-crome;* we have *nut-cromes* and many others. Belg. *crom*, uncus.

CROME, *v.* to draw with a *crome,*

CROODLE, *v.* to lie close and snug, as pigs, or puppies in their straw. A dimin. of *crowd* in our sense of it, q. v. w. c,

CROP, *s.*

1. Annual produce, as well animal as vegetable. We talk of *crops* of lambs, turkeys, geese, &c.

2. The craw of birds, metaphorically applied to other animals. L. sc. *crap.*

3. A joint of pork, commonly called the spare-rib. Teut. *krop*, stomachus.

CROPE, *v.* to creep slowly and heavily. Augm. of *creep.*

CROSS-EYE, *s.* that sort of squint, by which both the eyes turn towards the nose, so that the rays in passing to each eye, cross each other; and distinct vision is attainable only by much skill and habit in the squinter.

CROSS-PATCH, *s.* an ill-tempered fellow. *Patch* is a very old word of contempt in sh. &c. but used by us only in this combination.

CROTCH, *s.*

1. The meeting of two arms of a tree; or of an arm with the trunk; or of the limbs of the human body, below the waist.

2. A staff under the arm to support the lame.

CROTCHED, *adj.* cross, peevish, perverse. Doubtless for *crouched,* q. d. *crossed.*

CROTCH-ROOM, *s.* length of the lower limbs. It is said of one who has long legs, that he has plenty of *crotch-room.*

CROTCH-STICK, *s.* a stick having a crotch at the end. In all these words the general idea is *cross,* the name of which, is much alike in all modern languages from the Latin. The word *crotch* may seem to have come from the Ital. *croce,* as it easily might. From some derivations, however, the letter *c* appears to have sometimes had in the Saxon the soft sound of *ch* as it has in Italian. If so, the word may be our own. A. s. *cruce,* crux.

CROTCH-TROLLING, *s.* a method of trolling or angling for pike, used in the broads and rivers in Norfolk. The fisherman has no rod, but has the usual reel, and, by the help of a *cratch-stick*, throws his bait a considerable distance from him into the water, and then draws it gently towards him. It is much practised by poachers, as there is no rod, or "pole," to betray their intention.

CROUSE, *v.* to catterwaul. Not a corruption of *carouse*, as may seem at first sight, but far more expressively deduced from Fr. *courroucer*.

CROWD, *v.* to push, shove, or press close. To the word, in its common acceptation, number seems necessary. With us, one individual can crowd another. CH.

CROW-KEEPER, *s.* a boy employed to scare crows from new-sown land. On this poor word, no fewer than five sage commentators have wasted their critical powers to a very idle purpose. Lear, in his madness says, "That fellow handles his bow like a *crow-keeper*." A knotty passage! And the critics make a mighty coil about "*cow-keepers*, *crow-keepers*, and *scare-crows!*" But the boy himself would untie the knot at once. Besides lustily whooping, he carries an old gun from which he cracks a little powder, and sometimes puts in a few small stones, but seldom hits, and still seldomer kills a crow. In Shakspeare's time, it seems that the *crow-keeper* carried a bow, and doubtless "handled" it with as much awkwardness and as little success as the modern boy manages his gun. Tusser, speaking of keeping the birds from newly-sown lands, has these lines:

"Then stir about, Nicol, with arrow and bow,
Take penny for killing of every crow."

All is quite plain. Yet such puzzles as this have been known to "keep gravity out of his bed at midnight."

CROW-TIME, *s.* evening; when rooks fly back in great flocks, from their food to their trees.

CRUD-BARROW, CRUDDEN-BARROW, *s.* a common wheel-barrow, to be shoved forward. In P. L. we find the phrase *crowding* a barrow. *Crud* is the part.

CRUMBLES, *s. pl.* crumbs, dimin. The verb is common.

CRUMP, *v.* to eat any thing brittle or crimp; of which this word is an intens. L. SC.

CRUMP, CRUMPY, *adj.* brittle; dry baked; easily breaking under the teeth. Teut. *krimpan,* contrahere. BR.

CRUMPLIN, *s.*

1. A diminutive and mis-shapen apple.

2. Met. a diminutive and deformed person.

A. S. *crump,* curvus.

CRUNKLE, *v.* to rumple. Teut. *kronchelen,* corrugare.

CRUSH, CRUSTLE, *s.* gristle. Another form of the same word.

CRIMANY! *interj.* of sudden surprise.

CUCKOO-BALL, *s.* a light ball made of party-coloured rags, for young children.

CUCKOO-FLOWER, *s. orchis mascula* or *morio.* Lin.

CUCKOO-SPIT, *s.* the fine white froth on growing plants, which covers the little delicate larva of the *cicada spumans.* Lin. Otherwise *frog-spit* and

*toad-spit*. In L. sc. *gowk-spit*. The gowk is the
cuckoo. BR.

CUDDLE, *v.* to hug and fondle. Belg. *cuddegl.* L. sc.
BR.

CULCH, *s.* thick dregs or sediment.

CULP, *s.* a hard and heavy blow.  O. Fr. *coulp.*

CULPIT, *s.* a large lump of any thing.

CULVER, *v.* to beat and throb in the flesh.  As a
sore advances towards suppuration it "bulks and
*culvers.*"  In Suffolk it is pronounced *gelver,*

CULVER-HEADED, *adj.*  In common acceptation
it seems to mean thick-headed, stupid.  But this
must be an improper use.  It should rather mean
soft-headed, harmless "an it were any sucking
dove!"  The difference might be little or nothing
in point of stupidity.

CUMBLED, *part.* oppressed, cramped, stiffened with
cold.  "*Accombred* with cold." PR. PA.  Fr. *com-
bler.*

CUMBLY-COLD, *adj.* stiff, and benumbed with cold.
Intensely cold, if applied to weather.

C'UP, *v.*  Probably an abbreviation of "*come up.*"
It is usually addressed to beasts.  Ex. Come along,
*c'up.*

CUPBOARD-HEAD, *s.*  A most expressive designation of a head both wooden and hollow.  An adjective is sometimes formed from it.  Ex. "A stupid
*cupboard-headed* fellow!"

CUSHION-MAN, *s.* the chairman at the Quarter
Sessions; or at any other public meeting, where
there is the same distinguishing mark of presidency.

CUSTARD, *s.* the school-master's ferula, or a slap on

the flat hand with it. Mr. Pegge calls it a *custis*
But what can that mean? Our word, which is
most distinctly pronounced, may at least have had
originally a ludicrous allusion—" dant *crustula*
*blandi* doctores!

CUTE, *adj.* shrewd, quick in apprehension. " A *cute*
lad." Corruption of Lat. *acutus*, would etymologists be ready to say, with one voice. Yet it is not
so, but from A. s. *cuth*, expertus. JEN. W.C. BR.

CUTH'A, *v.* quoth he. It is an ancient form of expression, and was often spelt by old writers *quoth'a*,
and probably pronounced much like ours. It refers
to something that has been said by another person.
Thus in SH. Rom. and Jul. Romeo says, " One that
God hath made himself to mar." The nurse answers, " By my troth, it is well said: for himself to
mar, *quoth'a*."

## D.

DABBY, *adj.* moist and somewhat adhesive; sticking
to the skin like wet linen.

DABS, *s. pl.* dibbles. JUN. connects *dibble* with *dabble*.
It seems, indeed, to be a sort of diminution or refinement of it. If so, our *dabs* come very appositely
from Belg. *dabben*, lutum subigere.

DADDLE, *v.* to walk unsteadily as a child; following
his *dad*—" sequiturque patrem non passibus æquis."
Or, it may be a variation of *waddle*. Or even of
*tottle*, which may be understood as a dimin. of *tot-
ter*. *Tottle, toddle, doddle, daddle*, all are connected.

DAFTER, *s.* a daughter. Indeed, it is only the word *daughter* following in pronunciation the analogy of *laughter*. Why then insert it? Because there is recorded authority for it in this form, in the Register Book of a certain parish in Norfolk, which, through the blameable negligence of the curate, was kept many years by the parish clerk. All the female children baptised in above twenty years were *dafters.* The dates are, indeed, somewhat farther back than the retrospect of this work. But the pronunciation is still occasionally to be heard from some very old people.

DAG, *s.* dew.

DAG, *v.* to bedew. R. S. E. C.   W. W. R.   W. C.   BR.

DAG OF RAIN, Phr. A slight misty shower. Isl. *daeg,* imber.

DAGGY, *adj.* dewy; slightly moistened with rain.

DALLOP, *s.*

1. A patch of ground among growing corn where the plough has missed. T.
2. Rank tufts of growing corn where heaps of manure have lain.
3. A parcel of smuggled tea, varying in quantity, from six to sixteen pounds, and perhaps more or less.
4. A slattern, synonymous of *trollop.*
5. A clumsy and shapeless lump of any thing tumbled about in the hands.

DALLOP, *v.* to paw, toss, and tumble about carelessly.

DAME, *s.* Once an honourable designation of females of high rank; now applied only to those of

the lowest. It is almost obsolete even there. JEN.
says, that in the West it is applied to a farmer's
wife. In the East it would be very offensive.

DANGEROUS, *adj.* endangered. Ex. " Mr. Smith
is sadly-badly ; quite *dangerous.*"

DARNOCKS, DANNOCKS, *s. pl.* hedger's gloves ;
that for the left hand being made whole to grasp the
thorns, and for the right, with fingers to handle the
hedging-bill. It should rather be *Dornecks*, which
is the proper Flemish name of *Tournai*, a Frenchi-
fied name, long since universally substituted. Two
hundred years ago, it was celebrated for its coarse
woollen manufactures, principally of carpets and
hangings, mentioned in some of our old comedies.
Probably thick gloves were another article of importation. Our modern *dannocks*, indeed, are of
thick leather, and made at home by our own
glovers. Dan. *dorneck.*

DARK-HOUR, *s.* the evening twilight. The interval
between the time of sufficient light to work, or
read by, and the lighting of candles ; a time of
social domestic chat. Ex. " We will talk over that
at the *dark-hour.*"

DASH, *v.* to abash. Perhaps a better etymon than
any that has been offered for the word (in this
sense, at least, which is very common with us) is
A. s. *dwæs*, stupidus præ timore.

DAUBER, *s.* a builder of walls with clay or mud,
mixed with stubble or short straw, well beaten and
incorporated, and so becoming pretty durable. It
is used, particularly in Suffolk, to make fences for

farm-yards, &c. and even walls for mean cottages.
In Norfolk it is now difficult to find a good *dauber*.
W. C. BR.

DAUNT, *v.* to stun, to knock down. Exactly answer-
ing to its derivation, Fr. *dompter*.

DAUZY, DAUZY-HEADED, *adj.* dizzy; either
literally or metaphorically, as if confused, bewildered, thoughtless. PE.

DAZE, DAZLE, DAURE, *v.*

1. To dazzle.

2. To stun.

All these words, together with *dash*, are closely connected, and the same etymon may serve them all.
*Daze.* W. W. R. W. C. BR.

DAYMAN, *s.* a labourer hired by the day. "Jacque-
netta is allowed for the day-woman." SH. Love's
Labour Lost. In a statute of Edward III. he
is called a *dayar;* and in one of the Canterbury
Tales, a *day.* C. HAW.

DEAL-TREE, *s.* a fir-tree.

DEAL-APPLES, *s.* the conical fruit of the fir-tree.
There is an air of antiquity in this word. A. S.
*æppel,* seems to be a general name for all fruit,
eatable or not.

DEATHSMEAR, *s.* a disease fatal to children. This
word is imputed to us by all the collectors of Provincialisms; but a pretty extensive inquiry among
midwives, nurses, and other rustic gossips of much
experience and sagacity, has not produced any
living authority for it in either county. It does
not seem very likely that it ever did signify any
disease in particular, but the fatal termination of

any one. The collector might have heard an old nurse exclaim, "Ah! poor babe, 'tis in the *death-smear!*" i. e. in the *smore* or mist of death, on the point of losing its breath. Not that it is used even in that sense now. A. s. *smorau,* suffocare.

DEE, *s.* a die. *Pl. n. dees* or *dece.* A certain East Anglian sportsman, of no little celebrity in his day, a man of much simplicity of character, strangely combined with a great deal of shrewdness, having got into a party of black-legs at New-market, who meant to pigeon him, suddenly ex-claimed: " Hye, hye, here's a *dee* with tew douces!" His more adroit companions immedi-ately turned the charge upon him, and he was roughly handled for his fortunate or unfortunate discovery.

DEKE, DIKE, *s.* a ditch. A. s. *dice,* fossa. CH.

DEKE-HOLL, DIKE-HOLL, *s.* a hollow or dry ditch. Or *holl* may be used alone in the same sense.

DELF, *s.* a deep ditch or drain. From *v. delve.*

DELK, *s.* a small cavity, in the soil, in the flesh of the body, or in any surface which ought to be quite level. From *dell,* somewhat in the nature of a dimin.

DENE, *s.* din. o. E.

DERE, *adj.* dire, sad. Sir Thomas Browne. But it is o. E. CH. has it, and SH. Love's Labour Lost, " Deaf'd with the clamour of their own *dear* groans." Dr. Johnson observes that *dear* is for *dere.* And yet the words " own *dear*," may seem to come very nearly to the sense of the adjective φιλος in Homer; φιλον ητωρ, φιλον ομμα, φιλα *yourara.* It is a sense of close and particular endearment, in which certainly we often use those two words, in speaking of any thing we particularly cherish, as our beloved kindred or friends, or, as in Homer, the limbs or organs of our bodies.

DERELY, *adv.* direly, lamentably, extremely. Ex. " I am *derely* ill;" "*derely* tired," &c. Commonly, perhaps, but very absurdly, understood to be *dearly.*

DEVE, *v.* to dive. o. e. also, to dip.

DEVILIN, *s.* the species of swallow, commonly called the swift; *hirundo apus,* Lin. Named from its imp-like ugliness and screaming. JEN. *Sheer-devil.*

DEVIL'S-MINT, *s.* an inexhaustable abundance and succession of things hurtful or offensive, as if the devil himself were at work coining them.

DEVILTRY, DEVILMENT, *s.* any thing unlucky, offensive, hurtful, or hateful, in which the devil may be suspected of having some concern. The first word ought certainly to be *devilry,* for it would be an exact English form of the word *diablerie,* which has the same meaning. The second word looks like the French adverb *diablement,* transformed to an English noun.

DEVING-POND, *s.* a pond from which water is drawn for domestic use, by dipping a pail.

DEUSAN, *s.* a hard sort of apple which keeps a long time, but turns pale and shrivels. Hence the simile, " pale as a *deusan.*" Fr. *deux ans.*

DEW-BEATERS, *s. pl.* coarse and thick shoes whic resist the dew.

DEW-DRINK, *s.* the first allowance of beer to harvest men, before they begin their day's work.

DIBLES, *s. pl.* difficulties, embarrassments, scrapes. It may be a contraction of the Fr. *diableries,* or from N. Fr. *dibillé,* disabled.

DICK-A-DILVER, *s.* the herb periwinkle. *Vinca minor.* Lin. Is it so called from its rooting *(delving)* at every joint, and spreading itself far and wide.

DICKY, *s.* an ass, male or female.

DICKY-ASS, *s.* a male ass; the female being usually called a Jenny ass, or a Betty ass.

DIDDER, *v.* to have a quivering of the chin through cold. BR. Belg. *sitteren,* a sono, quem frigore trementes edimus. SK. G. A.

DIDDLE, *v.* to waste time in the merest trifling. An extreme dimin. of *dawdle.* BR.

DIDDLES, DIDDLINGS, *s.* young ducks, or sucking pigs.

DIDLE, *v.* to clean the bottom of a river.

DILLS, *s. pl.* the paps of a sow. A contraction, perhaps, of the foregoing word. At any rate they are connected.

DILVER, *v.* to weary with labour or exercise. It may not improperly be connected with *delving,* which is one effectual mode of producing fatigue.

DING, *v.*

1. To throw with a quick and hasty motion. Ex. "I *dung* it at him."

2. To beat or knock repeatedly. Ex. "I could not *ding* it into him." R. S. E. C.

DING, *s.* a smart slap; particularly with the back of the hand. Sui.-G. *dænge*, tundere.

DINGE, *v.* to rain mistily, to drizzle.

DIP, *s.* a sauce for dumplings, composed of melted butter, vinegar, and brown sugar. PR. gives us credit for this delicious hors d'œuvre.

DIRT-WEED, *s. chenopodium viride*, Lin. An expressive name for what generally grows on dunghills or other heaps of dirt. BR. *muck-weed.*

DISBURST, *v.* to disburse. The idea of *bursting* may naturally enough suggest itself to an illiterate person, on any occasion of expenditure. In using this word, then, he has a distinct meaning, which he would not have if he said *disburse,* of the proper signification of which he knows nothing.

DISCOMFRONTLE, *v.* seems to be a compound of *discomfit* and *affront,* in sense as well as in sound; the additional syllable at the end being intended to smooth and round it off with the liquid *l,* euphoniæ gratiâ.

DISOBLIGE, *v.* to stain or sully. A young miss is apt to *disoblige* her white frock by romping in the dirt with the boys, or by not taking proper care when she eats her tart. The cat may *disoblige* the carpet if she is not turned out of the room in time.

DO, *v.* Phr. " to do for." To take care of, provide for. Ex. " The children have lost their mother, but their aunt will *do for* them." The more correct sense of this phrase is widely different from ours. To " do for one," or to " do his business," means very generally and familiarly to dispatch him, to knock him on the head, or get rid of him in some other way. And so, indeed, it does with us. So that we have two opposite senses of *doing for*. To "do for," also sometimes means to manage the affairs of another as steward or agent.

DOATED, *part.* decayed, rotten; chiefly applied to old trees.

DOBBLE, *v.* to dawb; of which it seems a frequent.

DOCK, *s.* the broad nether end of a felled tree; or of the human body.

DOCKSY, *s.* a very gentle softening or dimin. of the foregoing in its second acceptation.

DOCTOR, *s.* an apothecary, who is invariably addressed and mentioned under this title.

DOCTOR OF SKILL, *s.* a physician, who never receives his proper title, but is as invariably styled *Mister.* It is fruitless to attempt to explain this commutation. Perhaps it may be on an equitable give-and-take principle; that the apothecary ought to be compensated for the implied denial of his skill, and the physician to feel himself sufficiently honoured by the express acknowledgment of it.

DODDY, *adj.* low in stature, diminutive in person. Probably from the common vulgarism *hoddy-doddy*, as we also shorten *hodmandod* to *dodman*.

DODGE, *s.* a small lump of something moist and thick, as of mortar, clay, &c.

DODMAN, *s.* a snail. *Hodmandod* is pretty general. We are content with a part of it. R. S, E. C.

DOER, *s.* an agent or manager for another.

DOGS, *s. pl.* andirons on the hearth where wood is the fuel. Carpenters also use *dogs* to support some of their heavy work. A word implying that the *dog*

is a beast of burthen, is certainly very odd and unaccountable in our language. It might do well
enough in that of Kamschatka or of the Esquimaux.
Horse would certainly suit us better. Indeed we
do use it in a similar sense, and even employ it in
some lighter labours. We make a *horse* bear our
shirts and stockings in the laundry, and our but-
tered toast by the parlour fire, and we load a poor
*dog* with logs and beams. It is vain to attempt
tracing the origin of such a strange expression. BR.

DOG'S-GRASS, *s.* the common *cynosurus cristatus*,
Lin. It is literally, "dog's-tail grass;" but we
have cut off the tail.

DOLK, DOKE, a larger and deeper *delk*, q. v. A. S.
*dolg*, vulnus.

DOME, DOOM, DUM, *s.* down; as of a rabbit, a
young fowl, &c. Dan. *dun*, pluma.

DONE-GROWING, *adj.* stunted in growth; short of
stature.

DOLE, *s.* a distribution of alms, in money, food, fuel,
or clothing. It is strange this word is not given at
all in T. J. nor definitely in Ash. A. S. *dælan*, dis-
tribuere.

DOOL, DOLE, *s.* a boundary mark in an uninclosed
field. It is very often a low post; thence called a
Dool-post. A. S. *dælan*, dividere. BR.

DOOR-STALL, *s.* a door post. The very Saxon
word. A. S. *dur-stodl*, postis.

DOP, *s.* a short quick curtsey. A. S. *doppetan*, mersare.

DOP-A-LOW, *adj.* very short in stature. Especially
spoken of females.

DOR, *s.* a cock-chaffer. The *meloloutha solstitialis*, Lin.

the larva of which does so much mischief to our
meadows and pastures, and the perfect insect is so
great an annoyance in summer evenings. A. S. *dora*,
fucus. R. S. E. C.

DORE-APPLE, *s.* a firm winter apple of a bright yellow colour ; supposed, I trow, pretty generally, to
be thus called because it is as hard as a *door.*   It is,
however, a corruption or perversion, in part translation of Fr. *pomme d'or.*

DORMER, *s.* a large beam.   It is observable that the
only authority given for it in T. J. is that of a Suffolk author, even the witty historian of Wheatfield ;
the nature of whose subject would of course lead
him often to prefer the words and phrases current
in his county.   The word is fairly our's.

DOSS, *v.* to attack with the horns, as a bull, a ram, or
a he-goat.   So it cannot be, as some suppose, the
same as *toss* ; because, though bulls can do so, the
other two horned animals can not.   Has it any connection with *dowse ?*   When the learned translator
of the three Greek Tragic Poets first came into
Norfolk as a curate, the farmer with whom he
lodged, completely posed his erudition, by telling
him, in pointing out to his observation a remarkably
fine bull, that he must soon make away with him, as
he had already "*dossed* three *mauthers.*"

DOSS, *s.* a hassock to kneel upon at Church.   Being
made of rushes and flags, which are also common
materials of baskets, it may be a contraction of
*dosser*, which occurs in O. E. in that sense ; and
being carried on the back came from Fr. *dos.*  CH.

DOUGH-UP, *v.* to stick together, as if with paste.

DOW, *s.* a dove. w.

DOW-HOUSE, *s.* a dove cote. Dowcot. sc. N.

DOW, *v.* to mend, in health. Of a sick man continuing
in the same state, it is said that he " neither dies
nor *dows*." May *dow* mean *do well?* " Doe or die,"
is an ancient military maxim or motto. Ray says,
*dow* or *daw* is, in " common speech," to awaken. In
what common speech? Are we to understand that
in his time it was a general word? PR. has "*die*
nor *do*." Of the etyma offered by Ray, the best
seems A.s. *dugan*, valere. w.c. w. w. R.

DOWLER, *s.* a sort of coarse dumpling. It seems
connected with *dough*.

DOWN-BOUT, *s.* a hard set-to; a tough battle.

DOWNFALL, *s.* a descent from the atmosphere.
Rain, hail, or snow. L. sc. *onfall*.

DOWN-LYING, *s.* a lying-in.

DOWN-LYING, *adj.* applied to a woman in her
travail.

DOWN-PINS, *s. pl.* those who in a jolly carousal
are dead-drunk. Metaphor from Nine-pins.

DOWNY, *adj.* low-spirited.

DRABBLE, *v.* to draggle. Ours is the better word.
A.s. *drabbe*, fæces.

DRABBLE-TAIL, *s.* a slattern, who allows her gar-
ment to trail after her in the dirt.

DRAGGING-TIME, *s.* the evening of the fair-day,
when the young fellows pull the wenches about.

DRAINS, *s. pl.* grains from the mash-tub, through
which the wort has been *drained* off.

DRANT, *v.* to drawl in speaking or reading; more
properly, perhaps, spelled *draunt* (pronounced like
aunt). It may be connected with *drone*.

DRANT, *s.* a droning or drawling tone. Ex. "He reads with a *drant.*" It may be from A.S. *dran,* fucus. JEN. *drean.*

DRAPS, *s. pl.* fruit in an orchard dropping before it is fit to be gathered.

DRAWK, *s.* the common darnel-grass. *Lolium perenne,* Lin.

DRAWLATCH, *v.* to dawdle tediously, and spend much time on little work.

DRAWLATCH, *s.* a tedious dawdling loiterer. Minshew explains *drawlatchet* a sort of nightly thief, from his drawing the latchets, or latches, of doors. He supposes the word to have been long obsolete in his time. Yet, lo! after two centuries more it still lives, very nearly in the same form, and not remote from the same meaning. For though we do not impute to a *drawlatch* any other dishonesty than that of wasting the time for which his employer pays him wages, it is easy to conceive that he uses a part of it in watching opportunities to pilfer; and, in so long a course of years, the word may easily enough have assumed a sense certainly not unconnected.

DREPE, *v.* to drip, or dribble. A.S. *drypan,* stillare. BR.

DREPING-WET, *adj.* so thoroughly soaked that water drips from the garments.

DRINDLE, *s.* a small channel to carry off water, a very neat diminutive of *drain.*

DRINGLE, *v.* to waste time in a lazy lingering manner. It has exactly the same sense as *drumble,* which Mrs. Ford uses in the "Merry Wives of Windsor," in rating her servants for not being

more nimble in carrying off the buck-basket. Had
that merry gossip been an East Angle, she must
have said *dringle*.

DROLL, *v.* to put off; to amuse with excuses.  Pron.
like doll.

DROPE, *v.* to run down like wax or tallow from the
candle, or perspiration down the face in violent
heat.  Intensive of *drepe;* but original Saxon.
A. s. *dropian,* stillare.

DROVY, *adj.* itchy ; scabby ; lousy ; or all three.  A
word of supreme contempt, or rather loathing.  It
is from the subst. *drove,* which we have not.  It
is o. e. and in a quotation among the commentaries
on sh. Hen. VI. from some contemporary author,
a *drove* is coupled with a *puzzel,* q. v.  A. s. *drof,*
cœnosus.

DROZE, *v.* to beat very severely.

DROZINGS, *s.* a hearty drubbing.

DRUG, *s.* a strong carriage with four wheels for conveying heavy loads of timber.  It has nothing to
do with dragging.  *Drugge* is o. e. synonymous
with *drudge.* B. A.

DRUGSTER, *s.* a druggist.  sc. N.

DUFFY-DOWS, *s. pl.* young pigeons not fully fledged.

DUDDLE, *v.* commonly used with the addition of
"up."  "To *duddle* up" is to cover up closely and
warmly, with an unnecessary quantity of cloaths.
Ex. "How he do *duddle* his self up."

DUGGLE, *v.* to lie snug and close together, like pigs
or puppies.  A. s. *dygle,* occultus.

DULLOR, *s.* a dull and moaning noise, or the tune
of some doleful ditty.  Certainly the same word as
*dolour,* by what rhetoricians call a metonymy of

cause for effect. Nothing more likely to produce moaning than dolour.

DUMP, *s.* a clumsy medal of lead cast in moist sand.

DUNDY, *adj.* of a dull colour, as *dundy-grey*, or whatsoever other colour is to be coupled with A. S. *dunne*, fuscus.

DUNK-HORN, *s.* the short blunt horn of a beast.

DUNK-HORNED, *adj.* sneaking; shabby. One of the numberless and merciless jests on cuckoldom; applied to the poor cornuto, with an insinuation that he would be glad, if possible, that his horns should escape observation and ridicule.

DUNT, *adj.* stupid; or dizzy. A dizzy calf with water in the head is said to be *dunt.*

DUNT, *v.* to stupify. Isl. *dunt*, ictus.

DUTFIN, *s.* the bridle in cart-harness.

DUZZY, *adj.* dizzy; an easy change of letters.

DWAIN, DWAINY, *adj.* faint; sickly. The verb *dwine* (unde *dwindle*) occurs in CH. and in BR. A. S. *dwinan*, tabescere.

DWILE, *s.*

1. A refuse lock of wool.
2. A mop made of them.
3. Any coarse rubbing rug.

It is certainly an awkward and rustic perversion of the word *doily.* Not, indeed, in its modern sense, of a small light cotton napkin, used at a dessert. But it may not be amiss to observe, that a young rustic lately caught, and taken into a country clergyman's family to be trained as a servant, called them *dwiles.* About 150 years ago, and probably long before, *doily* was a sort of woollen stuff, of

which, it appears from Congreve, that clothes were
occasionally, but rarely made. And so, we know,
they also were of drugget. Among its other uses,
*doily* might have beeen employed in our third
sense. In T. J. it is said to be named from its first
maker. It is more likely to be, by a very easy
change, from, Fr. *toile.*

DWINGE, *v.* to shrivel and dwindle. Apples are
*dwinged* by over-keeping. *V.* DWAIN, with which
it is certainly connected.

DYMOX, *s.* a sturdy combatant; a stout pugilist; a
champion. A good hearty constitutional English
word, probably a very ancient one, and not at all
likely to be peculiar to us.


# E.

E.A, *s.* water. A genuine Saxon word, unchanged.
It is to be found, with some variety of form, in the
proper names of places in all parts of East Anglia;
but in its own proper form, perhaps only in the
fen-country, at the south-eastern angle of the
county of Norfolk, and the adjoining part of the
Isle of Ely. Popham's *ea,* and St. John's *ea,* are
water-courses cut for the drainage of different
parts of the Bedford level into the Ouse above
Lynn. *Ea* brink is the beginning of a very sudden curvature of that river, from which point a
new cut was made at a prodigious expence, and
finished in the year 1820, to improve the outfall of
the fen waters into Lynn Harbour, by giving them

a straight direction.  It is commonly written and
printed, and generally pronounced by strangers
*eau,* as if the word had been borrowed from the
French, which it certainly was not.  The language
must have been strangely poor, which wanted to
borrow a name for one of the elements of nature!
and strangely fantastical, if, having one of its own,
of common origin, and very nearly of the same
form, it had preferred a foreign form.  In the
country it is invariably pronounced *ea*, and is most
strictly A. s. *ea*, aqua.

EACHON, *adj.* in speaking of two individuals we
commonly say *eachon (each one)* as in speaking of
more than two, *every one.*  It is o. e.  Indeed, in
common pronunciation it may sound like *eachin*, or
even *itchin.*  Ex. " I gave *eachon* of them half a
crown."

EAGER, *s.* a peculiarly impetuous and dangerous ag-
gravation of the tide in some rivers; caused as it
should seem, either by the vehement confluence
of two streams, or by the channel becoming narrower, shallower, or both.  Camden speaks of it,
at the meeting of the Avon and the Severn with
great fury, and calls it *higre.*  In T. J. it is said
to be " a tide swelling above another tide," observable in the river Severn.  The same thing has
been observed of other rivers, as of the Rhone and
Saone, but when once it is determined which shall
be uppermost in a channel sufficient for both, it
does not seem as if this would account satisfactorily for the continued violence and agitation of the
waters.  We have an *eager* in our river Ouse, many

miles above Lynn, near Downham-bridge, where
the waters seem to " stand on an heap " along each
bank, leaving a very dangerous sort of charybdis
in the mid-stream. Here can be no super-induced
tide, as there is no confluence, and we must endeavour to account for the phœnomenon in the several manners above-mentioned. Such a tide also
exists in the river Nene, between Wisbeach and
Peterborough, in the Trent, and in the Ouse near
York. A. s. *egor*, vehemens.

EASTERN-SUNDAY, *s.* We do not suppose this
festival to have any oriental connexion. It seems
to have been the heathen feast of the Saxon goddess *Eoster*, transferred, on the introduction of
Christianity, to a Christian solemnity. The adjective *eastern* means in Saxon formation, " of or
belonging to *Easter*." It is, however, often used
alone, substantively, subaud *Sunday* or *season*. It
may not be impertinent, though not exactly appo-
site, to remark here, that the female baptismal
name, *Esther* or *Hester* (by no means an uncommon one) is always pronounced *Easter;* no doubt
the name of the Saxon goddess, handed down
without interruption or change, and confounded
with that of the Persian queen.

EAVE-LONG, *adj.* oblique; side-long; along the
edges, skirts, or *eaves*, as we often call them, of in-
closed grounds, particularly when they deviate
from straight lines. Hence, " *eave-long* work," is
mowing or reaping those irregular parts in which
the corn or grass cannot be laid in exact parallel
lines. *V.* Scute. A. s. *efese*, margo.

EBBLE, *s.* the asp tree. It is a variation, scarcely amounting to corruption, of *abèle*, the name given by Evelyn, and all our botanists to the white pop- lar, another species of the same genus. They are *populus tremula* and *alba*, Lin.

ECCLES-TREE, *s.* an axle-tree. T. writes it *exle-tree*, and it is so in PR. PA. The metathesis is easy.

EDDISH, *s.* aftermath. Not in Johnson, but added by Todd, in different senses. This is ours. It is o. e. and v. d. Nay, indeed, the very Saxon word, for it appears that the *sc* in that language had the same power as in the modern Italian, that of *sh*. A. s. *edisc*, gramen serotinum. sk.

EITHER OF BOTH, Phr. either of the two. It is used by Bishop Saunderson, and is in PR. PA. "Neither of both," follows of course, which we also have. sh. in Love's Labour's Lost, has "either of neither," which is not by any means so gram- matical a phrase.

ELDERN, *s.* an elder tree. Properly, indeed, it *is* an adjective, with tree understood. It is as old as Piers Ploughman.

ELVISH, *adj.* peevish; wantonly mischievous. These senses are not given in the DICTT. under the word *elfish* or *elvish*. But certainly we have them in per- fect consistency with the character of the *elves*. Ex. "The bees are very *elvish* to-day."

END, *s.*
1. Part; division. Ex. "He has the best *end* of the staff." "It cost me the best *end* of an hundred pounds."

2. The stems of a growing crop. Ex. "Here is a
plenty of *ends*, however it may fill the bushel."

ENDLESS, *s.* intestinum cæcum; blind gut.

ENEMIS, *adv.* Of very obscure and and doubtful
meaning, like most of Sir Thomas Browne's words.
Hickes says it means *lest* (ne forté), and he derives it from Isl. *einema*, an adv. of exclusion, as
he says. It may mean, notwithstanding, from N.
Fr. *nemis.* Or it may be an adjective, signifying
variable, as *enmis* is in L. SC. which JAM. derives
from Isl. *ymiss*, varius. But as the word is quite
extinct, in is impossible to decide upon its meaning,
when it was in use.

ERRIWIGGLE, *s.* an earwig. If it be determined,
after Dr. Wallis and some other etymologists, that
*earwig* comes from *eruca*, in like manner as *periwig*
from *perruque*, our word is certainly a great improvement on that formation. For it is not only
deduced in like manner, but in the very same manner, to a letter. As from *perruque* comes *perri-
wig*, so from *eruque* (eruca) comes *eriwig;* and
the additional syllable makes it, very expressively,
a diminutive. It must not, however, be dissembled,
that a word thus happily formed, and even ele-
gantly finished, is exposed to so gross a corruption
as *arrow-wriggle* on *narrow-wriggle;* some persons
fancying, forsooth, that the little creature may be
so called because it is fond of wriggling itself into
narrow crevices. In PR. PA. it is *erewyggle.* In
the West it is called an *ear-wig.* JEN.

E'RY, *adj.* every. A very common elision. Ex. "My
e'ry-day clothes." T. B.

ESH, *s.* the ash-tree. Literally Saxon. A. s. *esc,* fraxinus. PR. PA. BR.

ETERNAL, *adj.* infernal; damned. By a pretty obvious association of ideas. Ex. " Oh, he is an *eternal* rogue!" o. e. In sh. Othello, Emilia says, " I will be hanged if some *eternal* villain," &c. So would an East Anglian vixen say; though, perhaps, not one of Emilia's condition.

ETHER, *v.* to wattle, or intertwine, in making a staked hedge. Otherwise to " *bond* a hedge," meaning, particularly, the finishing part at top, of stouter materials, which is to confine all the rest. A. s. *ether,* sepes. T. and BR. *edder.*

EVEN-FLAVOURED, *adj.* unmixed; unvaried; uniform. The word might possibly have a meaning, if it were properly applied; but in the only application I have happened to hear of it, it is perfectly nonsensical. It was currently used above thirty years ago in High Suffolk. " An even-flavoured day of rain;" meaning a day of incessant rain.

EVERY-EACH, *adj.* alternate; every other. Possibly from the o. e. *everich.* That word, however, is merely *every,* with the Saxon termination.

EXE, *s.* an axe. PR. PA. A. s. *ex,* securis.

## F.

FADGE, *v.*

1. To suit or fit. Two persons, two things, or two parts of the same thing *fadge* well or ill together.
2. To succeed; to answer expectation. o. e. " We.

will have, an this fadge not, an antic." ₃ʜ. Love's
Labour Lost.

A. s. *gefeagan*, accommodare.

FAGOT, *s.* a contemptuous appellation of a woman.
Ex. "A lazy *fagot*." ʙʀ. The French, always excelling us in politeness, have a sort of proverbial
saying, "Qu'il y a bien de différence entre une
femme et un *fagot.*" But then they explain it by
adding, "que la plus grande différence est qu'une
femme parle toujours, et qu'un *fagot* ne dit mot."
ʀᴏɢ.

FAIRY-BUTTER, *s.* a species of *tremella*, of yellow-
ish colour and gelatinous substance, not very rarely
found on furze and broom. ʙʀ. describes it as
growing about the roots of old trees. This must
be some other species; probably what is called in
some places witch's-butter; of coarser texture and
colour, by no means so suitable to those delicate
beings the fairies, as that which we name after
them.

FAIRY-RINGS, *s.* circles, or parts of circles in the
grass; distinguished, according to Mr. Brockett
and other writers, by darker colour and ranker
growth, in which, as many believed of old, and
some believe still, the fairies are wont to dance.
In our country, they are most observable where
the grass is short and fine; and the circular parts
are most distinguishable by the abundant growth
of a small esculent and well-flavoured fungus, called
the fairy-ring mushroom, *agaricus orcades*, Lin.

FALL, *v.* to let fall; to make to fall. ᴏ, ᴇ. "Mine eyes
*fall* fellowly drops," says Prospero in the Tempest.

" I shall *fall* that tree next spring," say we. In this instance, it is synonymous with *fell*, to which it is certainly of kin.

FALLALS, *s. pl.* flaunting and flaring ornaments. If any thing like derivation of the first syllable can be offered, it may suffice. The second follows as mere jingle. Lat. *phaleræ?*

FALSE-ROOF, *s.* the space between the cieling of the garret and the roof of the building. Where Grose picked up the *vaunce-roof,* which he imputes to us, and interprets a garret, it is impossible to conceive. No such word has been found by the most diligent inquiry. Perhaps his ear deceived him. But his imagination deceived him still more, when he fabricated the order from a Suffolk farmer to his *mauther,* which is almost as unintelligible to any farmer or *mauther* in that county, as it can be to any of his general readers, to whom he offers it as a specimen of our dialect !

FAMBLE-CROP, *s.* the first stomach in ruminating animals. To *famble* in o. e. signified to mumble or speak imperfectly. It may have sufficient connexion with *chewing* imperfectly, to afford some explanation of our word. Dan. *famler,* hæsitare.

FANG, *s.* a fin. From the fancied resemblance of their pointed ends to long teeth, but improperly ; for those teeth only are *fangs* by which an animal catches and holds its prey ; an use which probably no fish are able to make of their fins.

FANGAST, *s.* a marriageable maid. Sir Thomas Browne. The word is not now known, and is there-

fore given with Ray's interpretation and etymon.
A. s. *fangan,* capere, and *gast,* amor.

FAPES, *s. pl.* gooseberries. Variously called also *feaps, feabs, fabes,* and *thapes ;* all abbreviations of feaberries. But these names are with us applicable in the immature state of the fruit only. Nobody ever talks of a ripe *fape.* It is observable that the excellent market of our East Anglian metropolis is well supplied with *fapes* till the Guild-day; which is the Tuesday before June 22. On that day a *fape-tart* is an indispensable regale at every table; and after it, only gooseberries are to be found, whether ripe or unripe; perhaps, in minute strictness, when ripe they are goose-gogs. q. v. As it is one of the welcome first fruits of the year, sk. would derive it, not improperly from A. s. *feen,* gaudere. B. S. E. C. P. B.

FARE, *v.* to seem. Ex. " She *fared* sick ;" "they *fare* to be angry." PE.

FARE, *s.* a litter of pigs. *Farrow* is commonly used in this sense, but *fare* is the better word. A. s. *fearh,* porcellus. B. S. E. C

FARMER, *s.* a term of distinction commonly applied, in Suffolk, to the eldest son of the occupier of a farm. He is addressed and spoken of, by the labourers, as " the *farmer.*" The occupier himself is called master. A labourer speaking to the son would say, " Pray, *farmer,* do you know where my master is ? " Or one labourer would ask another, "Did my master set out that job ? " And would be answered, "No, my master did'nt, but the *farmer* did."

FARROW, *adj.* barren. A cow not producing a calf, is for that year called a *farrow* cow. Yielding no profit, she may be said to lie *fallow*. In Suffolk she would be called *ghast*.

FASGUNTIDE. *s.* shrove-tide; which is interpreted fasting-time. This is given by Blount, in his "Dictionary of Hard Words," 1680, as a Norfolk word. If it were so then, it is like many of Sir Thomas Browne's words of nearly the same age, very little, if at all, known now. Perhaps Blount was misinformed. The word, however, to do it justice, has somewhat of a Saxon air; and may have been in use. Indeed may be so still; though inquiry has not detected it.

FAT-HEN, *s.* a wild pot-herb, very well worth cultivation. It is as good as spinach if its grittiness be well washed off, and it be dressed in the same way. *Chenopodium album*, Lin.

FEATHER-PIE, *s.* a hole in the ground, filled with feathers fixed on strings, and kept in motion by the wind. An excellent device to scare birds.

FEFT, *v.* to persuade, or endeavour to persuade, says Ray in pref. to R. N. C. Yet he adds that in his own county, Essex, it meant, to "put off wares;" but that he was to seek for an etymon. So are we. But it is of no importance. It is one of Sir Thomas Browne's words become obsolete.

FEGARY, *s.* a whim, a freak, a toy. The same as *vagary*, o. E.

FEISTY, *adj.* fusty; but *fusty* is the corruption. *Feisty* is the original, and a most expressive word.

FEIST, FEISTINESS, *s.* fustiness. Ex. "This cask has a *feist* in it. " P. B. has this word, or as he

spells it *foist*, in its primitive Saxon sense, A. s.
*fist*, flatus ventris.

FELLOE, *s.* the felly of a wheel. A. s. *felga,* canthus.
O. E. B. TR.

FELT, *s.* a thick matted growth of weeds, spreading
by their roots, as couch grass. Ex. " This land
is all a *felt.*" *Felt* is a sort of manufacture made
by compacting and condensing the materials together without weaving, as that of which hats are
made. The metaphor is strong. Indeed, several
Saxon names of weeds have the prefix *felt* to their
names. A. s. *felt,* pannus coactilis.

FEN-NIGHTINGALE, *s.* a frog. Otherwise called
a March-bird. It is in that month that frogs are
vocal.

FEW, *adj.* little. It is a plural adjective, used with
a singular substantive in two instances only. We
talk of " a *few* broth " and " a *few* gruel." In
all other cases we use the word like other people.
But our usage is O. E. In a sermon at Paul's
Cross in 1550, a curious account is given of the
College commons at Cambridge in those days. " At
ten of the clocke they go to dynner, whereas they
be content with a peny pyece of byefe amongst
IIII, having a *few* potage made of the brothe of
the same byefe, with salt and otemele and nothing
els." Tempora mutantur! as our young academics
know, and so do their parents, to their cost. Indeed, in this instance, it is very reasonable they
should be changed. The usage is not only O. E. but
modern L. SC. They talk of " a *few* parritch."
And it is not unworthy of remark, that JAM. himself,

under the article "Bishop's-foot," says, "it is said the Bishop's foot has been in the broth when *they* are singed." It is moreover modern Northern English. BR.

FIE, *v.* to cleanse out a ditch, a pond, or any other receptacle of mud or filth. Otherwise *fay*, or *fey*. Isl. *fœgia*, purgare.

FIGHTING-COCKS, *s. pl.* the spikes of the different species of plantain, with which boys play a game so called. BR.

FILANDS, *s. pl.* field-lands, or rather *filde*-lands. O.E. Tracts of uninclosed arable land.

FILE, *v.*
1. To foil.
2. To defile; the simple for the compound, as in stry for destroy, and some others. O. E. and L. SC. W. W. R.
A. S. *fylan*, polluere.

FILL-BELLS, *s. pl.* the chain-tugs to the collar of a cart-horse, by which he draws.

FILL-HORSE, FILLER, *s.* the horse which goes in the shafts. In a regular team, the order is, the fore-horse, the lark-horse, the pin-horse, and the *fill-horse*. Perhaps more correctly the *thill-horse*, or the *thiller*. But *f* is very commonly substituted in pronunciation for *th*; as we sometimes call a thistle a fistle. SK. calls fill-horse "ultimus ordinis equorum." In Suffolk, the horses in a team are distinguished by the names of fore-horse, fore-lash, hand-horse, and *filler*.

FILLER, *v.*
1. To go behind.

2. To draw back. The figurative use is clear enough.

FIMBLE, *v.*

1. To touch lightly and frequently with the ends of the fingers. A gentle diminutive of *fumble.*

2. To pass through without cutting. Ex. " my scythe *fimble* the grass."

FIRE-NEW, *adj.* new from the fire ; newly forged. O. E. SH. *(passim.)*

FIRE-PAN, *s.* a fire-shovel. The word is in Johnson, but not in this sense, in which it seems provincial. Be that as it may, it is literally Saxon. A. s. *fyr-panne*, batillum.

FIT, *adj.* ready. Ex. " Come, stir, make yourself *fit*."

FITTER, *v.* to shift from one foot to the other. w. c.

FIVE-FINGERS, *s. pl.* oxlips. *Primula elatior.*

FIZZ, *v.* to make a hissing sound like fermenting liquors. Isl. *fisa*, sibilare.

FIZMER, *v.* to fidget unquietly, and make a great stir about some trifle, making little or no progress. Formed, perhaps, from the slight rustling noise produced by these petty agitations.

FLACK, *v.* to hang loose. Akin to flake.

FLACK, *s.* a blow, particularly with something loose and pliant.

FLACKET. *s.* a tall, flaunting wench, whose apparel seems to hang loose about her.

FLACKY, *adj.* hanging loose.

FLAG, *s.*

1. A portion of the surface of heathy land turned up by the spade, and heaped to dry for fuel. The more it abounds in roots of *ericæ*, &c. the better fuel it makes.

2. The surface of a clover lay of the second year,

turned up by the plough. The wheat for the next year's crop is dibbled into the *flag*.

FLAGELUTE, *s.* a very small rent or hole in a gar-ment. Perhaps from resemblance to the small per-forations in a *flageolet*.

FLAP, *s.* a slight stroke or touch, Ex. " I have got a *flap* of cold." The cold has touched or struck me. Belg. *flabbe*, colaphus.

FLAP-JACK, *s.*

1. A broad flat piece of pastry. *V.* APPLE JACK.

2. A flat thin joint of meat, as the breast of a lean sheep or calf. JEN.

FLAPPER, *s.* a young wild duck which has just taken wing, but is unable to fly far.

FLAPS, *s. pl.* large broad mushrooms.

FLARNECKING, *adj.* flaunting with vulgar ostenta-tion. Intensive of *flare*.

FLASH, *v.* To flash a hedge is to cut off the lower parts of the bushes which overhang the bank or ditch.

FLAZZARD, *s.* a stout broad faced woman dressed in a loose and flaring manner. It may be from *flash;* or perhaps a word of arbitrary fabrication.

FLEACHES, *s. pl.* the portions into which timber is cut by the saw. Another form of *flitch*.

FLEAK, *s.* a flake. The same word as N. supposes. We talk of "*fleaks* of snow." O. E.

FLECK, *s.* the down of hares or rabbits torn off by the dogs. Dryden has *flix* in the same sense. A. S. *flex*, linum.

FLECKED, FLECKERED, *adj.* dappled ; speckled with differences of colour. In SH. Romeo and

Juliet, it is applied to the different shades of grey in very early morning; which accords exactly with our use of the word. BR. Isl. *flecka*, discolor.

FLEET, *v.* to skim the cream from the milk. A. S. *flete*, flos lactis.

FLEET, *s.* a channel filled by the tide, but left very shallow and narrow at low water. This seems to be the proper sense; and the word is thus used at Lynn. But there appear to be some *fleets* on the Suffolk coast which do not answer this description, as Bawdsey Fleet. It seems, however, to be confirmed by the adjective; and those *fleets* may not now be what they were many centuries ago, when they received the name.

FLEET, *adj.* shallow. A dish or a basin; a ditch or a pond; or anything else of little depth, is said to be *fleet.* BR.

FLEETING-DISH, *s.* a skimming dish to take off the cream from the milk.

FLEGGED, FLIGGED, *part.* fledged. N. has *fligge*, which he says is " apparently for *fledge*." We are certain that it is. W. C. BR. *Fligge* (as of birds), PR. PA. Sui.-G. *flyga*, volare.

FLET-CHEESE, *s.* cheese made of skimmed milk. This is the name by which the celebrated Suffolk cheese is universally called in its native county.

FLETCHES, *s. pl.* green pods of pease; from some resemblance they are supposed to bear to an arrow. Fr. *fleche.*

FLET-MILK, *s.* the skimmed milk. SK. has *flotten* milk, and derives it from Belg. *vlieten*, cremorem lactis adimere. W. C. BR. Flet of milk. PR. PA.

.FLICK, *s.*

1. A smart stinging slap.

2. The outer fat of the hog, which is cured for bacon. In Suffolk this is called "*the flick,*" and the rest of the carcase " *the bones.*"

3. A flitch, either of bacon, or of sawn plank; and a better form it.

A. s. *flicce,* succidia. O. Fr. *fligue* de lard. BR.

FLIGGER, *v.* to quiver with convulsive motion. It is in CH. and in SH. where it is spelled *flicher,* and more properly, as it must come from A. s. *fliccerian,* motare alas. *Flicher* W. W. R. BR.

.FLIGGERS, *s. pl.* the common flag, *Iris pseudacorus,* Lin. so called from the motion of its leaves by the slightest impulse of the air.

FLIT, *v.* to remove from one house to another. Dan. *flytter,* commigro. CH. R.N.C. T.B. BR.

FLIZZOMS, *s. pl.* flying particles, or very small flakes in bottled liquors. The bees-wings, by which some persons of fine taste prove the age of their port, are nothing but *flizzoms.* R. N. C.

FLOP, *adv.* souse; plump; flat. Ex. " His foot slipped, and down he came *flop.*"

.FLUE, *adj.* shallow.

FLUFF, *s.* any light, flying, downy, gossamer-like stuff. A. s. *floh,* fragmen.

FLUSH, *s.* the stream from a mill-wheel. Teut. *flass,* fluxus.

FLUSH, *adj.* even; on a level. As a stream, unconfined, will rise to the level of that from which it was parted.

.FLY-TIME, *s.* the season in which flies are troublesome or mischievous.

FOG, *s.* long grass, growing in pastures, in late summer or autumn; not fed down, but allowed to
stand through the winter, and yielding early spring
feed.   By its length and thickness, the outer part
forms a cover or sort of thatch for the lower, which
is kept fresh and juicy, at least through a mild
winter.   This seems to entitle it to sx. derivation,
Ital. *affogare.*   R. N. C.   FE.   W. C.   BR.

FOGGER, *s.* a huckster; a petty chapman carrying
small wares from village to village.

FOISON, *s.* succulency; natural nutritive moisture, as
in herbage.   Ex. " There is no *foison* in this hay."
We do not use it in its general sense of abundance.
It is sometimes most perversely mispronounced *poison!* Fr. *foison.*   R. N. C.   L. SC.

FOISONLESS, devoid of foison.   SC. N.

FOKY, *adj.* bloated; unsound; soft and woolly.   Ex.
" a *foky* turnip,"

FOLD-PRITCH, *s.* a heavy pointed iron, to make
holes in the ground to receive the toes of hurdles.
A. S. *priccan,* pungere.

FOLLOW, *v.* to practice for a livelihood.   Ex. " He
*follow* jobbing, shoe-making, tailoring."   If it be
said that a man *follows* farming, or any more respectable occupation, it must be understood to be
on a narrow scale.   And in general, indeed, it
seems implied that he is not very likely to overtake
what he *follows.*

FOND, *adj.* luscious; fulsome; disagreeably sweet, in
taste or in smell.

FOOTING, *s.* sum paid down; or sometimes an enter-
tainment given, on entering upon a new office or
situation.

FOOTING-TIME, *s.* the time of recovery from a lying-in, of getting on *foot* again. R. S. E. Q.

FORCE, *v.* A strange sort of neutro-passive. Ex. "I *forced* to go." I was obliged, I could not help. It is O. E. It occurs in the curious gossiping Diary of Pepys.

FORECAST, *s.* forethought. PE.

FORECAST, *v.* to think before. It is an excellent quality in a servant to "*forecast* his work;" to think what he is to do next.

FORE-SUMMERS, *s.* the forepart of a cart. This kind of cart was some years ago much used in Norfolk, but it is now wearing out. A sort of platform projecting over the shafts was called "the *fore-summers.*"

FORFEITS, *s. pl.* SH. in Measure for Measure, mentions "*forfeits* in a barber's shop." They exist to this day in some, perhaps in many village shops. They are penalties for handling the razors, &c.; offences very likely to be committed by lounging clowns, waiting for their turn to be scraped on a Saturday night, or Sunday morning. They are still, as of old, "more in mock than mark." Certainly more mischief might be done 200 years ago, when the barber was also a surgeon. We have also *forfeits* in every inn yard, payable in beer, by those who dabble in the water cistern, carry candles into the stables, &c.

FORGIVE, *v.* to begin to thaw. By no means an inexpressive metaphor.

FORHINDER, *v.* to prevent. It is not synonymous with *hinder,* awkwardly eked out with another syllable. The Saxon *fore* has the same effect in Saxon words, as the Latin *præ*, or the Greek *προ*, in words derived from those languages. And, as the word *hinder* is synonymous with *let*, why is not *for-hinder* as good as *forlet*, which was formerly used by the best authors, though now it has disappeared from general use?

FORK, *s.* the lower half of the body. A long legged person is said to be "long in the fork."

FORLORN, *adj.* worthless; reprobate; abandoned. Ex. "a *forlorn* fellow," is one with whom nobody would have any concern. "A *forlorn* tyke," is a sad dog! the DICTT. give simply the sense of "destitute; forsaken," without implying any moral reason. Some of their authorities (*V.* T.J and N.G.) would very well bear ours, which is the true Saxon sense. A. S. *fore-loren*, perditus.

FOUR-EYED, *adj.* Applied to dogs which have a distinct mark over each eye, of a different colour; for the most part tan upon black; very common in in the smooth terrier, and the spaniel of King Charles's breed, as it is called. The late worthy president of the Linnæan Society, finding at Monaco, a dog so marked, and called from that circumstance, "*quattr' occhi*," notices it in his Continental Tour, as an ingenious aptness of nomenclature. Had his ears been more accustomed to the vulgar tongue of his native county, he would have found the very same at home. Let us, therefore, claim our share in our distinguished countryman's praise for ingenuity. One who wears spectacles is also said to be *four-eyed*.

FOURS, *s. pl.* the afternoon refreshment of labourers in harvest. Generally made a double plural *fourses*.

FOUTRY, *adj.* paltry; trumpery; despicable. The DICTT. have *fouty* as synonymous with the Fr. *fouteux*, and from a dirty Fr. derivation. Our's is the better word. It is most likely the *foutra*, often occurring in SH. one of the many Spanish words colloquially current in his time, but which have almost entirely disappeared. A surviving instance is worth preserving. " A *foutra* for thine office," says ancient Pistol to Justice Shallow, when he comes to announce the accession of King Hal. It was then become a *foutry* office.

FOY, *s.* a supper given by the owners of a fishing vessel at Yarmouth, to the crew in the beginning of the season. It is otherwise called a *bending-foy*, from the bending of the sails or nets, as a ratification of the bargain. It must be from Fr. *foi*.

FOZY, *adj.* very nearly, if not exactly the same, as FOXY, q. v. A. s. *woseg*, succi plenus.

FRACK, *v.* to abound; to swarm; to be thronged, or crowded together. Ex. "The church was *fracking* full;" "my apple-trees are as full as they can *frack*."

FRAIL, *v.* to fret or wear out cloth. Fr. *frayer*.

FRAME, *v.* to speak or behave affectedly; to shape the language and demeanour to an occasion of ceremony. " *Framed* manners " is L. SC.

FRAME-PERSON, *s.* a visitor whom it is thought necessary to receive ceremoniously. A. s. *frœmd*, extorris. The very word *frem'd* is in w. c. and BR.

FRAMPLED, *adj.* cross; ill-humoured. Mrs. Quickly

in Merry-Wives of Windsor, tells Falstaff that Mrs. Ford led a *frampold* life with her jealous husband." R. S. E. C.

FRAZLE, *v.* to unravel or rend cloth. In the north, a *frize* of paper is half a quarter of a sheet. PE.

FRAZLINGS, *s. pl.* threads of cloth, torn or unravelled. O. Fr. *fraisle*, fragil.

FRECKENS, *s. pl.* freckles. The ancient word. A. S. *fræcn*, turpitudo.

FREELI-FRAILIES, *s. pl.* light, unsubstantial delicacies for the table; frothy compliments; empty prate; frippery ornaments; almost any sort of trumpery meant for finery. It may have come (with a little license of decoration, well befitting it) from two words in Le Roux Dict. Com. *frelu*, to which he gives vaurien as a synonym, and *freluches*, niaiseries. To both he affixes v. l. for vieux langage.

FRENCH, *adj.* What the precise meaning may be (if any such it have) cannot be ascertained. It seems to mean, quite generally and indefinitely, as bad as bad can be. Any extreme provocation, severe disappointment, or keen distress, is enough to make one *French !* A word very comprehensibly Anti-Gallican.

FRENCHMAN, *s.* any man, of any country, who cannot speak English; as any one who does not understand East Anglain, is a shireman.

FRESH, *s.* home-brewed table beer, drawn from the tap.

FRESH, *adj.* tipsey. BR.

FRESHER, *s.* a small frog.

FRESHES, *s. pl.* waters flowing down rivers after

heavy rains, to the general outfall, and overflow-
ing the neighbouring country in their passage. BR.

FRIGHTFUL, *adj.* apt to take fright. Certainly
more distinctly expressive than *fearful*, which
would be generally used, yet the effect of substitution is very ludicrous. Ex. "Lauk! Miss, how
*frightful* you are!" says a homely wench, when
Miss screams at the sight of a toad or a spider.
CH. has *dredeful* in the same sense, which, to modern ears would sound more strangely still.

FRIMICATE, *v.* to play the fribble, to affect delicacy.
A word jocularly fabricated, perhaps, but not ar-
bitrarily, or without fair pretence to derivation.
*Fram, frem, frim*, is easy transition, *v. frame;* or
it may be from the Fr. *frimer*, which Le Roux has
in much the same sense, and calls it "mot de pay-
san." A home-bred East Anglian rustic might
think strange and outlandish persons, whether
Frenchmen or Shiremen, particularly given to *frimicate*.

FRIZE, *v.* to freeze. It forms its imp. and part. regularly *friz*. O. E. A. S. *frysan*, gelare.

FROG-SPIT, *s.* *V.* CUCKOO-SPIT.

FROISE, *s.* a pancake. O. E. Lidgate. Fr. *froisser*.

FROUZY, *adj.* blouzy; with disordered and uncombed
hair. In its more usual sense *frouziness* is offensive to the nose; not so with us, but to the eyes.

FROWY, *adj.* stale; on the point of turning sour from
being over kept. It is most commonly applied to
milk, or compositions of it. In the second passage
quoted in N. G. from SP. it is applied to grass in
pasture, ; and so it may be with us. This word,

and the preceeding, are both connected with *frow*, which, according to GR. signifies in the north, a slut.

FRUGAL, *adj.* the reverse of COSTLY, q. v. This word seems quite distinct from *frugal* in its current sense. Instances may, indeed, be produced in different languages, of the same word bearing even opposite senses, under different circumstances. The word sacer, in Latin is a very familiar one, sometimes meaning hallowed, sometimes accursed; which sense it bears in any particular passage, must be determined by the context or the occasion. But in each case its etymon is the same. On the contrary, our word, now under consideration, is likely to be of an origin very different from that of the common word, with which it agrees in every letter. "Good woman," quoth the village doctress, "is your child *costive?*" "*Costly!* Ma'am, no, quite the contrary, sadly *frugal* indeed!" So much for modern use. But have we any thing like authority for it in O. E.? We will have recourse to SH. In the Merry Wives of Windsor, Mrs. Page, on receiving Falstaff's love letter, ponders "What unweighed behaviour he could have picked out of her conversation." She presently concludes, "I was, then, too *frugal* of my mirth. Heaven forgive me!" She could not possibly mean too sparing. It would be nonsense; she must mean too free. The commentators are puzzled, and no wonder. Dr. Johnson says, he once thought "not" ought to be inserted before "too." But it seems his second thoughts were better, for he has not inserted it in the text. The puzzling word *frugal* stands alone in all the old editions. Now, without presuming to unsettle the derivation of the common word *frugal*, from the Latin *frugi* or *fruges*, or whatever may best please Vossius, or whom else it may concern, we may look at home for that of our *frugal* and Shakspeare's; and feel pretty confident that we find it, with only a very common change of one vowel. To adapt it to its Saxon origin, and to distinguish from a word of meaning so different, it might be spelled *frugle*. A. s. *frig*, liber.

FRUMP, *s.* a sour, ill-humoured person; more particularly an old woman.

FRUMPLE, *v.* to rumple; crease; or wrinkle.

FRUMPY, *adj.* having a sour and ill-humoured look; we do not include the ideas of mockery and insult as the DICTT. do.

FULL-DUE, *s.* final acquittance. Ex. " I shall soon have done with Mr. A; or I shall go away from B. for a *full-due*," for good and all.

FULL-FLOPPER, *s.* a young bird sufficiently feathered to leave the nest.

FUNK. *s.* touch-wood.

FURLONG, *s.* a division of an uninclosed cornfield, of which the several subdivisions are numbered in the map, and registered in the field book.

FURTHER, *adj. comp.* A word which can only be explained by examples of its use, which is very common. Ex. " If I do so I will be *further*;" meaning I will never do it. " I wish that fellow *further*;" i. e. I would I were well rid of him."

FUZZY, *adj.* rough and shaggy.

Milton Keynes UK
Ingram Content Group UK Ltd.
UKHW022022110923
428497UK00005B/176